Translated Texts

This series is designed to meet the need; eval history and others who wish to source material, but whose knowledge (to allow them to do so in the original language. Many important Late Imperial and Dark Age texts are currently unavailable in translation and it is hoped that TTH will help to fill this gap and to complement the secondary literature in English which already exists. The series relates principally to the period 300–800 AD and includes Late Imperial, Greek, Byzantine and Syriac texts as well as source books illustrating a particular period or theme. Each volume is a self-contained scholarly translation with an introductory essay on the text and its author and notes on the text indicating major problems of interpretation, including textual difficulties.

Editorial Committee
Sebastian Brock, Oriental Institute, University of Oxford
Averil Cameron, Keble College, Oxford
Henry Chadwick, Oxford
John Davies, University of Liverpool
Carlotta Dionisotti, King's College, London
Peter Heather, University College, London
William E. Klingshirn, The Catholic University of America
Michael Lapidge, Clare College, Cambridge
Robert Markus, University of Nottingham
John Matthews, Yale University
Claudia Rapp, University of California, Los Angeles
Raymond Van Dam, University of Michigan
Michael Whitby, University of Warwick
Ian Wood, University of Leeds

General Editors
Gillian Clark, University of Liverpool
Mary Whitby, Oxford

Front cover drawing: The church of St Hřip'simē, Vałarshapat (drawn by Gail Heather)

A full list of published titles in the Translated Texts for Historians series is available on request. The most recently published are shown below.

For full details of Translated Texts for Historians, including prices and ordering information, please write to the following:
All countries, except the USA and Canada: Liverpool University Press, Senate House, Abercromby Square, Liverpool, L69 3BX, UK (*Tel* +44–[0]151–794 2233, *Fax* +44–[0]151–794 2235, *Email* J.M.Smith@liv.ac.uk, http://www.liverpool-unipress.co.uk). **USA and Canada:** University of Pennsylvania Press, 4200 Pine Street, Philadelphia, PA 19104–6097, USA (*Tel* +1–215–898–6264, *Fax* +1–215–898–0404).

Translated Texts for Historians
Volume 31

The Armenian History attributed to Sebeos

translated, with notes, by R. W. THOMSON
Historical commentary by
JAMES HOWARD-JOHNSTON
Assistance from TIM GREENWOOD

PART II. HISTORICAL COMMENTARY

Liverpool
University
Press

First published 1999
Liverpool University Press
Senate House, Abercromby Square
Liverpool, L69 3BX

British Library Cataloguing-in-Publication Data
A British Library CIP Record is available
ISBN 0–85323–564–3 (two-part set)

Set in Monotype Times by
Wilmaset Ltd, Birkenhead, Wirral
Printed in the European Union by
Redwood Books, Trowbridge, Wiltshire

HISTORICAL COMMENTARY

INTRODUCTION

The basic annotation necessary for understanding Sebeos' text is presented in footnotes to the translation. Persons are identified, places located, titles explained. Ambiguous or obscure expressions are eluci-dated. Biblical citations and allusions are identified.

The historical commentary is intended to complement the footnotes. The text has been broken down into passages which deal with a single episode or with closely interrelated matters. These passages vary greatly in length, from a single, short paragraph to several pages. The historical commentary takes the form of extended notes on individual passages. This arrangement is intended to limit the number of times the reader will need to oscillate between the two parts of the book, as well as to impart a degree of independence and coherence to the individual notes. All citations of notes in this historical commentary are to individual historical notes.

A swift glance will already have shown the reader that a good deal may be said by way of commentary on a text with a high specific gravity which has not hitherto attracted the close, critical historical scrutiny which it deserves. I have striven to keep the notes within manageable bounds but subject always to the overriding need for clarity. They are by no means comprehensive in their coverage. Very little is said about the domestic history of Armenia, secular and ecclesiastical, or about its social order and institutional development at the end of antiquity. This will only be possible after a new round of sustained research, in which Sebeos' evidence is examined in association with that of other sources covering the same or adjacent periods. Instead, attention is directed primarily at Armenia's relations with the outside world (Persian, Roman and Arab) and the dramatic events in that wider world which had a major impact on Armenia. These are the principal themes of Sebeos' history and modern scholarship can provide the materials neces-sary for commentary. Here too, though, there has been some discrimina-tion: the quantity and quality of Sebeos' material on the last and greatest of the wars between the East Roman and Sasanian empires obtains the full treatment which it demands; so too does his detailed account of Arab expansion and the crisis in the Caliphate which was gathering force at the time of writing; but somewhat less is said of his patchier history of international relations in the late sixth century, which have been covered with exemplary thoroughness by Whitby, *Emperor Maurice*.

For the convenience of readers, the historical notes have been grouped together in three sections corresponding to three distinct phases in the period covered: I (**64–105**) introductory matter, Khosrov II's formal accession (590) and actual seizure of power with Roman backing (591), and the unpleasant consequences for Armenia of this Roman-Persian *rapprochement* (591–602); II (**106–134**) the last and greatest war between the East Roman and Sasanian empires in late antiquity, beginning with the *putsch* of Phocas (November 602) which sparked it off and ending with the deposition and execution of Khosrov (February 628) and Heraclius' triumphal entry into Jerusalem with the fragments of the True Cross which he had recovered from the Persians (March 630); III (**134–177**) a brief account of the life and doctrines of Muhammad followed by a narrative of the Arab conquests which becomes fuller as the author approaches the time of writing (spring–early summer 655), together with some additional material on the first Islamic civil war and its immediate context (added apparently in 661).

The historical commentary cannot entirely eschew philological matters. For a large amount of material is recycled from Sebeos in the chapters (ii.3–4) dealing with the end of the Sasanian empire and the rise of the Arabs in T'ovma Artsruni's *History of the House of the Artsrunik'*, completed at the beginning of the tenth century. The existence of this material is recorded at the head of notes dealing with the corresponding passages in Sebeos.

T'ovma undoubtedly made direct use of a manuscript of Sebeos, since a considerable amount of the recycled material is extracted *verbatim*. He was very selective, however, in his use of it. From sections I and II he confined himself to passages dealing with Sasanian dynastic history, high-level diplomacy, and the main episodes of warfare between the great powers. He was even more sparing in what he extracted from Sebeos' account of the origins of Islam. Apart from excising a great deal of other material, T'ovma seems to have limited his editorial intervention to abridgement of some passages and the addition of a prophecy of doom of his own composition, which he placed just before the decisive battle of Nineveh and the fall of Khosrov. There are very few places where T'ovma may be seen or may be suspected of tampering with the text (and then only in minor ways). So T'ovma's version of selected passages of Sebeos may be used, with reasonable confidence, as a means of controlling the very late manuscript on which the critical edition of Sebeos is based.

Considerable interest therefore attaches to a number of short passages (noted in Robert Thomson's translation of T'ovma) which have no parallels in the extant manuscript of Sebeos. Some of these passages supply important items of information (additional place-names, for example, or details about negotiations). They are well integrated into the material demonstrably taken from Sebeos. It therefore seems likely that the additional material presented by T'ovma was taken from his manuscript of Sebeos, which was, not unexpectedly, superior to that available to modern scholars. Note is therefore taken of all significant additional items of information which may have belonged to the original text of Sebeos.

The second issue confronted in the historical notes is that of chronology. Sebeos provides a solid framework of regnal dates, chiefly Persian until the fall of the Sasanian dynasty, then Roman and Islamic. Once the starting-point adopted for his calculation of Khosrov II's regnal years is established at June 589, there is no difficulty in fixing a rough location in time for most of the reported events. But a fair amount of investigation is needed to establish precise dates for a number of episodes (for example, for some of the campaigns fought in Armenia between 603 and 610). Some forays must also be made into Armenian domestic history, in order to establish key chronological points (notably, in the career of Smbat Bagratuni in Section I or those of his son Varaztirots' and of T'ēodoros Ṙshtuni in Sections II and III) and to draw up *fasti* of Persian and Roman governors in Armenia.

A third task, the most important, is that of elucidating the text. However elliptical, disjointed or obscure individual passages may be, it is important to try to understand the editorial processes to which they were subjected and to extract sense from the text. However surprising pieces of information or indications gained may be, they should be registered as evidence and treated as potentially useful for the reconstruction of history. Only after completing this process of interpreting and making sense of the text as we have it in the critical edition, can a fourth task be undertaken, that of calling on evidence supplied by other sources, with the twin objectives of assessing the strengths and weaknesses of Sebeos' History as history, and of identifying connections (perhaps taking the form of dependence on a common source) with other texts.

Fifth and finally, although it would save space simply to present Sebeos' evidence side by side with that of other sources, together with a necessary minimum of bibliographical references to the secondary literature, leaving judgements, historiographical and historical, to the reader, this would be an abnegation of duty on the part of the commentator privileged to subject Sebeos' text to critical historical examination for the first time. For it is important to demonstrate the many ways in which Sebeos' history contributes to a fuller understanding of the end of antiquity in the Near East. The wider readership whose attention is being drawn to the text, by its inclusion in the TTH series, is entitled to such a demonstration. A multitude of specific probes into the text should induce in readers, as in this commentator, considerable respect for Sebeos as scholar and historian.

I. SECTION I (64–105)

Introduction

Sebeos' coverage of the years 572–602 is patchy. He is mainly concerned with political upheavals in Sasanian Persia, along with some key episodes in the local politics of Armenia. He may touch lightly on other matters (for example Roman campaigns in the Balkans). Much else he simply passes by. Since there is a steady and variegated stream of information coming from two late sixth-century Roman sources, the *Ecclesiastical Histories* of John of Ephesus and Evagrius, and from a major work of secular history written a generation later by Theophylact Simocatta, Sebeos' contribution is, in the main, subsidiary on such aspects of Roman history as he covers. On Armenian and Sasanian matters, however, he provides much unique and valuable information.

Considerable difficulties confront the commentator who strives to establish something of the domestic history of the Sasanian empire (and of Sasanian policy towards Armenia) in this period. For there is a dearth of reliable information with which to compare and supplement Sebeos' account. Material from the *Khwadaynamag*, 'Book of the Lords', a Persian chronicle compiled in the reign of Yazkert III (632–

652), made its way via intermediaries into both the *Annals* of Tabari (completed in the early tenth century) and a huge verse epic, the *Shahnama* of Firdawsi (completed in 1010). Full account is taken of Tabari's work in the notes which follow, but the *Shahnama* (VII, 1–216 on Khosrov, Vahram and Vstam) is largely disregarded since it shows too much evidence of a fertile poetic imagination at work to inspire confidence in its value as a historical record. The only other useful sources of information drew their material from Christian milieux within the Sasanian empire – the near-contemporary *Khuzistan Chronicle*, and three later chronicles which incorporate earlier material, the *Seert Chronicle* (an eleventh-century Arabic translation of a Syriac ecclesiastical history written in the second half of the ninth century), *The History of the Caucasian Albanians* by Movsēs Daskhurants'i (tenth-century) and the *Georgian Chronicles* (a composite work originating in the late eighth century which received several subsequent accretions). In this first section (as in the two which follow), little attention is paid to a relatively copious but unreliable west Syrian historical tradition, deriving ultimately from a mid eighth-century chronicle which has been plausibly attributed to Theophilus of Edessa. A reconstitution (in translation) of part of a revised and amplified version written by Dionysius of Tel-Mahre in the first half of the ninth century may be consulted conveniently in A. Palmer, *The Seventh Century in the West-Syrian Chronicles* [*TTH* 15].

The chief aims of the historical notes are to elucidate what Sebeos says and to evaluate his material by comparing it with evidence supplied by these other sources. For the wider context and a soundly based reconstruction of the history of the East Roman empire and of its relations with Sasanian Persia in the late sixth century, the reader should turn to Whitby, *Emperor Maurice*. This has largely superseded the important earlier works of Stein, *Studien*, Higgins, *Chronology* and Goubert. They will only be cited exceptionally.

Literature: Whitby, *Emperor Maurice* 222–49; Rubin, 'Reforms' 234–6, 264–5; Howard-Johnston, 'The Great Powers' 171; Robinson, 'Conquest of Khuzistan'; Nautin, 'L'auteur'; Fiey, 'Icho'denah'; M.D., tr. Dowsett, xi–xx; Toumanoff, *Studies* 20–7; Conrad, 'Conquest of Arwad' 325–32, 346–8; *West-Syrian Chronicles* 85–104.

1: ch.7, **65–66**, *table of contents*. Sebeos gives a very odd account of his own work. It is uneven, suddenly switching from a bald list of major headings to a detailed enumeration of individual operations undertaken during Heraclius' two counter-offensives of 624–626 and 627–628. Then comes a second change of gear and change of manner, to the impressionistic and emotive, in the concluding reference to the Arab conquests. There is a second peculiarity: this table of contents does not, for the most part, tally with the actual contents of the text: thus it skips over events in the 590s which are treated in considerable detail in Section I; similarly there is no reference to the first two phases of Khosrov II's war against the Romans, although they loom large in Section II, the early campaigns, especially those fought in Armenia, receiving thorough coverage together with the fall of Jerusalem in 614 and Persian-Roman negotiations in the following year; the impression is also given that the text halts with the end of the initial phase of Arab expansion, after victory at Nihawand in 642 opened the way onto the Iranian plateau, whereas, in reality, it goes on to give an increasingly detailed account of international relations up to early summer 655; finally, there are allusions to episodes *which are not treated* in the extant text – namely the Persian conquest of Egypt and capture of Alexandria (619), Heraclius' dealings with the Turks (625–627), and a first Arab invasion of Atrpatakan (immediately after the battle of Nihawand).

Two partial explanations may be offered. First, Sebeos appears, unusually, to have written his introduction first rather than last, and not to have revised it subsequently. He makes it plain in his final sentence that he is presenting a plan, an account of the work which he wants to write. As happens to many authors' plans, it changed radically in the course of writing. Two important changes were probably deliberate – the extension of the chronological range to the time of writing and reduction of the geographical frame to Armenia and adjoining lands (which entailed excision of material pertaining to Egypt and the Turks). Second, it may be conjectured that Sebeos' original plan was largely shaped by the materials which he had to hand *at that stage*. The anomalous inclusion of a full summary of Heraclius' Persian campaigns is best explained on the hypothesis that Sebeos had acquired, at an early stage, a copy or a translation of the official history of those campaigns for which Heraclius had sought a wide circulation. The converse, lack of material, at that initial stage, on the 590s and much of the fighting over the following two decades, would explain the absence of those topics from his table of contents.

2: ch.8, **67**, *Peroz's defeat and death in 484*. The significance of this event is discussed above in Historical Background. The best account is that of Łazar P'arpets'i 154–7. For its significance and baleful consequences, see Greatrex 47–52.

3: ch.8, **67**, *forty-first regnal year of Khosrov I*. Until the death of the last Sasanian ruler Yazkert III in 652, Sebeos gives chronological definition to his history mainly by intermittent references to numbered regnal years of Sasanian kings. A reign was reckoned from the beginning of the calendar year in which a new ruler was formally installed. From the introduction of a new calendar modelled on that of Egypt in the first half of the fifth century BC, the Persian year consisted of twelve months, each comprising 30 named (but not numbered) days with five additional days tacked onto the end of the 12th month. These last were the solemn days of Farwardagin, on which the spirits of the departed were commemorated. No allowance was made for leap years, so that the calendar year slipped back from its original starting-point in spring one month every 120 years.

By the beginning of the sixth century, the calendar year, which began immediately after the commemoration of the dead with the Nawruz festival celebrating the reassertion of power by the forces of good in the visible world, was running eight months behind the seasonal year. At that time, in a single, surgical act of reform, the five additional days were transferred to the end of the eighth month, and the Nawruz festival was rescheduled to the first day of the ninth month. This brought about an appropriate but, in the long run, temporary, rough synchronization with the vernal equinox. The start of the calendar year was unaffected (save for the detachment of the Nawruz festival from its traditional place on the first day of the first month) and continued to fall in summer (July or June) throughout the sixth and early seventh century.

It was therefore from a date in the July or June preceding their actual accession to the throne that the reigns of Khosrov I and his successors were measured. The precise dates for accessions and notional starts of reigns falling within the scope of Sebeos' first section were as follows: Khosrov I, 13 September 531 (actual), 12 July 531 (notional); Ormizd IV, 7 March 579 (actual), 30 June 578 (notional); Khosrov II, 15 February 590 (actual), 27 June 589 (notional). Khosrov I's 41st year ran from 2 July 571 to 1 July 572.

Literature: Tabari, tr. Nöldeke 400–36; Higgins, *Chronology* 1–31; de Blois, 'Calendar'.

4: ch.8, **67–68** and ch.9, **70**, *opening of the Roman-Persian war of 572–591*. The circumstances leading to the outbreak of war in 572 and the disastrous failure of the Roman offensive in northern Mesopotamia in 573 are summarized above in Historical Background. Sebeos' coverage is narrowly focused on Armenia. Information unique to him is supplied on the Persian military response to the initially successful uprising in 572, but without reference to the wider context, namely the conclusion of two successive truces (for one year from the end of March 574 and, after a short gap, for three years from not earlier than July 575) which halted the fighting in the southern, Mesopotamian theatre of war but excluded Armenia. He also fails to report Roman offensive actions after 572, namely raids to Albania and the Caucasus in 575 and to the Caspian coast in winter 576–577, which complicated the situation for the Persian authorities as they sought to re-establish and secure their control over Armenia.

Sebeos' material deals with three subjects: (i) the initial rebellion of Persarmenia; (ii) Persian counter-measures; (iii) the role of the prince of Siwnik'.

(i) Roman sources confirm that the Emperor Justin II gave active encouragement to the Armenian insurgents with whom he was in contact from 569/570, and that he was ready to intervene in force in support of the rebels (an army, under the command of the Patrician Justinian [*PLRE* III, Iustinianus 3] was encamped at Theodosiopolis (Karin), close to the frontier, in winter 571–572). A context is also given for the assassination, by Vardan (and Vard), of the *marzpan* Surēn, who was under orders to construct a fire-temple at Dvin, capital of Persarmenia: he was opposed by the Catholicos, who mobilized 10,000 armed men against the project and led a deputation of nobles to protest to the *marzpan*; he, with only 2,000 troops, backed down, but returned with a much larger army, 15,000 strong, only to be confronted by twice as many Armenian soldiers as before; an armed clash ensued in which he was killed (probably in February 572). His death was the signal for a general uprising to begin. Sebeos is the only source to describe the fall of Dvin, capital of Persarmenia, to the rebels and their Roman allies, and the evacuation of the Persian garrison which had evidently surrendered on terms. The peoples of the Black Sea coast – Laz, Abasgians and

Alans – gave active support to the rebels, and the Iberians are reported to have gone over to the Roman side.

(ii) The immediate Persian response must be pieced together from snatches of information included later in a list of commanders and governors of Persarmenia (ch.9, **70**) as well as what is reported in ch.8, supplemented by scattered notices in Roman sources. Surēn's successor, Vardan Vshnasp, could do nothing more than try to contain the rebellion in 572. His successor, Mihran Mihrewandak (called Gołon Mihran in ch.9), probably remained equally on the defensive in 573, when Persian forces were concentrated in northern Mesopotamia. He is reported to have been in action there, losing a small engagement outside Nisibis in the spring. It was only after the collapse of the Roman offensive in the south and the fall of Dara later that year, and the subsequent agreement to confine the fighting in 574 to Armenia, that Mihran could set about restoring Persian authority in Persarmenia with a large force of Persian troops and Sabir Hun allies. Combining material from Sebeos' two chapters, we obtain the following sequence of events: (1) Mihran's entry into Armenia, prompting the civilian population to take refuge in castles and remote fastnesses (574); (2) advance into Iberia (probably late 574), where, in the plain of Khałamakhikʻ, Mihran's army was intercepted and decisively defeated by the Armenian rebel army: (3) Mihran's second, cautious advance into southern Armenia and seizure of Angł, in Bagrewand, a campaign probably to be dated to 575 which, it may be conjectured, inaugurated a programme of piecemeal pacification. On this conjectural chronology, the Roman raid transecting Transcaucasia in 575 may be interpreted as exploiting Mihran's defeat in Iberia late in the previous year.

(iii) The Persians had a committed local supporter in Philip prince of Siwnikʻ. The political disengagement of Siwnikʻ from the rest of Persarmenia originated in the fifth century. During the rebellions of 450–451 and 482–484, the then princes of Siwnikʻ sided actively with the Persians (Łazar Pʻarpetsʻi 57–68, 73–78, 83–86, 128, 140, 146, 149–153, 156, 159). The administrative transfer of Siwnikʻ from Persarmenia to Atrpatakan was a delayed consequence. It may perhaps be dated to the 530s when Khosrov I was engaged in wide-ranging administrative reforms. Philip prince of Siwnikʻ was evidently as active a supporter of the Persians as his forebears: the first of the two campaigns (*kṙiw*) in the course of which he fought two engagements (an attack on an unnamed city, the battle at Khałamakhikʻ) took place in 574 under the command of Mihran Mihrewandak who lost the battle (see above); the second may be placed in 579 during Varaz Vzur's brief tenure of the command when an evenly-balanced battle at the village of Ut'mus in Vanand ended in a Persian victory (ch.9, **71**).

Sources: T.S. III 9.3–11; Menander fr.16.1, 18.5; John of Ephesus II 20–22; Evagrius V 7; Theophanes Byzantius fr.3–4.

Literature: Whitby, *Emperor Maurice* 250–62; Rubin, 'Reforms'.

5: ch.8, **68–69** (with ch.9, **70**), *Khosrov I's expedition in 576*. After the renewal of the truce for a further three years from summer 575, Khosrov decided to speed up the process of restoring Persian authority in Armenia by taking personal command of a large expeditionary force. Sebeos gives an abbreviated account of the campaign, concentrating on his encounter with a Roman field army near Melitene, a subsequent crossing of the Euphrates and the loss of the royal baggage-train and travelling sacred fire. He supposes, mistakenly, that the encounter led to a full engagement of the two armies, and grossly exaggerates the scale of Persian losses on the campaign. He does, however, supply one nugget of information about Khosrov's route into Armenia, which involved his veering north from Bagrewand to Theodosiopolis instead of taking a direct route down the Arsanias (Aratsani) valley – perhaps an attempt (which failed) to take the city by surprise.

Much additional material is to hand in the Roman sources. Khosrov halted for a month near Theodosiopolis, then marched west, aiming for Caesarea in Cappadocia. The Roman general, Justinian (now *Magister Militum per Orientem*), conducted a brilliant defensive campaign. He blocked the road through mountainous terrain to Caesarea, forcing Khosrov to turn away into the north-east sector of the Anatolian plateau around Sebastea, which had been emptied of its inhabitants and their chattels (including, presumably, livestock). He thus drew the Persian army into a position where it could be encircled. Khosrov managed to escape but only by cutting loose from the road-system and taking to the hills, which entailed his jettisoning the royal baggage-train. He was not yet out of danger, since there was still the Euphrates to cross with a large Roman army ready to pounce as he did so. After a day-long confrontation with the Roman army in the plain of Melitene, he succeeded in carrying out this difficult operation under cover of darkness – attacking and disordering the more northerly of the two Roman corps facing him and setting fire to Melitene as a diversion before crossing the river.

Sebeos is not alone in exaggerating the scale of Persian casualties nor in associating the loss of the baggage-train with the confrontation/battle. Theophylact Simocatta and Evagrius both do so, although there are traces of conflation of two separate engagements in the latter's account. The distortion should probably be attributed to Roman propaganda.

Sources: Menander fr.18.6; John of Ephesus II 24, VI 8–9; T.S. III 12.6–14.11; Evagrius V 14.

Literature: Whitby, *Emperor Maurice* 262–7 (establishing 576 as the incontrovertible date of the campaign).

6: ch.9, **69–70**, *obituary of Khosrov I*. Khosrov enjoyed a very high reputation after his death, both for his feats of arms and for his domestic reforms. The following specific achievements are picked out: fortification of two Caucasus passes (independently documented in the case of the Pass of Chor at modern Darband); the occupation of Lazica in 541 (the misrepresentation of the voluntary submission of the king Goubazes as his capture may reflect Persian propaganda); the capture in 540 of Antioch-on-the-Orontes, the capital of the Roman Near East (which Sebeos has confused with Antioch-in-Pisidia); the subsequent construction of a new city near Ctesiphon, Veh-Antioch-Khosrov, where the captured population of Antioch was resettled; the capture of Dara in 573; the capture of Callinicum in 542; and an otherwise unreported raid into Cilicia, which, if it occurred, should probably be placed immediately after the fall of Antioch in 540, when it is known that the high command and senior clergy escaped to Cilicia. It is a rag-bag list of deeds, put in no particular order but corresponding in general to the truth. The tale of Khosrov's deathbed conversion, however, is fanciful. Other traces of wishful thinking on the part of Christians are to be found in John of Ephesus V 20 (wide reading about different religions led Khosrov to prize Christian writing and to show tolerance to his Christian subjects).

Literature: Hewsen, *AŠX* 122; E. Kettenhofen, 'Darband', *E. Ir.* VII 15–16; Christensen, *L'Iran* 363–440; Rubin, 'Reforms'; Howard-Johnston, 'The Great Powers' 191–2; Stein, *Bas-Empire* 485–94, 496–7; Morony, *Iraq* 139; Whitby, *Emperor Maurice* 257–8.

7: ch.9, **70-71**, *governors/generals of Persarmenia, 572-602*. Sebeos seems to have incorporated a pre-existing list into his text, fleshing it out with brief additional notices. The following *fasti* may be constructed:

(i) Vardan Vshnasp, appointed after the assassination of Surēn and in post for a year, February 572– winter 572/573.

(ii) Gołon Mihran (= Mihran Mihrewandak), probably already in post when he fought and lost an engagement near Nisibis in spring 573 (Theophanes Byzantius fr.4); his campaigns in Transcaucasia in 574 and 575 are discussed in n.4 above. His term of office was three years since Khosrov took over command of the northern theatre in 576 (n.5 above).

(iii) Tam Khosrov, one of the principal Persian generals in the first half of the war, was assigned to the Armenian theatre in 577 and 578 (Whitby, *Emperor Maurice* 267–9). His two campaigns are described more fully in Roman sources. In 577 Tam Khosrov won a decisive victory over a large Roman field army, under Justinian's command, which was operating in Armenia (John of Ephesus VI 10; T.S. III 15.8– 9). Sebeos supplies a general location for the battle, in the plain of Basean on the upper Araxes (the most exposed frontier district of Persarmenia). By this victory Tam Khosrov secured the Sasanian position in the north for the rest of the war. In 578 he took to the offensive, advancing west through the basin of Bagrewand (where the Arsanias gathers its headwaters), then cutting south across the Armenian Taurus and attacking the region of Amida. A diversionary raid into Roman Mesopotamia succeeded in removing the Roman army, commanded by Justinian's successor the future emperor Maurice, from his path in south-west Armenia (Menander fr.23.6; John of Ephesus VI 14; T.S. III 15.12–13).

(iv) Varaz Vzur, in post for one year, 579 (Whitby, *Emperor Maurice* 272). The close-fought battle which he finally won was probably part of a local cross-border conflict (Vanand, the district around modern Kars, was within easy striking distance of the Roman frontier), which took place in a year when serious diplomatic efforts were being made to bring the war to an end (Whitby, *Emperor Maurice* 271–2).

(v) The great Parthian and Pahlaw *aspet* or *asparapet* (as at ch.10, **73**, **75**), seven years, 580–586. He was executed, after his recall, on the orders of Ormizd (ch.10, **73**). He was the father of Khosrov II's mother and two sons, Vndoy and Vstam (see nn.9, 11, 18, 19 below). The victory which he won at Shirakawan (principal town of the district immediately to the east of Vanand) was probably of more than local significance. For in 581, Maurice, then *Magister Militum per Orientem*, launched a grand (but unsuccessful) offensive south of the Taurus, targeted on Ctesiphon, which was supported by a deep-probing attack in the north, to Dvin and Iberia (T.S. III 16.3–4; Menander fr.23.11 – see Whitby, *Emperor Maurice* 272–4). The northern operation ended in defeat, a defeat which may be equated with that reported by Sebeos.

(vi) Hrahat (Aphraates at T.S. II 3.3, III 5.15, 6.3 and 6), whose term probably began in 586 and ended with his death in 589 in command of one of two relief armies (his presumably being the Persarmenian) sent to Martyropolis which had been betrayed to the Persians soon after Easter that year. The campaign south of the Taurus in which he was involved may provisionally be identified with that of 586 described in detail by T.S. II 1–9: Hrahat commanded the left wing at the battle of Solachon, south of the Tur Abdin, which resulted in a serious Persian defeat; the countervailing success in which he was involved subsequently was probably the frustration of a Roman attack on Chlomaron, capital of Arzanene/Ałdznik‛ (Whitby, *Emperor Maurice* 280–4, 289). His victory in Bznunik‛ probably came in a cross-border raid.

(vii) Hratrin Datan, two years, 589–591, since he was in post at the time of Ormizd's deposition (February 590) and Khosrov II's restoration (summer 591) – *contra* Higgins, *Chronology* 35 who has his tenure end in March 590 on the questionable assumption that all appointees of Ormizd were replaced by Vahram on his seizure of power.

(viii) Vndatakan Khorakan, who may have held the post for several years, if the mutinous troops who killed him and went off to Gełum were joining in Vstam's 594 rebellion against Khosrov, which was centred on Gełum (**94–95** and nn.18–19 below).

(ix–xii) Merakbut, Yazdēn, Butmah and Hoyiman, none attested otherwise unless Yazdēn may identified with the famous Yazdin (for whom see Flusin, *St Anastase* II, 246–52) who held high office under Khosrov II and was, from around 600, the chief patron at court of Nestorian Christians. However, the only provincial governorship which Yazdin is known to have held (*Chron. Seert* 458, 524–5) was that of Beth Aramaye (Lower Mesopotamia) and the Mountain (the northern Zagros). These four names, together with Vndatakan Khorakan, reappear with variations in their spelling in a near-duplicate notice at **105** (discussed in n.23 below).

Literature: Stein, *Studien* 49–50; Higgins, *Chronology* 34–5; Whitby, *Emperor Maurice* (references incorporated above).

8: ch.10, **73–74**, *the campaigns and rebellion of Vahram Ch'obin, 587–589* (cf. T'.A. 85). The Turks (here as often elsewhere loosely designated by the name of their predecessors as Persia's principal nomad adversaries in the east, the T'etals, Hephthalites) eventually entered the fray against the Persians towards the end of the reign of Ormizd IV (579–590). Vahram Ch'obin, who was a member of one of the leading magnate families of Persia, the Mihran, and whose estates and local connections were centred on the region of Řeyy (near modern Tehran), was appointed commander-in-chief of the Persian forces opposing them. Sebeos, in tandem with other extant sources (principally Tabari), gives the impression that the operations in which Vahram drove the Turks beyond the Vehřot (Oxus) were carried out in a single campaigning season (dated by Tabari to Ormizd's 11th regnal year, 588/589). However, since emphasis is put on the gravity of the crisis facing Persia after the Turkish intervention in force, it is likely that it took at least two years (587–588) for Vahram both to mobilize a field army strong enough to face the Turks in open combat and then, as Sebeos alone reports in any detail, to reverse the initial gains which they had made in the region of Balkh and Herat.

Some damage appears to have been done to Sebeos' text, in the course of its transmission to the seventeenth-century manuscript, since a second victorious campaign by Vahram (589), into the eastern Caucasus, has been telescoped into the first, the Mazk'ut'k' have thereby been wafted far to the east beyond the Oxus from their actual Transcaucasian homeland (Hewsen, *AŠX* 121–2). Vahram appears to have been responding to an attack in force on Albania by an Iberian-led coalition of Caucasus peoples which the Romans had sponsored. At some stage, probably after Vahram's thrust north (which seems to have included an attack on Suania in the central Caucasus), a Roman army, subsequently reinforced from Lazica, intervened and succeeded in luring Vahram west and inflicting a defeat on him (its scale is evidently exaggerated by Theophylact Simocatta).

These two generally successful campaigns must have greatly enhanced the reputation of Vahram and are likely to have induced a certain trepidation in Ormizd. Ormizd, whose own posthumous reputation was that of an over-zealous upholder of justice and determined protector of the rights of the poor and the weak against the nobility, was in a relatively weak position *vis à vis* Vahram since he had not commanded Persian armies in the field. The eastern sources, Sebeos among them, show that mutual suspicion soured relations between the king and his great general. Vahram was nervous of the reaction of so autocratic a ruler. Ormizd's thanks for the share of the booty which Vahram sent him were far from effusive. Sebeos adds the interesting detail that Vahram had distributed the rest of the booty among his troops, so that Ormizd's demand for a larger share antagonized the whole army.

Such was the context for Vahram's decision to rebel, according to the eastern sources, and their version should be preferred to that of T.S. III 8.1–3, 10, who has Ormizd seize on Vahram's defeat at the hands of the Romans as a pretext for dismissing him from his command (although there is an echo of the eastern version in his later summary of Vahram's career, at III 18.12–14). Vahram now sought to divide his opponents. By introducing coins minted at Řeyy in the name of Ormizd's son, Khosrov, into circulation in the capital, he succeeded in casting suspicion on Khosrov, who fled from his father's court, at that time outside the capital, probably in the southern fringes of Media. He advanced with his army across the Zagros and took up a position on the Great Zab, thus separating the capital and the troops based there from the main army base on the Roman front, Nisibis. When the troops at Nisibis declared for the rebel, the regime of Ormizd was doomed. Before long the royal army holding the Great Zab ford and barring Vahram's way to Ctesiphon broke up in disorder when its commander was assassinated. All of this is passed over in silence by Sebeos who turns immediately from the inception of the rebellion to reactions in the court. He does, however, provide a unique notice about one consequence of the rebellion, namely an offensive launched by John Mystacon, the Roman commander in the north (*PLRE* III, Ioannes 101) who besieged Dvin (without success) and then invaded Atrpatakan.

Sources: T.S. III 6.6–8.3, III 8.9–8.12, III 18.4–IV 3.1; Tabari, tr. Nöldeke 268–73, 276; *Georgian Chronicles* 217–21; *Khuz.Chron.* 5; *Chron.Seert* 443–4.

Literature: Christensen, *L'Iran* 441–4; Toumanoff, *Studies* 382–6; Whitby, *Emperor Maurice* 290–1, 293–4.

9: ch.10, **75–76**, *overthrow of Ormizd, accession and flight of Khosrov II, 590* (cf. T'.A. 85). News of events on the Great Zab reached Ormizd and the court five days after their occurrence as they were travelling back to Ctesiphon. Three days later, on 6 February 590, a bloodless palace revolution brought about Ormizd's deposition, soon to be followed by blinding and death. His son Khosrov was informed and hurried back to be proclaimed king on 15 February. His position, however, was very weak, since the army sent north-west to shield the metropolitan area had dissolved. He tried to negotiate a deal with Vahram, offering him the second position in the realm, only to meet with a brusque rejection. Vahram's army then advanced to the inner line of defence around the capital, the Nahrawan canal. Morale was low among the defenders, who were evidently heavily outnumbered, and within a few days it was decided that the young king and a small entourage should flee. Khosrov made his way to the Euphrates and then, closely pursued by troops of Vahram's (who captured his uncle, Vndoy), followed the river valley until he crossed the Roman frontier near Circesium. Meanwhile Vahram entered Ctesiphon and was crowned on 9 March.

Sebeos' succinct account clarifies some important points about the coup. It had two clear stages. It was initiated in military circles, among the troops accompanying Ormizd as he was travelling between Media and Ctesiphon; but its execution was then entrusted to court magnates opposed to Ormizd, led by Vndoy whom the conspirators had released from prison. Khosrov may be cleared from any complicity in his father's death (as he is by Whitby) despite the contrary testimony of Theophylact Simocatta and Tabari, since Sebeos who had every interest in blackening his reputation breathes not a word of it. Finally Sebeos alone reports that Ormizd contemplated flight, to the Lakhm of Hira, adding the interesting detail (which confirms that he was returning from Media) that his route to Hira would have taken him across the Tigris well to the south of Ctesiphon, by the Vehkawat pontoon-bridge (which features again in the story of Khosrov II's deposition in 628 [ch.39, **127**]).

Sources: T.S. IV 3.2–6.5, 7.1–10.4, 12.1–12.7; Tabari, tr. Nöldeke 272–82; *Khuz.Chron.* 5–6; *Chron.Seert* 444, 465–6.

Literature: Whitby, *Emperor Maurice* 292–7; Higgins, *Chronology* 26–31; Morony, *Iraq* 147–150; Gyselen, *Géographie* 62.

10: ch.11, **76**, *Khosrov II's appeal for Roman aid, 590* (cf. T'.A. 85–6). Khosrov arrived on Roman territory after nightfall and camped ten miles from Circesium, from where he sent a message to the city-commandant announcing his arrival. He was admitted into the city at dawn the next day. From there he sent a letter to the emperor, which Theophylact

Simocatta claims to reproduce: he appealed to Maurice for help first as a fellow-ruler who would naturally be disturbed at the sight of a rebel destroying the established order in the neighbouring empire, and second on the grounds that the Romans needed the Persians to manage their sector of the outer world lest 'the fierce, malevolent tribes' might take control of Persia and 'thereby in the course of time gain irresistible might, which will not be without great injury to your tributary nations as well'. This letter, together with the commandant's report, was sent to Comentiolus, senior Roman general in the region, at Hierapolis in northern Syria, and forwarded thence to the capital. Khosrov was now received by Comentiolus with all due honour at Hierapolis (not nearby Khalab, modern Aleppo, as implied by Sebeos). Khosrov stayed at Hierapolis during the ensuing negotiations which reached a critical stage in early summer.

These were the circumstances (described in considerable detail by Theophylact Simocatta) in which Khosrov sent an embassy to Constantinople, probably in early summer 590, offering generous terms in order to secure Roman backing. Sebeos alone gives a detailed account of his terms, which he says were made in writing: by allowing himself to be designated Maurice's 'son', Khosrov acknowledged a degree of political subordination to the Roman empire; he agreed to return Persian gains in northern Mesopotamia, but his main territorial concessions were in Transcaucasia – the traditional balance of power in favour of the Persians would be redressed, Maurice being offered a roughly equal share both of Armenia and Iberia but Khosrov saving face by retaining the provincial capitals, Dvin and Tp'khis. Sebeos' information looks trustworthy. Corroboration is obtainable from Theophylact Simocatta who includes a vague reference to the territory offered by Khosrov towards the end of the speech which he concocts for the Persian ambassadors (the return of Martyropolis and Dara and 'bidding farewell to Armenia') and who has Khosrov designate himself Maurice's son at the end of his first letter. The cessions of territory were duly made after the defeat of Vahram (ch.12, **84**).

Sebeos disagrees with Theophylact Simocatta in suggesting that the decision to back Khosrov was taken against serious opposition, but the time taken by the negotiations (over three months, as Whitby calculates) provides indirect confirmation, suggesting as it does that the final terms were hammered out in the course of several rounds of negotiation at a distance.

Sources: T.S. IV 10.5–11.11, 12.8, 13.2–14.4; *Khuz.Chron.* 6–7; *Chron.Seert* 444, 466; Tabari, tr. Nöldeke 275, 282–4.
Literature: Whitby, *Emperor Maurice* 297–9, 304.

11: ch.11, **76–80**, *restoration of Khosrov II, 591* (cf. T'.A. 86–8). Khosrov moved to Constantina, one of the two main military bases in Roman Mesopotamia, when he received the emperor's favourable response, and began actively to undermine Vahram's regime. His uncles Vstam and Vndoy, the latter of whom managed to escape from prison, rallied support in Atrpatakan, under the watchful eye of John Mystacon, *Magister Militum per Armeniam*, who was mobilizing troops throughout Armenia. Towards the end of 590 the garrison of Nisibis changed sides and Martyropolis surrendered, events which gravely weakened the northern defences of Persian Mesopotamia. By spring 591, troops were massing against Vahram north and south of the Armenian Taurus.

Sebeos' figures for those in the northern theatre (15,000 from Armenia and 8,000 from Persia, all cavalry, from Atrpatakan) are plausible, but something is awry with the figure of 3,000 cavalry which he gives for Roman forces mobilized in the south. Apart from the testimony of several sources that Khosrov owed his restoration to the Roman troops backing him, there was no question of so small a force advancing into Persian territory and confronting Vahram's army. The figure may have been corrupted in transmission (say from 30,000 [infantry as well as cavalry] to 3,000) or, possibly, the troops in question may have been palace guards assigned to serve as Khosrov's retinue (T.S. V 3.7).

Of the strategy employed by the Roman commander-in-chief, Nerses (*PLRE* III, Narses 10), Sebeos says nothing, his attention being focused on the final stage of the campaign. It was, however, the preceding manœuvres which determined the outcome. The main Roman army, under the nominal command of Khosrov, advanced slowly towards the Tigris, taking control of Mardin and Dara on the way, paused, then crossed the river and pushed on south-east at a slow and deliberate pace as far as the Lesser Zab. This was a feint on the grandest scale, intended to detain Vahram in Mesopotamia until the point at which the Roman army could strike north-east and reach Atrpatakan before him. It also distracted attention from the approach of a small force, despatched from Dara to Singara, which came down the Euphrates valley and took over the metropolitan region for Khosrov as soon as Vahram hurried north.

The southern and the northern armies joined forces near Lake Urmia, before Vahram could intercept Nerses. Vahram, who was now outnumbered 2:3 (Theophylact Simocatta's total of 60,000 for those backing Khosrov [T.S. V 9.4] is close to that which may be calculated from Sebeos with the emendation proposed above [15,000 + 8,000 + 30,000]), was forced to retreat south-east, deeper into Atrpatakan. Sebeos now supplies information unique to him: in a desperate last throw, Vahram tried to redress the numerical balance, by winning over Musheł Mamikonean, commander of the Armenian army, and the other Armenian nobles. He offered substantial inducements in a letter, which there is no need to reject as spurious: Armenia would become a semi-autonomous kingdom and it would be enlarged to embrace all the territory which it had included at its maximum extent, including northern Mesopotamia and the whole of the Roman sector of Armenia with part of Cappadocia; Musheł, who was to be the king of what was to be a large western buffer state, was being offered a junior partnership in the Sasanian empire (the 'kingdom of the Aryans'), with the possibility of receiving subvention from Vahram. It was an extraordinary and alluring offer, but Vahram's all too evident weakness, it may be surmised, led Musheł and the Armenian nobles to reject it.

Sebeos' account of the defeat of Vahram tallies in essentials with that of Theophylact Simocatta (T.S. V 10.4–11.4). The battle lasted all day. The Roman troops were responsible for breaking the resistance of Vahram's army. Late in the day, Vahram's force of elephants was surrounded and captured, the animals then being presented to Khosrov. A great deal of booty was captured with Vahram's camp. Vahram himself escaped (Tabari confirms that he made his way to Turkish territory and that he was later put to death there).

Sources: T.S. IV 12.9–13.1, IV 14.5–V 11.9; *Khuz.Chron.* 7; *Chron.Seert* 466; Tabari, tr. Nöldeke 284–9; Garitte, *Narratio* chs93–95 (with commentary at 231–8).

Literature: Whitby, *Emperor Maurice* 298–303; Hewsen, *AŠX* 229–30.

12: ch.12, **80–84**, *growing antagonism between Musheł Mamikonean and Khosrov II* (cf. T'.A. 88). Sebeos preserves the only account of this episode, although there may be an echo at T.S. V 11.7 (a fleeting reference to the 'utter disrespect' shown by Khosrov to his Roman allies). The underlying cause is probably to be sought in changing attitudes among the Armenian nobility: expectations had probably been raised by Vahram's offer, initially in the inner circle around Mushel who were privy to it and then more widely, if, as seems probable, news of it leaked out; the map of Armenia was, in any case, about to be redrawn, under the terms of Khosrov's agreement with the Romans, and it was not unreasonable to hope or even to lobby for greater autonomy, especially within the reduced sector of the weakened Persian empire.

Relations between Romans and Persians remained good. John Mystacon, commander of the troops from Armenia, defused the crisis. The large share of the booty sent off under armed escort to Constantinople (**83–84**) probably more than covered the cost of funding the expedition (to which Khosrov referred, **80**). The Roman troops were rewarded individually for their services by royal largesse. The promised territorial concessions were duly made. Corroboration may be obtained from the skimpier accounts of *Chron.Seert* 466 (on all three points but only mentioning the two principal cities south of the Taurus restored to Roman control), T.S. V 11.3–6 (a large quantity of booty and a celebratory feast) and Tabari, tr. Nöldeke 287 (generous largesse). Mushel was given the honour of reporting the victory and delivering the booty gained to the emperor. He was not allowed to return. By this device restive elements in the Armenian nobility were deprived of their natural leader, and their efforts, described later in considerable detail, were easier to deal with.

13: ch.13, **85**, *Shirin and the position of Christians in Persia*. Shirin looms large in the romanticized versions of the history of Khosrov II's reign incorporated into several versions of the *Khwadaynamag* (cf. *Shahnama* VII 239–49, 321–9). Sebeos' brief portrait corresponds to that presented by other sources. She exercised considerable influence at court (her son, Mardanshah, was a serious contender for the crown at the end of Khosrov's reign) and her patronage was important in church affairs. She secured the Nestorian Catholicosate for her candidate Gregory of Prat in 605 and then, at his death in 609, probably played a part in Khosrov's decision to leave the see vacant and to favour the Monophysites over the Nestorians. For she had been won over to the Monophysite confession, at the same time as the influential court doctor Gabriel. She outlived Khosrov.

It may be true that there was a certain laxness in enforcing the rule prohibiting the conversion of Zoroastrians to Christianity in the early part of Khosrov's reign, especially if they were highly placed, but Shirin's influence is likely to have been less important than a desire to maintain good relations with the Romans. It was the severing of those relations at the end of 602 and the extraordinary series of Persian military successes over the following two decades which brought about a reversion to the strict enforcement of the prohibition. Macler was therefore surely right to identify the sentence in which a connection (false) is established between Shirin's death (misdated, since she was still alive in 628) and a number of martyrdoms (which preceded her death) as a later, ill-informed interpolation.

Literature: Christensen, *L'Iran* 475–6, 487–91, 493–4; Flusin, *St Anastase* II, 95–127.

14: ch.14, **85–86**, *miracle at Shawsh (Susa)*. There was no biblical or rabbinical authority for the popular belief, evidently deep-rooted, that Daniel was buried at Susa. An emotionally charged demonstration, backed by the double miracle reported by Sebeos, forced Khosrov to rescind his decision, so that Daniel's relics stayed in Susa. They are housed in a shrine on the bank of the Karka river, which replaced a medieval shrine destroyed by flood in 1869. The tomb, a large rectangular structure of green glass and ornate silverwork, stands in a brightly lit chamber, beneath a dome faced with mirrorwork. It is flanked by prayer-halls to north and south and approached from a courtyard on the east. Although the tomb itself is empty (the grave, unmarked, lies in a crypt below), it is an object of intense devotion, involving both prayer and physical contact. The cult of saints flourishes in the Islamic Republic of Iran.

There is plenty of evidence in other sources to show that Maurice was a devout and active Christian. He is known to have acquired other relics (the meagre bedding of John the Faster, patriarch of Constantinople, which he used in Lent, and the cap of the Nestorian Catholicos Sabrisho). He was frustrated in another attempt to acquire a relic of a venerated civic saint (St Demetrius at Thessalonica).

Literature: A. Netzer, N. Sims-Williams, P. Varjavand, 'Danial-e Nabi', *E.Ir.* VI, 657–60; Whitby, *Emperor Maurice* 21–3.

15: chs15–17, 21, **86–90**, **94**, *the Vahewuni incident and its consequences, 594–595*. Sebeos devotes considerable space to what seems at first sight to be a set of relatively insignificant episodes. The Vahewunis and their

allies join Musheł Mamikonean and Smbat Bagratuni as central players
in the first part of his history and ensure that it remains centred on
Armenia and the fate of its nobility at home and abroad. There is little
difficulty in following the story, despite the long digression towards its
end on Roman recruitment and religious policy which provoked discontent among Armenians in the 590s. The incident itself may be placed in
the period autumn 594–spring 595, since one of the consequential
events, the mobilization of an Armenian force by the Persians (presumably at the beginning of the campaigning season) and Khosrov's invitation to its leaders (including some involved in the incident) to attend on
him, is dated to his sixth regnal year (June 594–June 595).

The overriding concern of Maurice's regime, after 591, was to reverse
the gains made by Avars and Slavs in the Balkans in the previous decade,
by re-establishing Roman military pre-eminence and reasserting
Roman authority over the Slavs who had colonized the northern and
central Balkans. Regular troops were transferred to the west as soon as
peace was restored in the east, with Khosrov securely installed on the
Persian throne. More, though, were needed and the Roman authorities
naturally looked to Armenia with its high reputation as a nursery of
fighting-men. Precisely what system or systems of recruitment were
introduced is unclear, save that they respected Armenian lordship and
sought to raise troops in the form of noble-led contingents. There was
evidently an element of compulsion which aroused resentment.
Enlistment began at the moment of victory over Vahram, when Musheł
Mamikonean led a first 400-strong contingent west, escorting the
Roman share of booty to Constantinople (**83–84**). Before long an inten-
sive recruiting drive was under way (the subject of ch.18, **90–91**) and the
troops raised were deployed in the Balkans under the command of
Musheł. By the second half of 594, after some three years of such recruitment, resentment had grown and was ready to express itself in action.

The Machiavellian scheme to gut Armenia of its manpower, attributed to Maurice, is, almost certainly, Sebeos' retrospective interpretation. Maurice's letter, unlike the majority of other documents quoted or
summarized in the text, is evidently an editorial concoction. It cannot,
however, be denied that the Romans would have found it easier to
manage their much enlarged sector of Armenia if they were able to
siphon off a significant percentage of its military manpower. But there
was no question of tampering with the traditional social order. The nobility had to be *managed*, the Romans being forced (because of their need

for recruits) to adopt a tough stance. At a later stage, as part of this strict regime, they were ready to take considerable risks in their determination to root out any dissident element among the nobles in their sector (as is witnessed by their campaign deep into the mountain fastnesses south of Lake Van, to stamp out Vahewuni opposition).

The Persians adopted a different policy, encouraging Armenian nobles and their military followings to enlist by offering substantial cash inducements. It was the arrival of an official, the auditor (financial administrator) of Vaspurakan (a new term designating the rump of Persarmenia retained by the Persians after 591), with a large sum of money for distribution among potential Armenian recruits, some from the Roman sector, which sparked off the crisis. Sebeos hints that the decision to seize the money and to initiate a general rising against both empires was taken on the spur of the moment. This is confirmed by the leaders' subsequent indecision and disagreement. No preparations seem to have been made to obtain the help of the North Caucasus Huns for which they hoped. The solidarity shown by the two empires, which prevented the trouble spreading, also seems to have surprised them.

Sebeos traces their movements and actions as they reacted to circumstance: (i) a march north to Nakhchawan in the Araxes valley; (ii) at the appearance of the Roman army of Armenia under the command of Heraclius, father of the future emperor (*PRLE* III, Heraclius 3), who joined the Persian army operating against the rebels, three of the rebel leaders (Mamak Mamikonean, Kotit lord of the Amatunik' and Step'anos Siwni) and others unnamed submitted to Persian authority; (iii) the remaining three (Atat Khorkhoṙuni, Samuēl Vahewuni together with T'ēodoros Trpatuni, who, like them, reappears later in the Roman sector) continued north with their contingents, aiming for the land of the Huns; (iv) the pursuing Roman and Persian force caught up with them, on the bank of the river Kur in Albania, and compelled them to submit to one or other great power – this was the stage at which Atat Khorkhoṙuni made his peace with the Romans, was summoned to court and assigned to the Balkan theatre; (v) the Vahewunis and T'ēodoros Trpatuni must also have submitted at this stage, but soon caused trouble again, attempting to assassinate a Roman *curator* near Karin (Theodosiopolis); (vi) when they failed, they took refuge in the formidable mountains south of Lake Van, but were hunted down and killed by a Roman force – T'ēodoros Trpatuni who managed to escape to the Persian court was handed back and tortured to death; (vii) meanwhile those Armenian nobles who had answered the Persian call to arms, including the three rebel leaders who had submitted to the Persians, were awaiting royal instructions about their deployment; (viii) those instructions, received probably in spring 595, were for the nobles to go Khosrov's court, after which their contingents were sent off and stationed at Ispahan.

16: chs17–18, **90–91**, *Mushel Mamikonean in the Balkans, 593–598*. The formidable striking power of the nomad Avars, in combination with the plentiful manpower of Slav tribesmen, posed a serious threat to the Balkans from the beginning of Maurice's reign. In two rounds of warfare the Avars devastated much of the middle and lower Danube valley (summer 583 and autumn 586), and went on to invade the plain of Thrace (south of the Haemus range) in 587 and 588 (Whitby, *Emperor Maurice* 140–55). At the same time Slavs were beginning to settle in large numbers south of the Danube. Peace was made with the Avars at the end of 588, at considerable expense to the Roman treasury, but Slav raiding continued.

The Roman counter-offensive in which Mushel Mamikonean and the Armenian troops took part may be identified with that initiated in 593 under the supreme command of Priscus (temporarily replaced by Peter in 594). The aim was to deter Slavs from crossing the Danube by punitive raids across the river and to impose Roman authority on those who had settled to the south, working up the Danube from east to west. Considerable success was achieved in a series of campaigns, Sebeos' 'fierce war over the face of that land' (Whitby, *Emperor Maurice* 158–62). But the military balance swung against the Romans when the Avars intervened in force in autumn 597, once again sweeping down the Danube valley. The Roman army in which Mushel and his Armenians were serving was probably that commanded by Comentiolus which crossed the central Haemus in 598 to cut the Avars' line of retreat up the Danube but was then itself intercepted, after a rapid march, by the full Avar army. Heavy losses were suffered in the ensuing fighting retreat over the Haemus. These were the circumstances in which Mushel and many other Armenians died (Whitby, *Emperor Maurice* 127–8, 162–3).

17: ch.20, **91–93**, *career of Smbat Bagratuni I (the abortive rebellion against the Romans of 589)*. Sebeos includes a fair amount of biographical material about Smbat. This first chunk, like the three which follow, is laudatory in tone. The most likely source, as has been suggested in Part I in 'Sebeos as Historian', is a lost encomiastic biography, which emphasized the physical strength, courage and piety of its subject.

This first extract, as Whitby, *Emperor Maurice* 127, 291 suggests, has been introduced at the wrong point in Sebeos' text. For the abortive rebellion in the Roman sector of Armenia in which Smbat took a leading part is independently dated by T.S. III 8.4–6 to 589, shortly before Vahram's march south across the Zagros. It follows that the first, urgent quest for troops to serve in the Balkan theatre long predates the recruiting drive of the 590s. Whitby (115–19, 145–8) places it in winter 586–587, after a disastrous autumn in the Balkans when the Avars swept down the Danube valley, capturing several important cities in their path, while Thessalonica was coming under intense pressure from a large force of Slavs. There was therefore an urgent need for reinforcements to be despatched 'in great haste' and Armenia surely joined Italy as one of the chief suppliers. This would provide the best explanation for the unexpected appearance in the Balkan theatre in 587 of John Mystacon, who is otherwise only known to have held commands in the east and in particular in Armenia. At that early stage, the Romans seem to have relied more on inducements and less on compulsion than in the 590s.

T.S. III 8.7–8 confirms that Smbat was put into the arena to face the wild beasts and that his life was then spared after appeals from the crowd. The Armenian biography has improved the story, and clearly indicates that, his ordeal over, Smbat was restored to imperial favour. Sebeos, who picks and chooses his material, now refers cursorily to Smbat's second disgrace and leaves him serving as a tribune in Africa. This incident and the next phase of Smbat's career, which saw him return to Armenia (where he appears in Sebeos' next extract), were probably covered fully in the lost life.

18: chs22–24, **94–96**, *rebellion of Vstam, 594–599/600*. Sebeos' chronology becomes rather flaccid in chapters 22–26, the events in each being placed loosely at the time of those recounted in the previous chapter. The start of Vstam's rebellion, however, can be fixed more precisely because of a connection established with the earlier set of notices dealing with the Vahewuni affair. Incidental remarks (in ch.22) reveal that the troops mobilized in Persarmenia in spring 595 and their noble leaders (**88**, **94** with n.15 above) accompanied Khosrov on his campaign against the rebels. The campaign should therefore be dated to 595. This points to 594 as the year in which Vstam rebelled and gathered support. Corroboration is to hand in *Chron.Seert* which places the open warfare between royal and rebel forces in 594/595 (in the fifth year of Khosrov's reign, which, on its reckoning [erroneous], began in 590/591).

Sebeos' account of the origins of the rebellion parallels that of the most detailed surviving version of the *Khwadaynamag*, that of Dinawari, written in the ninth century. Additional material is supplied by a substantial but condensed notice in *Khuz.Chron.* and a passing reference in *Chron.Seert* (à propos of the future Nestorian Catholicos Sabrisho whose appearance in a vision encouraged Khosrov to engage Vstam's forces). Like Dinawari, Sebeos has Khosrov take (delayed) revenge on those responsible for his father's death, Vstam being warned in time and taking refuge in the western Elburz mountains (Gelum [Sebeos], Delum [Dinawari]). *Khuz.Chron.*, on the other hand, suggests that the young king was asserting himself against the uncles who had played a vital part both in bringing about his restoration and then conso- lidating his hold on Persia, and who had then been rewarded with high office, Vstam being posted to command the army on the Turkish frontier (i.e. in Khurasan), Vndoy becoming the senior minister at the centre. Too much criticism of Khosrov's policies by the latter leads to his arrest and execution.

The course of the rebellion may be pieced together from these four sources. Vstam gathered supporters from all over the empire (Dinawari) and assembled an army of which the core consisted of Elburz highlanders (Sebeos, *Khuz.Chron.*, Dinawari). Coming down onto the plateau, in the area of Řeyy (Sebeos, *Chron.Seert*), he sent out raiding forays, directing them through Media to the borders of Mesopotamia (Dinawari). Khosrov, however, mobilized a considerably larger army (which oper- ated as three independent corps, in the opening phase of the campaign [Dinawari], and, according to Sebeos, included Roman as well as Armenian contingents), and forced Vstam to abandon open warfare after defeating him in battle. Sebeos' location of this battle near Řeyy should probably be preferred to Dinawari's (by Hamadan in Media, where Vstam retreats from Řeyy before the battle). The next phase of the rebellion lasted several years, since the death of Vstam is securely dated to 599/600 (n.19 below). Safe in the fastnesses of the western Elburz, Vstam set about broadening the territorial base of the rebellion. First, he won over the troops stationed in his home region of Komsh ('the land of the Parthians') on the south side of the eastern Elburz. Then, after receiving reinforcements in the form of rebel Armenian troops from Ispahan, he extended his authority over the whole length of the Elburz range. The rebellion of four Elburz provinces, which is reported separately by Sebeos, was surely not spontaneous but engineered by Vstam. Royean and Zrēchan (Persian Royan and Zalexan) lay south of Gełum; Amał (Persian Amul) was further east, close to Taparastan (Persian Tabaristan) which lay on the north flank of the eastern Elburz and west of Vrkan.

Sources: *Khuz.Chron.* 8–9; *Chron.Seert* 481–2; Dinawari, summarized in Tabari, tr. Nöldeke 478–82.

Literature: Marquart, *Eranšahr* 124–5, 129–31, 136; Gyselen, *Géographie* 44, 49–50, 58–9, 81–2; Tabari, tr. Nöldeke 478–87.

19: chs24–27, **96–100**, *career of Smbat Bagratuni II (599/600–606/607) and the end of Vstam's rebellion (601)*. Sebeos' second extract from the postulated biography of Smbat has him in favour with Khosrov. How he achieved this position, whether or not he had Roman authorization to go to Persia, must remain uncertain since Sebeos has skipped over a decade of Smbat's life (589–599/600). His appointment as governor (*marzpan*) of Vrkan (Persian Gurgan), between the Elburz and Kopet mountains at the south-east corner of the Caspian, can be precisely dated to 599/600, since his retirement after eight years in the post is dated to Khosrov's 18th regnal year (606/607). By 599/600 Vstam was preparing to mount a second open challenge to Khosrov, and had obtained the backing of two Kushan client-rulers beyond the north-eastern frontier (for which see n.21 below). Vrkan was of crucial strategic importance since it was wedged between the Elburz range and Khurasan ('the regions of the east'), which was now actively supporting Vstam. Smbat's appointment (partly directed, it may be suggested, at weakening the resolve of the rebel Armenian troops) was a signal mark of royal favour.

Vstam's death at the hands of one of his Kushan allies (designated a Turk in *Khuz.Chron.*) may be dated with reasonable confidence to Smbat's first year in post, probably in the first half of 600. The rare examples of the coins which he issued from the outbreak of his rebellion end in his seventh year (599/600 if 593/594 was the first). Further corroboration may be obtained from Dinawari. For if his chronology of Khosrov's reign lags one year behind the true reckoning, as does

Tabari's, the only date which he gives in his full account of Vstam's rebellion – Khosrov's tenth regnal year (598/599 +1) – would correspond
exactly to the first year of Smbat's governorship (599/600). It should be
noted, though, that Dinawari attaches it to the start rather than the end
of the rebellion.

This was not the end of the rebellion, though. For although Smbat
had previously won a victory over some of the rebel Elburz highlanders,
he and his Persian colleague were now defeated in Komsh (despite
having superior numbers) by the men of Gelum and their Armenian
allies, as they made for the fastnesses of the western Elburz. He returned
to the attack in the following year (601) in Taparastan. This time he was
victorious, and it is implied by Sebeos that the rebels, even if some held
out, were of little significance thereafter.

Sebeos' account of Vstam's rebellion is superior to those of the other
sources. Whereas they compress a complex series of events apparently
into a single year (the deaths of Vstam and Vndoy are reported side by
side in *Khuz.Chron.*), focusing either on the 595 campaign (*Chron.Seert*
and Dinawari) or 600 (*Khuz.Chron.*), Sebeos provides the crucial dating
indications and distinguishes several phases in the rebellion.

Sources: *Khuz.Chron.* 8–9; Dinawari, summarized in Tabari, tr.
Nöldeke 479–80.

Literature: Marquart, *Eranšahr* 71–4; Gyselen, *Géographie* 50, 53,
84; Tabari, tr. Nöldeke 485; Whitby, *Emperor Maurice* 305–6; Göbl 53,
80 and pl.13; Sellwood, Whitting and Williams 150–1 and ill.59.

20: ch.27, **100**, *career of Smbat Bagratuni III (retirement in Armenia,
606/607–614)*. The life of Smbat quarried by Sebeos combined a
secondary theme of piety with the primary theme of Smbat's heroic
exploits and generalship. In the preceding episode, Smbat's acquisition
of a piece of the True Cross is woven into the story of his conflict with
the rebel forces after Vstam's death. Now religion comes to the fore, as
Smbat uses his influence at court to get permission to rebuild the cathedral at Dvin, to have his candidate installed as Catholicos in 606/607,
and to override the objections of the local Persian garrison commander
and of the *marzpan* of Armenia to the siting of the cathedral. The cathedral which took many years to build (it was only completed in the
Catholicosate of Komitas, 609/610–628 [**112**]) was built on the site of its
predecessor, dating from the middle of the fifth century, which had been
burned down in 572 (**68**). It had the same long three-aisled nave, but the

east apse was turned into a triconch and the surrounding porticoes were removed to make way for two side apses.

Literature: Khatchatrian, *L'Architecture Arménienne* 55–8; Garitte, *Narratio* 254–77.

21: chs28–29, **100–104**, *career of Smbat Bagratuni IV (supreme commander of Persian forces in the east, retirement at court and death, 614–616/617).* This is the fourth, last and most substantial extract from the postulated biography of Smbat. A selective account of operations in the east, focusing on Smbat's personal role, is framed by detailed notices about his audiences with Khosrov before and after his tenure of the eastern command. Information unique to Sebeos and of great historical interest is supplied both about Sasanian court ceremonial and the geopolitical position of Persia in the second decade of the seventh century.

(i) *Smbat's two audiences at Great Dastakert.* No other extant source of demonstrable authority, in Armenian or any other language, can match these two notices of Sebeos' for the detail given about honours and powers granted by a Sasanian king to an individual (at the first audience) or the signal marks of favour shown towards him in the special protocol devised for his reception (on his return from the east). The honours took the form of two titles (the Armenian *tanutēr* and the Persian honorific name, Khosrov-Shum) and investiture with insignia of five sorts: a hat, probably the low square cap which Khosrov II and his entourage wear in the reliefs of boar and stag hunts at Taq-i Bustan rather than the rounded tall hats worn by courtiers in early Sasanian reliefs; a robe, probably a caftan, richly decorated, of the sort illustrated on late Sasanian silver plates and in the Taq-i Bustan boar hunt; a bejewelled collar and a necklace, two traditional marks of status; finally several silver cushions, symbolic indications of a given degree of precedence at royal feasts and hence of court rank, evidently high in Smbat's case. Extraordinary powers were granted to him: together with the supreme command in the east, he was given delegated authority to appoint *marzpans* (provincial governors with military powers), and was granted simultaneously a probably lucrative civilian office in charge of a central financial ministry. His special status was made manifest by the presence of royal guards in his entourage and by the use of royal trumpets.

Sebeos' Great Dastakert, where this investiture ceremony took place, is called simply Dastakert by Theophanes, who describes it as Khosrov's main residence from the fall of Dara (in 604) until his precipitate flight to Ctesiphon-Veh Ardashir on 23 December 627 when Heraclius' army was approaching. Only part of the outer shell of the town has been found, 107 kilometres from Ctesiphon. Sarre and Herzfeld, who make the identification and ascribe its construction to Khosrov II, describe the extant stretch of its defences as 'the most powerful walls of baked bricks preserved in the Near East', the curtain wall being 16.6 metres thick with semi-circular towers at 17.7 metre intervals which project 10.2 metres. The outer hall of the palace, in which Smbat was received, was, it may be assumed, an *ayvan*, a large vaulted hall, open on one side, a characteristic feature of Sasanian palaces.

It was presumably to Great Dastakert that Smbat returned in triumph after his second campaign. The whole court and the royal guards were sent out a day's journey to escort him to the palace. His mount was a horse from the royal stables 'with royal équipage'. It may be conjectured that he changed from the horse to the richly caparisoned elephant for the ceremonial entry into the town and the procession to the *ayvan* of the palace. There he greeted the king, kissing his hand *before* doing obeisance. The acme of his career came with his designation as the third-ranking noble of the court.

(ii) *Date*. There may have been some indication in the lost life of the time spent by Smbat in Armenia after his retirement in 606/607 (perhaps in the form of notes about the start of successive springs, like that heading this notice), but, if so, it has dropped out in the process of excerpting. The date of Smbat's recall may, however, be inferred from that given later for his death, the twenty-eighth year of Khosrov's reign (June 616–June 617). The operations conducted by Smbat in the east seem to have occupied two campaigning seasons, with a formal inquiry into what had gone wrong in the first taking place in the intervening winter. Turkish forces were involved in the first campaign but not in the second. Smbat then returned for his second audience and spent a short time at court before his death. The campaigns may then be dated either to 614 and 615, Smbat's death occurring probably soon after June 616, or, marginally less likely, to 615 and 616, with his death coming in winter 616–617 or the following spring. It follows that Smbat spent at least seven years in retirement (607–613).

(iii) *The campaigns and their context*. There had been a significant change in the geopolitical position of the Sasanian empire in the 550s, when the Turks emerged as the dominant power in central Asia, east and west. Between 558 and 561 Persia's chief nomadic antagonists since the middle of the fifth century, the Hephthalites, were eliminated as an independent political entity in a joint Persian-Turkish campaign. Thenceforth the spheres of influence of the two powers abutted directly onto each other, and the Persians had to take as much account of the menacing presence of the Turks in the north as of the East Roman empire in the west. Sebeos, like Movses Daskhurants'i in his reports on episodes involving the Turks in the affairs of Transcaucasia 626–629, refers to the existence of a single supreme Turkish ruler, 'the great *Khak'an*, king of the regions of the north' (*contra* the consensus of modern scholarly opinion). He implies thereby that authority across the huge expanses of the Turkish empire was divided among several *khak'ans* but that one had acknowledged seniority or primacy. Chinese sources, which provide fuller coverage of events within China's horizon of vision, confirm that there was an overarching unity in the Turkish world, highlighting those episodes when the western *khak'an* intervened directly in China's steppe frontage (582–587 and 597–603). It follows that the formidable military resources of the central Asian steppes could be concentrated for major joint actions in east or west.

This is what seems to have happened in the second phase of the first campaign fought by Smbat as commander-in-chief of Persian forces in the north-east. So swift was the Turkish intervention and on such a scale that one must suppose that their forces were already mobilized and waiting in reserve, ready to pounce once the Kushans had provoked Persia into taking military action and had appealed for aid. If this hypothesis is correct, the army which Smbat had assembled, including a nucleus of Armenian cavalry removed from their regular station in Vrkan (where they had been serving since 599/600), was lured out into the north-east. Smbat and his immediate entourage of three hundred men, probably his staff and personal guards, were caught and trapped in an isolated fortified village in Khurasan. Smbat himself managed to escape only for a relief force, commanded by Datoyean, to suffer a crushing defeat during the evacuation of the trapped men. At this point Persian defences seem to have collapsed and Turkish forces swept over the Iranian plateau, coming close to Reyy and Ispahan in the west. It was at a time of their choosing that the Turks withdrew, the great *Khak'an* issuing the order to the field commander, the *Chembukh*. The inquiry instituted by Khosrov after this *débâcle* pinned the blame on

Datoyean and exonerated Smbat. He was able to salvage his reputation
in the second campaign when the Turks were conspicuous for their
absence. On their own the Kushans were no match for his army which
had received substantial reinforcements, and, after a victory in the field
(transformed by the biographer into the personal feat of Smbat),
Persian forces were able to launch a grand counter-raid into Kushan
territory west and north of the Hindu Kush.

Explanations for the Turkish act of aggression in 614 or 615 and for
their disappearance from the scene in the following year are hard to
find, for lack of evidence. Wider geopolitical circumstances may,
however, provide part of the answer to the first question (on the assumption that news travelled at reasonable speed and reasonably accurately
across Eurasia and hence that the great *Khak'an* was aware of developments in the sedentary empires flanking the steppes). Khosrov's commit-
ments in the west grew rather than diminished after his forces made the
vital break through the inner line of Roman defence on the Euphrates in
610. By 614 the Roman Near East lay at his mercy, there being no
prospect of serious orthodox counteraction from the Roman field army
after its decisive defeat in 613. In 614 his forces occupied northern
Palestine and captured Jerusalem. In 615 they struck through Asia
Minor and reached the Bosphorus. The Turks, it may he suggested, took
advantage of a thinning of Persian frontier forces in Khurasan, at a time
when they judged there was no possibility of substantial troop transfers
from the west. Khosrov had to resort to the desperate expedient of
calling an old, experienced general out of retirement and sending him
east with a scratch force.

Chinese sources provide the explanation for Turkish disengagement
in the second campaigning season. The great *Khak'an* K'i-min died in
the course of 614 and his son and successor, Shi-pi, reoriented Turkish
foreign policy. His priority was to consolidate the Turks' position *vis à
vis* China, now that the position of the Sui dynasty was weakening. The
new policy was announced by a dramatic act – a surprise attack in force
when the emperor was inspecting China's northern defences which
almost succeeded in capturing the emperor and led to his being besieged
for over a month in the city of Yen-men close to the frontier. This inaugurated several years of Turkish involvement in Chinese affairs. Smbat's
second campaign, which seems to have benefited from the shift of
Turkish forces from west to east consequent on this change of policy,
should therefore be dated to 615 rather than 616. The need to do every-

thing he could to revive his prestige in the Iranian heartland of his empire after the *débâcle* of 614 would also help to explain Khosrov's decision to launch a second offensive, in the west, aimed at the Roman capital, in 615.

(iv) *The Chembukh and Chepetukh.* This seems to be one and the same title, a mangled version of the title borne by the second-ranking Turkish *khak'an*, the *Yabgu Qagan*. It is rendered more accurately as *Jebu Khak'an* by Movses Daskhurants'i, who describes the holder as viceroy of the king of the north when, in 625, he welcomed Heraclius' proposal of a military alliance. Two years later, like Sebeos' *Chepetukh*, he led a large Turkish army through the Darband pass and invaded Transcaucasia. The degree of deformation to which the Turkish title has been subjected may be partly explained by its transmission across two language frontiers – from Turkish to Persian (the Persian forms are *Jepik*, *Jabbu* and *Sinjepuk*) and from Persian to Armenian.

(v) *The Kushans.* The inhabitants of a broad swathe of fractured country beyond the north-eastern frontier of the Sasanian empire, centring on the mountain ranges which splay out from the Hindu Kush, were called Kushans, after the name of the dynasty which had ruled an empire comprising those territories, a strip of land on the north bank of the Oxus and the north Indian plain, for nearly two centuries before the rise of the Sasanians. Sebeos mentions that several Kushan kings issued the appeal to the Turks during the 614 campaign, but then reports that a single king, at one point designated king of the Hephthalites, commanded their forces in 615. The temptation to emend Sebeos' text by deleting the plural from the first reference to kings should be resisted. For the first passage casts light on the political organization of the Kushans, the second on the military command during a particular campaign, which had to be in the hands of a single individual. In any case, two named Kushan kings feature in a previous episode (**97**).

Several valuable pieces of information are supplied about the Kushan lands in the period following the destruction of Hephthalite power. First, authority was dispersed (as was to be expected in what is now Afghanistan) among a number of local rulers. Second, one of them was the leader of the Hephthalites, at least some of whom had been allowed to stay, probably reduced to a status equal to their former subjects, in the lands which they had once ruled. Third, the Oxus formed the divide between that part of former Hephthalite territory which had been allocated to the Persians, after the destruction of the Hephthalite state by joint Turkish-Persian action, and the larger share appropriated by the Turks. Fourth, although the Kushans were subordinated to Persian authority (hence their later 'rebellion' which Sebeos mentions in the post-script to this passage), they were not integrated into the Sasanian empire nor were their lands reorganized into provinces. The outermost region of directly governed Persian territory remained Khurasan, with Marg and Margrot (Persian Marv and Marv-rud) acting as isolated forward bases in the steppes. Fifth, the Turks were careful to observe constitutional niceties in 614, refraining from crossing the Oxus and entering Persia's Kushan protectorate until they had received the Kushans' appeal for help.

(vi) Appended to the account of the last phase of Smbat Bagratuni's career is an apparently free-floating notice about a later rebellion of the Kushans and their participation in a Turkish-led invasion of Transcaucasia. This attack (and the negotiations which led to it) is described in considerable detail by Movses Daskhurants'i. It took place in 627 and was indeed intended to aid the emperor Heraclius in his second northern counter-offensive against the Persians. The Turkish army invaded Albania, then turned west into Iberia and laid siege to the main town, Tp'khis. There it was joined by the Roman army commanded by Heraclius and a summit meeting was held between emperor and *Yabgu Qagan*, to plan future joint action. Turkish preoccupation with China in the preceding decade may be indicated in the epithet 'Chinese' used of the *Yabgu Qagan*.

This notice carries Sebeos' foray forward yet deeper into the future. Its positioning in his text is surely not accidental but to be explained by an origin in the lost life of Smbat. There it would have served an obvious function, supplying a coda to Smbat's final exploit, demonstrating that the campaign of 615 not only obtained very high honours for him but achieved a durable success in the east, since it compelled the Kushans to respect Persian authority for more than a decade to come.

Sources; Theophanes 321–3; M.D., tr. Dowsett 83–8; Liu Mau-tsai I 65, 71.

Literature: E.H. Peck, 'Clothing IV. In the Sasanian Period', *E.Ir.* V, 745–52; Adontz/Garsoïan 214–18 (cushions); Dentzer, 'L'iconographie iranienne'; Gignoux, 'L'organisation administrative sasanide'; Sarre and Herzfeld, *Archäologische Reise* 76–93; D. Huff, 'Architecture III. Sasanian', *E.Ir.* II, 329–333; Marquart, *Eranšahr* 58–67, 71–4, 75–7, 80, 87–91; Stein, *Bas-Empire* 517–18; D. Sinor, 'The establishment and dissolution of the Türk empire', *Cambridge History of Early Inner Asia*, Cambridge, 1990, 297–310; Barfield, *Perilous Frontier* 131–45; Golden, *Khazar Studies* I, 187–190; A.D.H. Bivar, 'The History of Eastern Iran', *C.H.Iran* III, 1, 191–217; E.V. Zeimal, 'The Political History of Transoxiana', *C.H.Iran* III, 1, 247–9; Gyselen, *Géographie* 85, 88.

22: ch.30, **104–105**, *flight and death of Atat Khorkhoŕuni, 601/602.* Sebeos' narrative is clear but leaves us in the dark about Atat's motives. Some conjectures may, however, be offered on the basis of circumstantial evidence. Atat was serving with his troops in Thrace (his despatch there in 595 is reported at **88**) when he was summoned to the palace. It is unlikely that apprehension at what lay ahead in the Balkans deterred him from resuming his command, since, by the date of this episode (a year before Maurice's fall on 23 November 602, therefore late in 601 or, possibly, early in 602), the worst of the Balkan fighting was over and the Romans had inflicted a decisive defeat on the Avars (n.24 below). The importance evidently attached to his recapture (Maurice being ready to go to the brink of war to do so) suggests that the root cause was political, that he was involved in machinations against Maurice (this would also explain his subsequent eagerness to return, once Phocas had seized power).

A valuable glimpse is given into Roman internal security measures. Official authorization was required to cross from Europe to Asia (presumably across the Dardanelles), and movements within Asia Minor and western Armenia were monitored by road-blocks (the troops of various cities whom Atat encountered in eight or ten places). The general alert issued by the imperial authorities is unlikely to have outstripped Atat and his retinue who had a head start and were travelling at high speed. Hence there is no reason to suppose that special security measures were in force. Atat presumably remained in attendance at Khosrov's court, probably at Great Dastakert, once he had been rescued from Nakhchawan. Hence his procuring Arabian horses, for a second planned flight which would have taken him across the desert.

Literature: Whitby, *Emperor Maurice* 306–7.

23: ch.30, **105**, *Persian and Roman governors of Armenia, 591–602.* This list of Persian governors is a doublet of that given previously at **71**. To judge by the similar note included about the death of the first of them, Vndatakan (Ni)khorakan, it was taken from the same source – probably a list kept in the Catholicosate. It is hard to explain the divergences in the spelling of names, unless Sebeos was working fast and relying on memory when he slipped in this second notice. This would help account for the substitution of Dvin for Gaṙni as the site of the mutiny and the wrong total (thirteen years) given for the period of peace.

The Roman governors, holding the command of *Magister Militum per Armeniam*, were John Mystacon (already in post during the Persian civil war, 589–591 [**74, 77, 82, 83**]), Heraclius (in post in 594–595 when he concerted operations with the Persian authorities against the Vahewuni rebels and, jointly with Hamazasp Mamikonean, dealt effectively with their second rising in the Roman sector [**88–89** and n.15 above]; he was father of the emperor Heraclius) and Sormēn (not attested otherwise).

Literature: *PLRE* III, s.v. Heraclius 3, Ioannes 101, Suren.

24: ch.30, **105**, *planned transfer of Armenians to the Balkans, 602*. The great disturbance which prompted Priscus to hasten back to Constantinople may safely be identified with the military revolution, led by Phocas, which overthrew Maurice. Priscus evidently supported the change of regime, since he prospered under Phocas, holding the key metropolitan command of *Comes Excubitorum* throughout the reign and marrying a daughter of Phocas. A date late in 602 is thus obtained for Maurice's plan to introduce Armenian colonists into Thrace. The military service to which the 30,000 households scheduled for relocation were to be liable was not likely to be as onerous as in the past. For concerted action by the field armies commanded by Priscus and Comentiolus in 599 had countered the successful Avar attack of 598 (n.16 above) with an offensive into the Avar heartland north of the Danube. With the Avars on the defensive and Roman power impressed on the Slavs who had settled south of the Danube by the campaigns of 593–596, Maurice was able to consolidate the Roman position in 600 and 601, and now planned to reinforce it by introducing the Armenian colonists, while simultaneously taking the war to the Slavs on the north bank of the Danube, in winter when they would be more vulnerable (the first campaign of this sort was ordered for winter 602–603).

It is likely that Maurice intended to disperse the Armenian households in a number of separate military colonies, perhaps to oversee important concentrations of Slav settlers, perhaps to control strategic points. The Byzantine historian may be tempted to view Maurice's scheme as a precursor of a future general system under which estates were allocated to individual households on condition of hereditary cavalry service by one of their members. However, the terms under which the Armenians were resettled are not specified by Sebeos, and, even if individual households received individual land-grants, there is no reason to suppose that a new general principle of military recruitment was being established. The Armenians were probably viewed as latter-day *foederati* or *laeti*, foreigners who were subjected to special arrangements. In any case it is hard to find concrete evidence of a general system linking military service to tenure of particular estates before the tenth century.

Literature: *PLRE* III, s.v. Priscus 6; Whitby, *Emperor Maurice* 164–8; Haldon, *Seventh Century* 244–51.

II. SECTION II (106–134)

Introduction

Contemporaries, whether directly involved or far removed from the field of conflict, took a close interest in the last great war between the East Roman and Sasanian empires (I. Historical Background, above). A fair amount of what they saw and heard has survived in written form. The range of texts supplying information is impressive, although their quality is variable. At first sight, Sebeos should be ranked with the best of them. For his account is one of the longest and abounds with detailed information (above all precise chronological indications). It also fills a gaping hole left by other accounts concerning events in the Armenian theatre in the first phase of the fighting, and provides a Persian perspective to balance the Roman viewpoint which predominates otherwise. But no text should be used until it has been appraised properly. That is one of the principal tasks undertaken in this section of the historical commentary.

The process of appraisal is relatively simple, although in practice rather laborious. Information supplied by each notice in Sebeos' account can be compared with corresponding material in sources of demonstrable worth. Each successive test contributes to our understanding of Sebeos' working-methods and helps us reach a general view on his reliability. The principal sources which are taken as authoritative and used as external controls are the following:

(i) The *Chronicon Paschale*, a Greek text written by an official working in the Constantinopolitan patriarchate, concludes with a section covering a series of episodes of the war. This last section of contemporary history consists almost entirely of documents or extracts from documents, and as such is a source of inestimable value. It is one of two chronologically precise and accurate texts which can be used to check Sebeos' dates. It also reproduces a document, the Senate's letter to Khosrov written in 615, against which to test the accuracy of Sebeos' version of the Roman negotiating position that year (presented in the form of a speech from Heraclius to the general commanding the Persian army at Chalcedon).

(ii) Embedded in an apparently ill-organized universal chronicle which comes down to the year 724, written in Syriac and completed in 727, is a distinctive body of material taken from a source of high quality composed around 640 (excerpts translated, with discussion, in *West-Syrian Chronicles* 5–24). The *Chronicle to 724* is the second text packed with precious, trustworthy chronological indications, which can act as a control on Sebeos. It also provides an important item of information on the peace negotiations of 628–629.

(iii) The poet George of Pisidia watched the war from a privileged position. Like the anonymous author of the *Chronicon Paschale*, he was an official in the patriarchate at Constantinople. He was a protegé of the patriarch Sergius, and at times benefited from the emperor's patronage. In his secular poems he deals with two episodes of the war in considerable detail, as well as presenting a general *encomium* of Heraclius (in the *Heraclias*). He provides valuable material for the reconstruction of events and enables us to breathe something of the atmosphere of the time. Although there is little overlap between the subject-matter of the two narrowly focused poems (the military exercises held in Bithynia in 622 and the siege of Constantinople in 626) and what is covered by Sebeos, the *Heraclias* supplies enough information to enable us to check Sebeos' information on the opening of Heraclius' first counter-offensive in 624.

(iv) The *Chronicle* put together by Theophanes, an abbot of aristocratic extraction, probably between 811 and 814, presents the fullest historical narrative of the war in Greek. Although much of the material on the first two phases derives, at two removes, from an unreliable west Syrian source (probably Theophilus of Edessa – see Introduction to Section I above) and Theophanes can be shown to have been an overbold compiler, all too often seeking spurious chronological precision by cavalier editorial decisions, he incorporates material of the highest quality on Heraclius' two counter-offensives in the third phase. This material, which, in my view (Howard-Johnston, 'Official History'), is taken from a history of the war commissioned by Heraclius soon after its end, can be used as a control on Sebeos' apparently disjointed notices. Even so there are difficulties in placing some of Sebeos' reports in a defined context and making sense of what he says. It should be noted that Theophanes' dating by years from Creation lags one year behind reality from some time in the reign of Phocas (after 603) until at least 659 (*The Chronicle of Theophanes Confessor*, tr. C. Mango and R. Scott (Oxford,

1997), lxiv–lxvii). All his dates have been adjusted in this commentary to take account of this systematic discrepancy.

(v) The *History of the Caucasian Albanians* by Movses Daskhurants'i (already encountered in Section I) incorporates detailed information about the war taken from an early source of considerable value. With its attention focused on Caucasian Albania (what is now ex-Soviet Azerbaijan), it documents Heraclius' steppe diplomacy and the intervention of the Turks in the war. It can be used as a second point of comparison for judging Sebeos' account of the third phase.

These five texts, together with Sebeos, provide most of the material upon which any reconstruction of the war must be based. But a considerable amount of supplementary information can be garnered from a wide variety of other sources. As in the case of the five principal sources, they too can be used to check the quality and coverage of Sebeos' account. Most useful for this diagnostic purpose are the following: the *Life* of St Theodore of Sykeon (died 613), written by his disciple George; the *Life* of St Anastasius the Persian (martyred shortly before the fall of Khosrov in February 628), composed in 629–630 together with an account of the recovery of his relics from Mesopotamia, probably written by the same hand in 632 (Flusin, *St Anastase* I, 40–91, 98–107); a short, slight history covering the period from Phocas' *coup d'état* in 602 to 769 (with a gap from 641 to 668), written probably in his youth by the patriarch Nikephoros, which contains valuable material on international relations; the two east Syrian chronicles which have been exploited in Section I, the *Khuzistan Chronicle* (covering roughly the same period as Sebeos, with a taste for gossip and wide-ranging interests in both ecclesiastical and secular history) and the *Seert Chronicle* (largely but not entirely preoccupied with church and monastic history); the *Georgian Chronicles*; a set of texts on the siege and sack of Jerusalem in 614 and the deportations which followed, which bear the stamp of Roman propaganda (Strategius); the *Annals* of Tabari, the premier Abbasid historian, who quarried high quality material on the fall of Khosrov from the Persian *Khwadaynamag*, 'Book of Lords'; and, finally, the secular component of the history written by Dionysius of Tel-Mahre in the first half of the ninth century, a text in general of dubious value for the first half of the seventh century but with nuggets of reliable information (long extract translated, with discussion, in *West-Syrian Chronicles* 85–221).

Editions/translations: listed by author/title in Bibliography, I. Texts.

Literature: cited editions / translations; works cited in Introduction to Section I; Whitby, 'A New Image'; Flusin, *St Anastase* II, 131–40 (Strategius); Howard-Johnston, 'Al-Tabari'.

25: ch.31, **106**, *Phocas' coup, 602* (T'.A. 88). Phocas' seizure of power (he was crowned on 23 November 602) is correctly placed in Khosrov's 14th year (which began in June 602) but occurred just after the end of Maurice's 20th (August 602). Sebeos is probably right to suggest that the mutinous Balkan troops not only chose Phocas as their leader but designated him their candidate for the throne from the first. For he was raised on a shield, a ceremony which had long since acquired clear imperial connotations. The rumour that Maurice's eldest son, Theodosius, managed to escape is registered by John of Antioch and Theophylact Simocatta, and taken to be true by both east Syrian chronicles. No tangible evidence of Theodosius' death was produced by Phocas' regime as in the case of Maurice and his five other sons (whose severed heads were put on public display outside Constantinople, according to *Chron. Pasch.*). The statement that the army returned to its station in Thrace, which is unique to Sebeos, indicates, if true, that Phocas remained committed to Maurice's Slav pacification programme.

Sources: J.A. 36–7; T.S. VIII 6–15; *Khuz. Chron.* 15–16; *Chron. Seert* 517–20; *Chron. Pasch.* 693–4; Dionysius 119–20.

Literature: Whitby, *Emperor Maurice* 24–7.

26: ch.31, **106**, *disturbances in the Roman empire, 608–610.* This is a muddled and misleading notice. Sebeos has leapt forward to the gathering political crisis of 608–610, and has reversed the true order of events. In reality the crisis was triggered by the rebellion of Heraclius senior (father of the future emperor) in 608 and culminated in an outbreak of rioting in the capital as it came under attack from a fleet led by Heraclius junior in October 610. The two key intermediate stages were the take-over of Egypt and widespread disturbances in the other provinces of the Near East. It looks as if Sebeos has decided to bunch together information which reached him about Roman domestic history in Phocas' reign, and has then taken liberties as he devised his own succinct presentation. There are also two errors of detail: (i) Heraclius senior's command has been changed from Africa to 'the regions of Alexandria'; apart from the oddness of this expression, the following statement that he took over the land of Egypt by force clearly implies that it was not part of his allocated command; (ii) Bonus, a key figure in Heraclius' regime (*PLRE* III, s.v. Bonus 5), has been confused with Bonosus (*PLRE* III, s.v. Bonosus 2), whom Phocas sent to bring the Near East under control and whose brutal methods were denounced by the opposition; the evident exaggeration of the scale of the slaughter instituted by him in Sebeos' account derives ultimately from Heraclian propaganda.

Literature: Olster, *Usurpation* 101–138; Borkowski, *Alexandrie II* 23–43; Dagron/Déroche, 'Juifs et chrétiens' 18–22.

27: ch.31, **106–107**, *Persian actions in Roman Mesopotamia in 603* (cf. T'.A., 88). Sebeos returns to the immediate consequences of Phocas' coup: Nersēs, probably still *Magister Militum per Orientem* (*PLRE* III, s.v. Narses 10), rebelled against the new regime, installing himself and his troops in the heavily fortified city of Urha (Edessa), which was within striking distance of the Persian frontier; the following spring (603) the Persians invaded Roman Mesopotamia in force, laid siege to Dara and came to his aid. *Khuz.Chron.* and *Chron.Seert* confirm that Khosrov took personal charge of these operations, thus breaking with the recently established convention that the king should keep his distance from operations in the field. It signalled his public commitment to the cause of avenging his benefactor Maurice, as well as his confidence in the outcome, now that civil war was disrupting Roman defensive preparations. The scale of the operations, the evident high priority assigned to the capture of Dara and above all the presence of the king indicate that the main body of the Persian army was concentrated in the south. It follows that the force allocated to the Armenian theatre, whose fate is described in ch.32, had a subsidiary probably diversionary function.

The account of Khosrov's victory outside Edessa, his subsequent entry into the city and Nersēs' formal presentation of Theodosius as legitimate pretender to the imperial throne is unique to Sebeos. The rubbishing of the pretender as Nersēs' stooge should not be taken too seriously. The story looks very much like a piece of black propaganda from Phocas' regime, putting its own gloss on a ceremony which did take place. There is an inherent implausibility in the suggestion that both Khosrov and the Edessan public were duped in this way by Nersēs. Rather more credence should be attached to the Persian version, best represented in *Khuz.Chron.*, that Khosrov had crowned Theodosius, whether genuine or impostor, in Ctesiphon before setting off for Nisibis and the frontier and had put the Persian forces nominally under his command. If this was closer to the truth, the ceremony in Edessa probably had a constitutional function: a high-ranking Roman field commander, appointed by the emperor Maurice and loyal to him, was placing his fugitive son or putative son formally and publicly under Khosrov's protection; he was thereby inviting Khosrov to intervene in Roman affairs and restore the legitimate pretender to the Roman throne.

Corroboration that the siege of Dara was protracted is provided by *Chron.724*, where its fall is dated to 604, as well as by the important chronological co-ordinate given at **108** below (Dara was still under siege at the opening of the second season of campaigning in Armenia). Sebeos' figure of one and half years may therefore be preferred to the dating of *Khuz.Chron.* (the city falls in Khosrov's 14th regnal year, i.e. before the end of June 603), and the contradictory indications of *Chron.Seert* (the siege lasts nine months, until shortly before the death of the Nestorian Catholicos Sabrisho [securely dated to summer 604]). For the most part Khosrov probably directed siege operations from the comfort of Nisibis nearby, where, according to *Khuz.Chron.*, he gave an audience to the aggrieved *rad* (judge) of Syarazur.

Theophanes supplies some more information on the circumstances of Nersēs' death: 'the other army' which attacked and captured Edessa consisted largely of troops transferred from the Balkans in winter 603–604 after Phocas negotiated a peace treaty with the Avars; Nersēs managed to escape from Edessa to Hierapolis; later he gave himself up in return for a guarantee of safety which was soon disregarded.

Sources: Theophanes 291–3; Dionysius 120–2; *Khuz.Chron.* 16–18; *Chron.Seert* 498–504, 520; *Chron.724* 17.

Literature: Whitby, 'The Persian King'; Flusin, *St Anastase* II, 106–110, 120–1.

28: ch.32, **107–109**, *operations in Armenia in 603 and 604*. This notice, like those which follow on later Persian offensives in Armenia in the first phase of the war, is unique to Sebeos. Unless there are obvious signs of confusion in the story presented or elements which are hard to square with what is reported of events elsewhere in other sources, the information will be treated as trustworthy.

In the north Persian forces were mobilized soon after news came of Phocas' coup, in the difficult conditions of an Armenian winter, and menacingly close to the Roman frontier, which now ran just to the west of Dvin. This looks like a move intended to deceive the Romans into expecting the main attack in spring 603 in the north, with the object of preventing them from sending reinforcements to Mesopotamia. The Roman regional field army duly mobilized in its turn, taking up a position in the western sector of the large alluvial plain of Dvin, on the frontier or very close to it. The decisive victory which it won demonstrated what Roman forces could achieve if they were not divided.

The strategic balance in Armenia shifted dramatically in the second campaigning season. The Romans were on the defensive from the first in 604. Their prime object seems to have been to protect, insofar as possible, the large plain in Vanand and Shirak, one of three rich agricultural areas in the sector of Persarmenia ceded to them in 591 (the other two, Bagrewand and Basean, were to come under attack in 605). The population of 33 villages was evacuated to the fortress of Erginay (modern Arkina) on the river Akhurean, the only natural line of defence in Shirak. The regional army, its numbers perhaps depleted (it may well have contributed to the reinforcements rushed to Mesopotamia that year), camped nearby, at first to the east of the river, then on its west bank. The Persians were evidently deploying a larger force in this theatre than in 603 (hence Nersēs was left to fend for himself in the south), it being imperative to reverse the defeat of 603.

Literature: Hewsen, *AŠX* 69 (map xxiv), 210–11, 214–15, 218–19; Sinclair, *Eastern Turkey* I, 425.

29: ch.32, **109–110**, *Senitam Khosrov's campaign in Armenia in 605*. The arrival of a new commander signals the start of a new campaigning season. There are two juxtaposed notices. The first covers operations which took place in southern Armenia, where a Roman force defended Bagrewand, the elongated plain where the Aratsani river (modern Murat Su) gathers its headwaters. These are treated in exceptional detail, probably because the Roman general at the centre of the story was an Armenian, Tʿēodos Khorkhoṙuni, and his behaviour had a decisive influence on the outcome. Then comes a brief notice summarizing the main achievements of Senitam Khosrov that year: (i) defeat and expulsion of the Romans from Basean, the fertile plain through which flows the upper Araxes; and (ii) acquisition of four named places, each of which is designated a walled town (*kʿalakʿ*) – Angł (captured in the course of operations in Bagrewand), Gaylatukʿ (at the north-west extremity of Gogovit, across the mountains to the north-east of Bagrewand), Erginay (captured but not garrisoned in 604), and Tskhnakert in Mesopotamia (near Dara). The succinct presentation of this notice is what might be expected of a government bulletin. Such a provenance would also account for the demonstrable exaggeration of the importance of the places captured: Erginay is classified as a fortress, *berd*, in the preceding fuller passage in which it features (**108**), while Angł is described four times as a fortress as against once as a town in the first of these two notices (**109–110**).

The second notice makes it clear that Senitam Khosrov was assigned the supreme command along the whole western frontier after Khosrov relinquished it at the end of the 604 campaigning season. His presence in the north shows that Armenia remained the main theatre of combat in 605. In the south the war appears to have subsided, the Persians only making one gain (Tskhnakert) which consolidated their position around Dara.

Senitam Khosrov launched a two-pronged offensive, along each of the natural lines of attack across Armenia. A clue to his strategy is supplied by the linking phrase which introduces the second notice: this places the battle in Basean after the invasion of Bagrewand, a sequence which is confirmed by the order in which the three Armenian gains of the year are then listed. The following reconstruction may be proposed. The initial thrust south of Mount Ararat into the Aratsani valley was a subsidiary operation entrusted to a subordinate commander (we would expect Senitam Khosrov to have been named had he been the general who detained T'ēodos Khorkhoṙuni after the capitulation of Angł). Apart from the rich prize of Bagrewand itself, this attack brought immediate military benefits: it diverted attention from the Araxes valley where the main blow was to be delivered, raised the disturbing possibility that the Roman forces in Basean might be outflanked, and cannot but have had a depressing effect on their morale. The main Persian army, presumably under the direct command of Senitam Khosrov, then advanced up the Araxes valley, defeated the Romans in Basean and drove them back over the Araxes-Euphrates watershed which had formed the pre-591 frontier. Victory in the field was followed up by the extension of Persian authority into the hinterland of Bagrewand and, probably, by the installation of garrisons at three key strongholds listed as the year's gains in Armenia. Bagrewand, Gogovit and Shirak were thus being brought under permanent Persian control.

The detailed account of operations in Bagrewand calls for some additional comments. As in 604, the Romans took up two defended positions, which were not far apart, in the hope of catching the Persians between two fires. A village on the bank of the Aratsani was taken over, remodelled and incorporated into the perimeter of what became a heavily fortified camp. Nearby lay a fortress, which, it may be assumed, was secured by a detachment from the army. A clear distinction is drawn between the camp with its fortification (*amrut'iwn*) and the fortress (*berd*) which is also designated a city (at the time of its capitulation). In the event the Romans were easily overcome by a lethal combination of surprise and treachery in the high command.

It was naturally the permanent fortress which the Persians garrisoned after the departure of its Roman defenders. At this stage the fortress is at last given a name, Angł, and duly reappears in the list of gains given by the second notice as the walled town of Angł. It follows therefore that something is amiss in the opening sentence of the first notice which identifies the village where the fortified camp was established as Angł. It may be suggested that a few words have dropped out between 'the village' and 'called Angł', the phrase originally reading 'the village called *X near the fortress* called Angł'.

Literature: Hewsen, *AŠX* 69 (map xxiv), 210–11, 213–14, 215–16, 218, 265; Sinclair, *Eastern Turkey* I, 398–401, II, 226–8.

30: ch.33, **110–112**, *renewal of Persian offensive operations in 607.* Sebeos supplies unique information (mainly about events in Armenia) and a general framework within which specific events reported by other sources may be arranged. A key date is given, the 18th regnal year of Khosrov (June 606–June 607), for the start of the second offensive (datable therefore to spring 607), which involved co-ordinated attacks in great force north and south of the Taurus. No other source reports the recruiting campaign, datable to the preceding year (606), which enabled the Persians to sustain action on this scale, or the last two battles fought in Armenia, the first in 607 at Du and Ordru on the old Persian-Roman frontier, the second probably in 608, which repelled a Roman counter-attack on the plain of Karin (Theodosiopolis). The information about Theodosiopolis' capitulation in 607 and the deportation of its population in 609/610 is also unique to Sebeos.

The account of military operations is highly selective, attention being focused on the Persians' prime targets in each theatre, Urha (Edessa) in

Mesopotamia and Karin (Theodosiopolis) in Armenia. The capitulation of Edessa (dated to 609 by *Chron. Pasch.* and *Chron.724*) was rapidly followed by that of the other cities of Mesopotamia, and, in August 610, by a military thrust into northern Syria. Two of the cities captured soon after Antioch are named in other sources (Apamea and Emesa). The Persian-sponsored pretender was deployed to good effect in Armenia, endorsement of his claims by a deputation of leading citizens providing the reason or pretext for Theodosiopolis' capitulation. Once Theodosiopolis was secured and a garrison installed, Persian forces were able to range far and wide over Roman Armenia, taking the key stronghold of Citharizon (Dzit'aŕich) in the south, which commanded the Arsanias valley and an important pass across the Armenian Taurus, and capturing three other strongholds as they advanced west into the north-east segment of the Anatolian plateau. The new general, Shahēn, whose arrival in Armenia signals the start of the next campaigning season (608), probably concentrated at first on consolidating Persian control over western Armenia, before making a new forward thrust into Cappadocia (the fall of Caesarea is securely dated to summer 611).

Sebeos' presentation of events in Armenia may be faulted on two counts. He breaks up the chronological order by bunching together information concerning Theodosiopolis, and, by confining his coverage to notable gains, he gives the impression that the invasion of Cappadocia took place much earlier than it did.

Sources: *Chron. Pasch.* 699; *Chron.724* 17; Dionysius 127 (cf. Theophanes 299); *Khuz. Chron.* 24; Garitte, *Narratio* ch.112 (with commentary 261–3); *Vie de Théodore* ch.153; Nikephoros ch.2.

Literature: Howard-Johnston, 'Procopius'; Bryer/Winfield, *Pontos* I, 20–39.

31: ch.34, **112–113**, *seizure of power by Heraclius (October 610), embassy to Khosrov and military action in 611–612* (cf. T'.A. 88–89, including additional passage giving Heraclius' message to Khosrov in direct speech). A set of four well-ordered notices provides information, some of it unique to Sebeos, on key events. (i) Heraclius' enthronement (5 October 610) is placed, correctly, in Khosrov's 22nd regnal year (June 610–June 611). The constitutional position is reported correctly: the elder Heraclius, governor of Egypt as well as north Africa since 609 (n.26 above), was formal leader of the revolutionary forces; it was by virtue of the consulship which he had assumed when he first rebelled and with the backing of the Senate that he installed his son, the younger Heraclius, on the throne. Sebeos is wrong, however, to suggest that there was no resistance to the new regime (it centred on Phocas' brother Comentiolus [*PLRE* III, s.v. Comentiolus 2], army commander on the northern front, and was confined to Asia Minor in the following winter). (ii) The embassy sent to announce Heraclius' accession to the Persians with the customary gifts was evidently intended to put out peace feelers. Roman weakness was acknowledged in the solicitous tone adopted, as Sebeos notes, in Heraclius' letters. Khosrov severed diplomatic relations in the simplest and most brutal of ways, and reiterated (presumably to his own court) his backing for Theodosius. (iii) Heraclius supervised the operations, of summer 611, which penned Shahēn's force back into Caesarea. The unnamed general to whom he delegated the subsequent blockade was Priscus, one of Maurice's senior generals who had been a pillar of Phocas' regime. He may have held the lucrative post of *curator* (head of a *domus divina* or group of imperial estates). But it is surprising to find him so designated in a military context. It is possible that the title assigned to him by Sebeos is a corruption of the grand court dignity *curopalate*, which Domnitziolus, nephew of Phocas, is known to have held (*PLRE* III, s.v. Domnitziolus 2) and which Heraclius bestowed on his brother Theodore (*PLRE* III, s.v. Theodorus 163) after Priscus' disgrace. (iv) The break-out of Shahēn and his men from Caesarea after a year's blockade was a serious blow to the prestige of the new regime and led to the immediate disgrace of Priscus.

Sources: *Chron.Pasch.* 699–701; G.P., *In Heraclium ex Africa redeuntem*; J.A. 37–8; *Vie de Théodore* chs153–154; Nikephoros chs1–2; Theophanes 295–9; Dionysius 126–7.

Literature: Grierson, 'Consular Coinage'; Kaegi, 'New Evidence'; *PLRE* III, s.v. Priscus 6; Kaplan, *Les hommes* 140–2.

32: ch.34, **113**, *Shahēn's expedition to Pisidia (617) and a list of Persian governors of Armenia (612–627)*. The first of these two notices is out of place. While it may be tempting to associate the capture of Melitene with Shahēn's first thrust to the west (608–611), this cannot be true of the second stage of the campaign which saw him meet Shahrvaraz in Pisidia. So deep a double invasion of Asia Minor was only feasible once the Persians had reached the sea beyond Antioch (late in 610) and had taken firm control of Cilicia (in 613). If the two senior commanders involved are tracked through the second phase of the war, a date may be conjectured.

The years 614 and 616 may be ruled out since Shahrvaraz was fully occupied in Syria and Palestine, dealing with inter-confessional violence in Jerusalem in 614 (n.34 below) and responsible, it may be surmised, for the restoration of order in Palestine in 616, which enabled the acting head of the Jerusalem patriarchate to authorize the reoccupation of monasteries in the Judaean desert (n.35 below). Shahēn, as will be seen in note 37 below, was in Asia Minor in 615 but in the north-west rather than the south-west, from where he was urgently recalled to deal with a Roman counter-attack in Armenia. The first year when both generals could have been present in Pisidia is therefore 617. This is a more likely date than 618 when the Persians were probably fully engaged in preparing for the invasion of Egypt which took place in 619 (*Chron.724* 17). The double attack may perhaps be envisaged as a massive feint designed to draw Roman attention away from Egypt. Some corroboration for the earlier date is provided by the fire-damage observed at Sardis for which a *terminus post quem* of 615/616 can be obtained from coins sealed in the destruction layer.

Juxtaposition of this notice with a list of Persian governors of Armenia may suggest an explanation of this editorial error. Sebeos includes three such lists in his text, the first and longest covering the period 572–602 (**70–71** with n.7 above), the second a doublet for the years of peace 591–602 (**105** with n.23 above). The five senior commanders named in the course of the narrative of operations in the years 603–612 in the northern theatre probably fill the gap before the tenure of Shahrayenpet (first mentioned at **111**), who heads the third list. His immediate predecessor seems to have been Shahēn (mentioned immediately beforehand at **111**), the hand-over perhaps taking place soon after Shahēn's return from Caesarea in 612. Sebeos appears to have confused this with a later episode when Shahēn was summoned to court from somewhere else and was given his orders for 617.

The hypothesis that active military commanders and governors of Armenia form a single series, if it is accepted, leads to an unsurprising further conclusion: at a time of war civil administrative powers and military command were combined in this important frontier region of the Sasanian empire. This was certainly true of the last two governors in the list, of whom something is known: Shahraplakan (Sarablangas at Theophanes 308–10) took up his appointment in 625 and was engaged in the unsuccessful operations against Heraclius of that year (n.39 below); Ěṙoch Vehan (Razates at Theophanes 317–19) was appointed in 627, pursued Heraclius across the Zagros in October and was killed at the battle of Nineveh on 12 December (**126** with n.42 below).

It is hard to know what to make of the enigmatic phrase about an engagement fought and won by Shahrapłakan in Persia. It could refer to fighting in Atrpatakan in 625, but no Persian victory that year is recorded in any other source.

Literature: Foss, 'Persians' (proposing a different chronology for Persian attacks on Asia Minor and crediting them with causing lasting damage to urban life); Foss, 'Sardis'.

33: ch.34, 114, *Philippicus' counter-thrust into Armenia, 615.* Philippicus (*PLRE* III, s.v. Philippicus 3), senior general and brother-in-law of Maurice, retired to the monastery which, together with his wife Gordia, he had founded at Chrysopolis in 594, *after*, not before, the death of Maurice. He was recalled to active service by Heraclius immediately after his seizure of power, and was sent to negotiate with Phocas' brother Comentiolus in Asia Minor in the winter of 610–611 (n.31 above). The counter-stroke described by Sebeos may be identified with that reported in the *Life* of St Anastasius: the saint served on Shahēn's campaign to Chalcedon in 615 (n.37 below) and returned to the east with the Persian army, when Shahēn was drawn back in pursuit of Philippicus who had entered Persian territory. Sebeos fills in the details missing from the brief notice in the *Life*: Philippicus' diversionary campaign was directed at the administrative heart of Persarmenia in the Araxes valley; he stayed put, close to Vałarshapat, until the very last moment, when Shahēn's army, after a long forced march, was poised to attack; then he slipped away to the north, passed round the back of Mount Aragats (a huge, relatively low volcano [4,090m], which is Mount Ararat's pendant to the north of the Araxes), and sped west over the plain of Vanand, past Karin (Theodosiopolis) and down the upper Euphrates valley. The Persian army was too exhausted to pursue him closely. Instead Shahēn rested his men and then withdrew back to the base, south of the Taurus, from which he had set off on his expedition to Chalcedon.

The Roman viewpoint of Sebeos' notice points to use, direct or indirect, of a Roman source. Sebeos fails to relate it to his

Armenian/Persian material and introduces the notice extracted from it at the wrong place in his account.

Flusin is ready, after some hesitation, to identify as one and the same the episodes reported by the *Life* and Sebeos. He is also ready to countenance *two* attacks by Shahēn on Chalcedon in successive years, the second of which resulted in its capture – attaching too much weight to the presence of two notices to this effect in adjacent year-entries (615/616 and 616/617) in Theophanes' *Chronicle*. The notices are better interpreted as doublets referring to a single episode, that of 615.

Sources: *Chron.Pasch.* 695; *Vie de Théodore* ch.152; Flusin, *St Anastase* I, 48–9; Theophanes 301.

Literature: Hewsen, *AŠX* 69 (map xxiv), 214–15, 217–18; Flusin, *St Anastase* II, 83–93.

34: ch.34, **114–116**, *Persian occupation of Cilicia, submission of Palestine and fall of Jerusalem, 613–614* (cf. T'.A. 89 on the fall of Jerusalem). Events are reported in chronological order. Much of the information given is unique to Sebeos. Without it, the modern historian would be hard put to piece together a crucial military episode in the war and to make sense of Persian policy in Palestine:

(i) Heraclius' eight-month-old son, Heraclius Constantine, was crowned co-emperor on 22 January 613.

(ii) Later that year Heraclius took personal charge of a second major counter-offensive, intended to dislodge the Persians from their north Syrian bridgehead. It can be securely placed after the disappointing end of the Caesarea blockade in 612 and before the Persian advance into Palestine late in 613 (which took place, according to Sebeos, some months before the start of the Jerusalem crisis, itself securely datable to April/May 614 [see below]). Apart from an incidental reference in the *Life* of St Theodore, there is no other description of the Persians' victory outside Antioch and their subsequent advance into Cilicia despite a reverse suffered by the vanguard. Heraclius abandoned orthodox warfare for several years.

(iii) Sebeos' is the only connected and relatively dispassionate account of the Persians' entry into Palestine. He distinguishes between a military advance to the provincial capital, Caesarea, which was occupied, and a much wider extension of political authority. The latter was achieved bloodlessly. With no prospect of rescue by a Roman field army and with growing internal problems, as the Jews of Palestine came out openly in support of the Persians and there were outbreaks of communal violence, the authorities in Palestine had no choice but to submit voluntarily. The arrangements made for the remote control of Jerusalem through a small military/political commission may have been replicated at other large population centres.

(iv) The Jerusalem crisis has been examined closely by Flusin. Sebeos is, as might be expected, more candid and more dispassionate than Strategius, a monk of the St Sabas lavra at the time, whose account, written originally in Greek, only survives in Georgian and Arabic translations. While Strategius blames the circus factions in general terms (Sebeos' 'the youths of the city'), Sebeos details the actions of theirs which provoked the crisis, first their killing of the members of the Persian commission in Jerusalem, then their instigation of a pogrom which led the Jews to appeal to Shahrvaraz at Caesarea for help. The principal disagreement between the texts is chronological, Strategius dating Shahrvaraz's capture of the city 20 days after the start of the siege on 13 or 15 April (i.e. 3 or 5 May), Sebeos offering two alternative dates, 19 May (28th Margats') and 9 April (ten days after Easter which fell on 30 March in 614). If Easter is taken to be a slip for Ascension (8 May in 614), as suggested by RWT (footnote 429 to **115**), Sebeos' two dates almost coincide (18 and 19 May). Flusin hesitates between the two chronologies, but preference should probably be given to Sebeos', since it has the backing of the Palestine-Georgian liturgical calendar (commemorations of 'the fire of Jerusalem' on 17 May and 'the devastation of Jerusalem' on 20 May) and *Chron. Pasch.* (a notice of the author's own composition laments the fall of Jerusalem which is loosely dated to June 614, probably the time when the news reached him in Constantinople). It may perhaps be inferred from the relatively unemotional tone of Sebeos' notice that it derives from a Persian source, possibly a copy of a communiqué kept in the archives of the Catholicosate at Dvin.

(v) The following notice about Persian behaviour after the fall of the city probably had a different, Christian, provenance. Hence the stress on the 17,000 dead (apparently corrupted to 57,000 in T'.A. and inflated to a body-count of over 60,000 in some versions of Strategius and 90,000 in Dionysius). The search for the fragments of the True Cross, involving the torture of clergy, is also reported by *Khuz. Chron.* and Tabari.

(vi) Sebeos is silent about events after the sacking of the city. The screening of the surviving population outside the city, in which Jews sought out hitherto undiscovered ringleaders of the pogrom, and the deportation to Mesopotamia of a considerable number of people, including the patriarch Zacharias and those with useful trades, are reported by Strategius and the east and west Syrian sources. Whether Shahrvaraz reverted to his policy of managing Jerusalem and the rest of Palestine at a distance from his base at Caesarea or now introduced a garrison into Jerusalem is left unclear.

Sources: *Chron.Pasch.* 703–5; *Vie de Théodore* ch.166; Strategius; Garitte, *Calendrier* 67; *Khuz.Chron.* 24; Tabari, tr. Nöldeke 290–1; Dionysius 128; Theophanes 300–1; Sophronius, *Anacreontica* xiv.

Literature: Mango, 'Temple Mount' 3–4; Dagron/Déroche, 'Juifs et chrétiens' 22–6; Flusin, *St Anastase* II, 78–9, 129–71.

35: chs34–35, **116–118**, *reconstruction in Jerusalem 614–616/617* (cf. T'.A. 89). The change of policy on the part of the Persians, which also resulted in improved conditions for the deportees, was probably a response to pressure from the important Christian communities of Mesopotamia and their powerful patrons at court who included Shirin. Less value should be attached to the explanatory note introducing Modestos' letter to Komitas than to the text of the letter itself. For the letter looks like an authentic document, translated into Armenian from a Greek original (hence the transliteration of the Greek terms for archbishop and metropolitan rather than their Armenian equivalents in the heading). Its accuracy can be tested by reference to the specific sites where reconstruction is reported to have taken place: the list (Holy Sepulchre, Golgotha, the 'mother of churches' at Sion, and the church of the Ascension) tallies exactly with that given by Antiochus, another monk of the St Sabas lavra, in a letter written probably late in 616 (cf. also the commemoration of Modestos' building work in the Palestine-Georgian liturgical calendar). Modestos' letter is datable relatively early in the period of Persian occupation of Palestine: this is implied by the opening, with its reference to the arrival of a group of Armenian pilgrims (apparently the first to reach Jerusalem since the city's sack) and the consolation which they gave; hence there is no reason to doubt the date indicated by the positioning of the letter and Komitas' reply in Sebeos' text, between the fall of Jerusalem in 614 and the discovery of the relics of St Hṙipsimē at Vałarshapat in 616/617 (**121**).

The start of reconstruction in Jerusalem may probably be associated with the imposition of direct Persian rule over the whole of Palestine. This can tentatively be dated to the first half of 616 (on the hypothesis that it brought about the restoration of order in the vicinity of Jerusalem, which allowed Modestos to authorize the St Sabas monks to reoccupy their lavra two years and two months after the fall of the city). Modestos' letter is carefully phrased. The best possible gloss is put on Persian actions. The blame for setting fire to the holy places is transferred (rightly or wrongly) to the Jews and the impression is given that reconstruction of the named key sites was largely complete at the time of writing. This is highly unlikely, if the letter was written, as it appears to have been, within a year of the start of the work. It is also contradicted by Modestos' final plea for help in rebuilding the sites of the Passion, which implies that much remained to be done. There is also a studious vagueness about the measures taken against the Jews: Sebeos seems to have been misled into supposing and suggesting, in his introductory note, that all Jews were expelled from Jerusalem, whereas two sentences in the letter imply rather that it was Jews wishing to move into Jerusalem who were being banned from doing so and who then tried to bribe their way in.

The Persian authorities were, it seems, trying to strike a balance between Christians and Jews in Palestine. They had no choice but to strive their utmost to do so, since otherwise they ran the risk of alienating one of two important interest groups in Mesopotamia, either the Christians or Babylonian Jewry. Modestos' letter, which receives some corroboration from other, inferior sources, shows that their policy was to maintain the *status quo* in Jerusalem. There were two strands to their policy: in the first place, Jews with established residence were allowed to stay in Jerusalem but others were banned from migrating and settling in the city (the demolition was also ordered of a small synagogue which had been built on the esplanade of the Temple Mount); second, in an effort to regain the esteem of Christians in Palestine and elsewhere, a programme of rebuilding damaged Christian shrines was instituted and the news of it was disseminated through inscriptions.

Sources: Antiochus Monachus; Garitte, *Calendrier* 110–11.

Literature: Mango, 'Temple Mount' 4–6; Flusin, *St Anastase* II, 97–118, 171–80; Dagron/Déroche, 'Juifs et chrétiens' 26–8.

36: ch.36, **118–121**, *Komitas' letter to Modestos*. There is no reason to doubt the authenticity of this letter, which picks up and elaborates the theme of consolation running through Modestos' letter and touches on the two main items of news reported by him, the rebuilding programme (mentioned near the beginning) and the restrictions put on Jewish immigration into Jerusalem (alluded to at the end). There is nothing original in Komitas' general line that disaster is an admonition from God and therefore presupposes an underlying affection for mankind which will show itself in due course as forgiveness. It was indeed the principal theme of the sermon delivered by the patriarch Zacharias to the deportees from Jerusalem (Strategius XIII 21–76).

An important historical inference may be drawn from the reference to Mount Sinai: by the time the Armenian pilgrims made their journey (perhaps at Easter 617), the Persian authorities had succeeded in establishing good order in the desert beyond Palestine. This must have entailed instituting stable relations of clientage with Beduin tribes along the desert frontage of the sown lands. It is unclear whether the antecedent Roman system was reactivated or a new Persian scheme was put in its place.

The joy expressed in the introductory paragraph seems incommensurate with the news just received from Jerusalem. Indeed the status of the paragraph is rather puzzling: it is not a historical notice composed by Sebeos, like that introducing Modestos' letter, but looks like an extract from some other contemporary text. If this were so, it might be prudent to attend to the chapter heading (which is present in the manuscript) and to attribute the short extract to a quite separate letter addressed by Komitas to Heraclius when he was in Jerusalem – i.e. on the occasion, in March 630, when he restored the True Cross to the city. This would explain its exultant tone. Sebeos would, on this hypothesis, be guilty of a serious error, in associating two quite unrelated documents.

37: ch.38, **122–123**, *Persian advance to Chalcedon (615), Roman peace proposals* (cf. T'.A. 89–91, including an additional passage [quoted in footnotes 492 and 493 to **122–123**] in which Heraclius offers land, walled cities and treasures to the Persians, and some additional information [probably incorrect, see n.33 above] about subsequent events). This is an important and revealing notice. It deals in the main with an expedition led by Shahēn which reached Chalcedon (it is unclear whether or not the city was occupied) and with the successful efforts of Heraclius to re-open diplomatic communications with Khosrov. The episode is securely dated to 615 by *Chron.Pasch* , which gives a brief summary of events and then appends the text of a letter subsequently sent by the Senate to open formal negotiations. A notice in the *Short History* of Nikephoros is embellished with direct speech (from Shahēn) in the revised and stylistically upgraded version of the chapters. The episode also features in the *Life* of St Anastasius, since he took part in the expedition, serving in the cavalry. Little attention should be paid to Theophanes' two notices, which report the expedition, with different outcomes, under two years. On three key points of substance, Sebeos' version tallies with that of the other trustworthy sources: a Persian army reached Chalcedon; gifts were presented to the Persians; and Heraclius negotiated with the Persian general from a ship offshore.

Sebeos has, however, topped and tailed this notice with material relating to a later episode, the siege of Constantinople in 626, when the Persians and Avars made concerted attacks. For it was in 626 that Shahrvaraz (named as the commander by Sebeos) led a Persian army to the Bosphorus, with the intention of capturing Constantinople (as stated by Sebeos in the opening paragraph). That was also the occasion when the Persians were known to be eager to send a force across the straits – to link up with their Avar allies on the European shore. The contemporary documentary report reproduced in *Chron.Pasch.* leaves no doubt about the extent of Roman concern on this score, but then breaks off for three days, leaving the reader in the dark about what actually happened. This *lacuna* is partially filled by Sebeos' notice that an attempt was made by the Persians but that it failed and heavy losses were incurred.

Sebeos amplifies the bald statements of other sources about Heraclius' gift-giving, distinguishing between the presents given to Shahēn and senior officers ('the princes') and largesse to the Persian troops, which took the form of a donative and seven days' provisions (presumably fresher and more alluring than their usual rations). The speech which Sebeos put into Heraclius' mouth provides important information about his negotiating stance, about the concessions which he was ready to make so as to open communications with Khosrov. Its value may be gauged by comparing it to the negotiating stance later adopted by the Senate when it wrote a carefully phrased letter of apology and introduction to accompany the Roman embassy, once Khosrov agreed to receive one. The full text of the letter is reproduced in *Chron.Pasch.*

According to Sebeos, Heraclius was ready to make extraordinary political concessions. These are clearly indicated in a few key sentences.

On the one hand, he insisted on the right to existence of the Roman empire ('my empire'), which God had established, but, on the other, he stated unequivocally that Khosrov could install a candidate of his choice on the imperial throne. In effect, Heraclius was offering to stand down and to allow the Roman empire to become a Persian client-state. The very fact that it was the Senate, not Heraclius, which subsequently negotiated with Khosrov, confirms that Heraclius had not made his continuing tenure of office a precondition. Naturally he received backing from the Senate, which, in the key section of its letter, begged Khosrov 'to consider Heraclius, our most pious emperor, as a true son, one who is eager to perform the service of your serenity in all things'. Both concessions are made in this sentence: Khosrov is allocated the right of choosing the emperor (the Senate merely recommends Heraclius) and that emperor will be a client-ruler, a 'son' rather than a 'brother' of the Sasanian king, who will do his bidding.

The Senate also noted, in an earlier passage, that Heraclius had avenged Maurice and had rescued the empire from Phocas. What was an overt argument in favour of Heraclius' candidature, in the letter, reappears in the speech in Sebeos as an argument against prolongation of the war: Khosrov's expressed aim of seeking vengeance for the blood of Maurice has been achieved by Heraclius' father. This tell-tale detail, correctly representing the older Heraclius as the constitutional leader of the rebels (see n.31 above), argues strongly for the authenticity of the material conveyed in the speech. It is a point which is also noted in the Senate's letter (Phocas was ousted by Heraclius together with his late father). Finally the pleading tone of the speech (Heraclius requests mercy from Khosrov) corresponds to that running through the letter.

What then are we to make of this notice? Its core consists of material of high quality, deriving presumably from a well-informed Roman source, but a serious editorial error has occurred – the conflation of two distinct Persian thrusts into the Roman metropolitan area. This conflation or combination of episodes appears to be a rare instance of interventionist editing on Sebeos' part, which has gone horribly wrong. One can only suppose that he could not conceive of the Persians launching two major offensives on separate occasions against the metropolitan region. He could also have been misled by his source, *if* (but this takes us into the realm of pure conjecture) chronology were disregarded for dramatic effect and the two expeditions were juxtaposed as the two moments of gravest crisis for the Romans.

Sources: (i) (615) *Chron. Pasch.* 706–9; Nikephoros, chs6–7; Flusin, *St Anastase* I, 48–9; Theophanes 301; (ii) (626) *Chron. Pasch.* 716–26; G.P., *Bellum Avaricum*; Theodore Syncellus; Nikephoros, ch.13; Theophanes 316; Dionysius 135.

Literature: (i) *Chron. Pasch.*, nn. 442–4; Flusin, *St Anastase* II, 83–93; (ii) *Chron. Pasch.*, nn. 457–80; Howard-Johnston, 'Siege'.

38: ch.38, **123–124**, *Persian ultimatum, preparations for Heraclius' first counter-offensive* (cf. T'.A. 91–2). Distinct but related material has been combined in this section of text. A notice (**124**) about the installation of Heraclius' son Heraclius Constantine as co-emperor, at a time when he was a baby (securely dated to 22 January 613 by *Chron. Pasch.* 703–4), perhaps presented in a cast-back in Sebeos' source, introduces a fleeting and incomplete reference to the constitutional arrangements made for the period of Heraclius' absence from Constantinople. Formal power was vested in Heraclius Constantine, a ten-year-old boy in 622 (this must be the meaning of Sebeos' vague phrase about confirmation of his imperial status), but executive authority was delegated to two regents.

Heraclius' departures from Constantinople in 622 and 624 have also been confused. It was in 622 that he celebrated Easter in the city (it fell on 4 April) and left the next day, to supervise preliminary training manœuvres in Bithynia and then to conduct operations against the Persians in Asia Minor (G.P., *Expeditio Persica*). That was the year when he appointed a regency council of two (the Patriarch Sergius and Bonus, *Magister Militum Praesentalis* [*PLRE* III, s.v. Bonus 5]) to run affairs in the name of Heraclius Constantine during his absence (Theophanes 302–303; cf. M.D., tr. Dowsett 78). There were eunuchs (but no wife) in his entourage: they joined in the rescue of a ship which had run aground during the sea-crossing to Pylae, on the south side of the Gulf of Nicomedia (G.P., *Expeditio Persica* I 205–8). After spending 623 preoccupied with western diplomacy, Heraclius next left the city by sea on 25 March 624, well before Easter (15 April) which he celebrated in Nicomedia with his family. He is very likely to have passed through Chalcedon since it lay on the most direct route, across the Bosphorus and then overland, to Nicomedia. This time he was accompanied by a wife (Martina, whom he had married in autumn–winter 623–624, according to Nikephoros, ch.11) and his destination was indeed the east (*Chron. Pasch.* 713–14). Having combined elements from two different episodes, Sebeos seems to have solved the resulting chronological problem by plumping arbitrarily and mistakenly for the 34th regnal year of Khosrov (622–623).

The main body of this section of text is concerned with preparations for Heraclius' first counter-offensive. It leads directly into Sebeos' account of operations in 624, and it deals with a connected series of events revolving around a Persian ultimatum – the ultimatum arrives, is made known to court and patriarch in Constantinople, is placed on the altar in St Sophia, and finally is used to stoke up anti-Persian feeling in the army. Shorn of the extraneous elements which Sebeos has included, the notice supplies two unique items of information about the preparations for war in 624: first that the army was mobilized in Cappadocia, at Caesarea; second that much play was made of a highly offensive Persian diplomatic note, received apparently not long before Heraclius left the capital. While there is no reason to reject either item, one may legitimately ask whether the diplomatic note was an authentic Persian document, since it was so eagerly publicized by Heraclius and its phrasing was well calculated to heighten anti-Persian sentiment. It is more plausible to view it as a successful piece of Roman disinformation, designed to bring about the effect it achieved: insults thrown at Heraclius (senseless, insignificant, leader of brigands) were gratuitous and likely to be counter-productive; anti-Christian invective came ill from a ruler who now governed most of the east Christian world; and Old Testament citations, from Isaiah and the Psalms, would seem to betray a Christian hand at work in the drafting.

Literature: Oikonomidès, 'A Chronological Note'; Howard-Johnston, 'Heraclius' Persian Campaigns'.

39: ch.38, 124–125, *operations in 624 and 625* (cf. T'.A. 92–3). Sebeos' account, highly abridged though it be, provides considerably more topographical detail than any other extant source. There was yet more detail about the operations of 624 in Sebeos' original text, to judge by T'ovma Artsruni's version: this makes it clear that Gandzak was sacked, mentions three other places or areas which were attacked (Ormi, Hamadan and May [Media]), and adds that Heraclius, after overthrowing the great fire altar called Vshnasp, 'filled the lake opposite the pyraeum with corpses'. On key points, geographical and military, corroboration can be obtained from document-based material presented by Theophanes, from George of Pisidia's summary of Heraclius' achievements in the *Heraclias* and from Movsēs Daskhurants'i. There are, however, serious gaps in the coverage of operations in 625, which make it hard to relate what is reported by Sebeos to the fuller version in Theophanes.

The main features of the 624 campaign have been caught: Heraclius did indeed take a northern route through Armenia, crossing the Euphrates, attacking and capturing Dvin (G.P., *Heraclias* II 160–6); the invasion and devastation of Atrpatakan and Media is likewise corroborated by M.D., tr. Dowsett 79 and Theophanes 307–8, the latter noting that he camped outside Gandzak before sacking a fire-temple at Thebarmais (called Dararstasis by G.P., *Heraclias* II 167–230); Sebeos correctly names the fire which was extinguished there – it was Adur Gushnasp, venerated in the fortified fire-temple complex at modern Takht-i Sulaiman, set in a bowl of mountains in a remote valley and holding within its *enceinte* a mysterious green-blue lake, deep, warm, mineral-rich. Confirmation is to hand for other key points in Sebeos' account: the recall of Shahrvaraz from Roman territory (Theophanes 306; M.D., tr. Dowsett 79); the appointment of Shahēn to command a scratch defensive force (Theophanes 306); the flight of Khosrov (Theophanes 307; M.D., tr. Dowsett 79); Heraclius' withdrawal north to Albania (Theophanes 308 and M.D., tr. Dowsett 79–81 who add that he spent the winter there).

Heraclius' generalship showed to best advantage in the campaign of 625, in the course of which he succeeded in defeating three pursuing Persian armies in detail. Sebeos makes no mention of the first of these armies into the field, that commanded by Shahrapłakan who was sent to keep watch on the Roman army in winter and who shadowed it in the opening operations of spring (Theophanes 308–9; M.D., tr. Dowsett 81). But he alone reports Khosrov's strategic dispositions for 625, which were apparently predicated on the assumption that Heraclius would be returning home: Shahrvaraz's army was sent north-east from Nisibis (where it had probably spent the winter) across Armenia (a movement also noted by Theophanes 309) to take up a position commanding a northern route of withdrawal from Albania; Shahēn's was deployed far to the south, ready to strike across the Bitlis pass should Heraclius opt for a southern line of retreat through Armenia.

In the event, Heraclius opted to attack and, after a delay occasioned by the reluctance of his men, set off south from Albania. There was now a danger that the army of Shahrapłakan behind him might unite with that of Shahrvaraz which was close at hand. The victory which Sebeos reports was probably that won by Heraclius over Shahrapłakan's pursuing force which he harried day and night until its morale broke. After this, he resumed his march south, defeated first Shahrvaraz (who had now been joined by Shahrapłakan) and then Shahēn in major engagements, reversed the direction of his march, halted (probably in Albania) to cover the withdrawal of his Laz and Abasgian allies, marched south-west past Tsłukkʻ, crossed the Araxes not far from Nakhchawan (as reported by Sebeos), and finally turned west, making for Lake Van (Theophanes 309–11; M.D., tr. Dowsett 81).

Sebeos' coverage is very selective. He omits most of the year's action, leaping from the opening battle to the long march from Albania to the region of Lake Van at the end of the campaigning season. Persian troop numbers given in this and the following section of text (discussed in the next note) are more credible than those given for Heraclius' army or the detachment sent off on an operation in winter 625–626.

Literature: M. Boyce, 'Adur Gushnasp', *E.Ir.* I, 475–6; Schippmann, *Feuerheiligtümer* 309–57; Herrmann, *Iranian Revival* 113–18; Manandian, 'Marshruty' 134–46; Hewsen, *AŠX* 60 (map x), 60A (map xi), 61 (map xii), 62 (map xiv), 66A (map xix), 67 (map xx), 67A (map xxi), 69 (map xxiv), 157–9 (Tigranakert), 193 (Tsłukkʻ), 253–8 (Pʻaytakaran), 262 (Gardman); Howard-Johnston, 'Heraclius' Persian Campaigns'.

40: ch.38, **125–126**, *surprise attack on Shahrvaraz's headquarters in winter, 625–626.* This minor operation was of little military consequence but probably had a marked effect on the balance of prestige between Heraclius and Shahrvaraz and on the mood of their respective armies. Much is made of it by Theophanes as well as by Sebeos. There is a common storyline to the two accounts, although each has details missing from the other. Both begin by noting that the main body of the Persian army was dispersed for the winter, and then turn to the planning of a surprise night attack (the initiative lies with Heraclius from the first according to Theophanes, who may well be guilty of clumsy abridgement here). Both note that Heraclius selected the best men *and horses* for the operation. Sebeos gives more precise information about Shahrvaraz's dispositions (headquarters at Archēsh, dispersed cantonment in Ałiovit, vanguard at Ałi). Theophanes, by contrast, only mentions the site of the first engagement (with the Persian vanguard), which he calls Salbanon. In both versions, the operation involves two actions: first the annihilation of the Persian vanguard, except for one man who manages to escape and warn Shahrvaraz; then the attack on Shahrvaraz's headquarters, which results in a heavy death-toll (somewhat exaggerated by Sebeos), mainly because the Romans set fire to the buildings where the Persians were holding out. Both sources report that Shahrvaraz barely managed to escape, Sebeos commenting on the sorry state of the horse which he rode, Theophanes on his own sorry condition, undressed and unshod. Each includes a graphic scene missing from the other's account: in Sebeos' case it is that of the arrival of the lone survivor from the first engagement and Shahrvaraz's initial reaction of incredulity and anger; Theophanes gives a fuller account of Persian resistance at Archēsh (from the rooftops) and the effects of the fire in the second engagement. Both end by noting the booty captured by Heraclius, Theophanes detailing some of the choicer items of Shahrvaraz's equipment which were netted.

The simplest and most plausible explanation for the marked similarities between Sebeos' and Theophanes' versions of this episode is that they drew directly or indirectly on a common source. Shared material would also help explain some of the parallels between their accounts of the later stages of Heraclius' second counter-offensive (see n.42 below). If there were such a common source, a conjecture may be offered as to its identity – namely, a history of Heraclius' Persian campaigns, commissioned from George of Pisidia and based in the main on Heraclius' war despatches. There would be nothing very remarkable in Heraclius' sponsoring a written memorial of his achievements and ensuring it a relatively wide dissemination.

Source: Theophanes 311–12.

Literature: Hewsen, *AŠX* 62A (map xv), 165–7; Howard-Johnston, 'Heraclius' Persian Campaigns'; Howard-Johnston, 'Official History'.

41: ch.38, **126**, *Shahrvaraz's pursuit of Heraclius, 626*. Sebeos now leaps to the operations of spring 626. He is right to present Shahrvaraz as driving Heraclius west. Theophanes gives a detailed account of Heraclius' retreat, which took him through northern Mesopotamia (past Amida) and Cilicia, across the Taurus and finally, veering northeast, to Sebastea. There is a glaring omission from this passage: nothing is said about the co-ordinated thrusts by Persians and Avars which culminated in a ten-day siege of Constantinople (29 July–7 August); it is not made clear that Constantinople was Shahrvaraz's ultimate objective nor that a second Persian army, commanded by Shahēn, invaded Asia

Minor from Armenia (it was intercepted and defeated by the expeditionary force, either under Heraclius' or, according to Theophanes, his
brother Theodore's command). Mistakenly believing that the 615 and
626 Persian advances to the Bosphorus formed part of a single offensive
(n.37 above), Sebeos has removed the second episode from its proper
place and has combined it with the first. He plugs the resulting gap in
626 with a note, evidently displaced from the following autumn / winter
(626 / 627), about measures taken to rest and re-equip a weary army
(surely Heraclius') in a region safe from enemy attack.

A somewhat similar phrase (also probably dislodged from its proper
place) is to be found much earlier in T'ovma Artsruni's version of
Sebeos – at the end of the brief report about a naval attack on
Constantinople (which took place, in reality, in 626), which is appended,
as in the extant manuscript of Sebeos, to the account of Shahēn's 615
campaign to Chalcedon. He notes that the Persians, after losing 4,000
men (specified as cavalrymen) in the naval engagement, 'had no more
enthusiasm for that undertaking, but spread out and occupied the whole
land'.

Sources: Theophanes 312–15; M.D., tr. Dowett 81; T'.A. 91.

42: chs38–39, **126–127**, *Heraclius' invasion of Mesopotamia, 627–628* (cf.
T'.A. 93–4, who gives more detail about Khosrov's mobilization, naming
two of the guards regiments sent as reinforcements before the battle of
Nineveh, adds a figure [4,000] for the Persian survivors of the battle,
and enumerates the booty gathered by Heraclius from Khosrov's
palaces [passage quoted below]). Sebeos' account of this dramatic last
episode of the war tallies in its key elements with that of Theophanes,
which undoubtedly consists in the main of material excerpted and
condensed from Heraclius' war despatches and reaching him in the
form of an official history. Most other sources deal cursorily with it
(M.D., *Georgian Chronicles*, *Chron. Seert*, *Khuz. Chron.*, Tabari,
Dionysius). However, unlike Theophanes and Movsēs, Sebeos passes
over the earlier operations of Heraclius and his Turkish allies which
culminated in the siege of Tp'khis and picks up the story as Heraclius
enters Armenia, marching south. Thenceforth the two accounts complement each other. Sebeos may not mention the Turkish force which
accompanied the Romans as far as the Zagros mountains and guaran-
teed their safety, but he supplies valuable geographical detail about the
line of Heraclius' march and notes that the Persian general Řoch Vehan

(Razates in Theophanes) only set off in pursuit when Heraclius entered Atrpatakan. The route which Sebeos specifies provides the explanation for this dilatoriness on Řoch Vehan's part: it looked at first as if Heraclius was doing the sensible thing and returning to Roman territory, making a long detour to the south through Shirak to Gogovit where he could be expected to turn west, to reach the natural thoroughfare leading towards Asia Minor which is formed by the valley of the Aratsani. Instead Heraclius turned *south-east* when he reached Gogovit, crossed Her and Zarewand at the head of Lake Urmia, entered Atrpatakan and then struck south aiming for Mesopotamia. It seems to have taken as long for the news of Heraclius' change of direction to reach Řoch Vehan as it took Heraclius and his men to cover the distance from Gogovit to the border of Atrpatakan. Řoch Vehan then strove to make up the lost ground by forced marches; but he only succeeded in drawing close (reaching Gandzak) when Heraclius halted at Chamaetha on 9 October and rested his troops for a week.

The principal features of subsequent operations are presented in both texts: the march south to Mesopotamia which Heraclius had reached by 1 December when, Theophanes reports, he crossed the Great Zab; the decisive battle of Nineveh (dated to 12 December by Theophanes); the victorious advance of the Romans on Ctesiphon; the devastation of Khosrov's palaces (T'.A.'s version adding that Heraclius 'seized the many stored treasures, an incalculable booty of gold, silver, and clothing, very many animals, and a multitude of prisoners as numberless as the sand of the sea', which amounts to a neat summary of the lengthy tale of booty-gathering told by Theophanes); and the final bold winter recrossing of the Zagros, back to Atrpatakan (its start is dated to 24 February in Heraclius' dispatch of 8 April which is reproduced in *Chron. Pasch.*). There is considerably more detail about most operations in Mesopotamia in Theophanes' despatch-based account, but Sebeos provides some invaluable supplementary information.

With the help of details given by Theophanes about the crossing of the Great Zab, it is possible to elucidate an obscure, apparently corrupt, passage in Sebeos according to which *they* (i.e. the Persians) turned west on reaching Asorestan while *he* (i.e. Heraclius) went to Nineveh. Both were actions of Heraclius, according to Theophanes. After reaching the Tigris valley below the Great Zab, he turned north-west (Sebeos' west), crossed the river on 1 December and camped near Nineveh. His intention seems to have been to hold the line of the river, but the Persians found and used another crossing. Nothing is reported about the movements of the main body of either army from this point until their engagement near Nineveh ten days or so later, but it may be conjectured that the Persians established a secure bridgehead on the west bank of the river, thereby forcing Heraclius to concentrate his troops closer to the river. Theophanes confirms that the Persians were awaiting reinforcements before engaging the Romans, puts the number of reinforcements at 3,000, but denies that they arrived before the battle.

Sebeos' account of the battle itself is superior to Theophanes', which simply focuses on episodes (doubtless improved in the writing) involving Heraclius and his horse. The sudden transformation of retreat into attack under the cover of mist is typical of Heraclius' generalship. The scale of Persian losses may be exaggerated by Sebeos, but he gives more detail about the treatment of Persians taken prisoner (numbering 4,000 according to T'ovma Artsruni) and places the battle and subsequent operations in their proper strategic context. The Persian army in the west, under the command of Shahrvaraz, did indeed remain a formidable fighting force and it was reasonable to be apprehensive about its intervening. Sebeos is surely right to suggest that anxiety on this score was the prime reason for Heraclius' decision to undertake a second, hazardous, mid-winter crossing of the Zagros.

Finally the two sources complement each other about Khosrov's movements, Theophanes reporting his hurried flight from his favourite palace of Dastakert to Ctesiphon, Sebeos his subsequent arrival at Vehkawat. This was a district in the central flood-plain south of Ctesiphon. Shielded by the formidable defences of the capital to the north and the Tigris to the east (once the pontoon-bridge had been dismantled), Khosrov was safely out of the Roman's army reach. This bridge, which appears to have crossed the Tigris into Vehkawat, should be distinguished from that linking the two halves of the capital, Veh-Artashir on the right bank and Ctesiphon on the left.

Sources: Theophanes 317–23, 324–5; *Chron. Pasch.* 729–30, 731–2; M.D., tr. Dowsett 85–6, 88–9; *Georgian Chronicles* 223–8; Nikephoros, chs12, 14; *Chron. Seert* 541–2; *Khuz. Chron.* 28; Tabari, tr. Nöldeke 293–6; Dionysius 137–8; Flusin, *St Anastase* I, 86–91; Strategius xxiv.

Literature: Manandian, 'Marshruty' 146–53; Hewsen, *AŠX* 64A (map xvii), 66 (map xviii), 69 (map xxiv), 176–9; Morony, *Iraq* 147–51; Flusin, *St Anastase* II, 265–81; Howard-Johnston, 'Heraclius' Persian Campaigns'.

43: ch.39, **127**, *the deposition and death of Khosrov, February 628* (cf. T'.A. 94–5, adding some direct speech and three pieces of information [the royal household falls into the conspirators' hands as well as the royal stable, it is a thick myrtle bush under which Khosrov hides, and he is imprisoned and abused by some nobles before being executed]). Heraclius' victorious sweep through Mesopotamia exacerbated a growing internal crisis. War-weariness had set in. Resentment had been engendered by Khosrov's autocratic manner and the heavy taxation needed to fund the war. Kawat, Khosrov's eldest son, made contact with a leading disaffected magnate, the former supreme commander of Sasanian forces. The latter gathered support for a coup at court and in the higher echelons of the army, sent a deputation to inform Heraclius of the conspirators' plans, and put them into action on the night of 23–24 February 628.

The coup is reported, in considerable detail, in extant sources of proven worth (*Chron. Pasch.*, Theophanes, M.D. and *Khuz. Chron.*, to which Tabari may be added since he is in general agreement with them). These corroborate all the key points in Sebeos' succinct account: (i) Khosrov had returned to the capital some time before the coup; (ii) Kawat had been left with the royal household in Vehkawat (at the palace of Aqr Babil, according to Tabari); (iii) Khosrov showed a callous disregard for the welfare of his troops; (iv) the conspirators' first open move was to seize by night the bridge linking the two halves of the capital (but the western half, Veh-Artashir, has been corrupted into Vehkawat); (v) it was by the bridge, in the night, that Kawat was formally proclaimed king; (vi) deserted by those around him, Khosrov hid in the garden beside the palace but was discovered and arrested; (vii) Khosrov and all his sons except Kawat were executed.

Surprisingly, Sebeos refrains from giving a date for what was a pivotal event in his history, but he supplies an interesting piece of information which is not recorded otherwise – the spiriting of Khosrov's horses out of the royal stable. These may have been the mounts (mentioned by M.D.) used by the prisoners whom the conspirators released at the start of the coup.

Sources: Theophanes 325–7; *Chron. Pasch.* 727–9; M.D., tr. Dowsett 89–92; *Khuz. Chron.* 29–30; Tabari, tr. Nöldeke 296, 351–83. Cf. Strategius xxiv; *Chron. Seert* 551; Nikephoros ch.15.

Literature: Christensen, *L'Iran* 492–6; Howard-Johnston, 'Heraclius' Persian Campaigns'.

44: chs39–40, **127–129**, *reign of Kawat, February–October 628* (cf. T'.A. 95–6). Sebeos gives the fullest account of the new government's peace proposals. Key points can be corroborated from documents reproduced at the end of *Chron. Pasch.*, Heraclius' exultant despatch of 8 April 628, a copy, mutilated towards the end, of the letter he had received from Kawat, and the fragmentary start of Heraclius' reply. The Persian ambassador, Phaiak Chosdae, a secretary with the rank of Ṙashnan, only reached Heraclius' camp at Gandzak on 3 April, having been held up by heavy snowfalls in the Zagros mountains. No preconditions were put forward on the Persian side. In his letter, Kawat simply stated his determination to make peace with the Romans and other neighbouring peoples, announced his intention of releasing all prisoners and made it very plain, by repeated references to Heraclius as his brother and to the brotherhood of the Romans, that he intended to restore traditional relations of equality between the two powers. His offer to abandon Roman territory suggests that he envisaged a restoration of the traditional balance of power on the ground, presumably the arrangements which had prevailed from 387 (with one major modification, the allocation of Lazica to the Roman sphere, agreed under the terms of the treaty of 561) rather than those imposed by Maurice in 591 which had shifted the balance of power in Transcaucasia decisively in the Romans' favour.

While welcoming these proposals and returning prisoners and booty in his hands (a reciprocal gesture of goodwill not reported in other sources), Heraclius gave a clear sign that negotiations would be tough by calling Kawat his child in his formal reply (Nikephoros – cf. also Oikonomidès, 'Correspondence', who conjectures that Heraclius used the term *huiotes*, sonship, in his letter, of which only a narrow, vertical strip survives). The return embassy was headed by Eustathius, as Sebeos reports (*PLRE* III, s.v. Eustathius 12). It was a measure of Kawat's trust (or weakness) that he allowed Eustathius to be present when he had a letter drafted instructing Shahrvaraz to evacuate Roman territory. This incident and Shahrvaraz's subsequent refusal to obey are only reported by Sebeos.

It is probable that Heraclius did return home, as noted by Sebeos, i.e. to Constantinople, since he announced, in his despatch of 8 April, that he was setting off through Armenia.

Kawat's reign is variously given as lasting six or eight (*Chron. Seert*), seven (*Chron. 724*, M.D.), and eight months (*Khuz. Chron.*, Tabari). If the date of his son Artashir's assassination, 27 April 630, given later by Tabari, is accepted along with the 18 months generally agreed for Artashir's reign, the correct figure would be eight months. Kawat's plan for economic revival involved tax reductions (M.D. and *Chron.Seert*).

Sources: *Chron.Pasch.* 727–37; Nikephoros ch.15; M.D., tr. Dowsett 92; *Chron.Seert* 551–5; *Khuz.Chron.* 30–1; *Chron.724* 18; Tabari, tr. Nöldeke 383–5; Dionysius 138.

Literature: Blockley, 'Division'; Stein, *Bas-Empire* 516–21; Oikonomidès, 'Correspondence'; Flusin, *St Anastase* II, 282–5; Howard-Johnston, 'Heraclius' Persian Campaigns'; Sellwood, Whitting and Williams 159–63 and ill. 68–70.

45: ch.40, **129–130**, *Heraclius' agreement with Shahrvaraz, Shahrvaraz's putsch, 629–630* (cf. T'.A. 96–7, who rearranges Sebeos' material, placing Shahrvaraz's assassination [correctly] after the return of the True Cross to Jerusalem). There is no hint here of any earlier political understanding, such as that alleged to have been reached by Heraclius and Shahrvaraz in 626 by *Chron.Seert*, Tabari and Dionysius. The allegation should probably be rejected as a piece of deliberate disinformation, circulated to further Roman interests as the war reached a climax in 627–628. By 629, however, both Heraclius and Shahrvaraz had compelling reasons for reaching an accommodation: Heraclius had no choice but to deal directly with the commander-in-chief of the Persian occupation forces if he were to recover the lost provinces of the Near East, while Shahrvaraz needed to strengthen his position now that he was at odds with the government in Ctesiphon. The initiative therefore may have come equally well from either Heraclius as Sebeos claims or Shahrvaraz (the version of Nikephoros). Negotiations were evidently far advanced when the two parties met at Arabissus in the Anti-Taurus in July 629, since the Persian evacuation had begun in June.

The terms of the agreement may be pieced together from the principal sources. Here, as on several previous occasions, material once present in Sebeos, which appears to have dropped out of the extant manuscript, may be retrieved from T'ovma Artsruni's version (T.'A. 96). Heraclius in effect invested Shahrvaraz with the Sasanian crown and made his political support manifest by sending a small military force with him to Ctesiphon. Shahrvaraz, for his part, undertook to evacuate Roman territory up to an agreed frontier and to return the fragments of the True

Cross, a symbol of victory which Heraclius would use to project himself as the sole effective defender of Christians of all confessions throughout the Near East (nn.47–48 below). War reparations are also mentioned by Nikephoros, who adds that the emperor and his candidate for the Sasanian throne bound themselves together by a marriage alliance. *Chron.724* states unequivocally that 'the Euphrates was recognized as the frontier between them', implying thereby that Shahrvaraz had insisted on retaining some of the territory beyond the traditional post-387 frontier which he and his troops had conquered, i.e. the Roman provinces of Mesopotamia and Osrhoene which lay east of the Euphrates (with their principal cities, Amida and Edessa). Corroboration is obtainable from T'.A., who enables us to restore Sebeos' sentence about the territorial agreement as follows: 'Khoŕeam agreed and gave over to Heraclius, emperor of the Greeks, Jerusalem, Caesarea in Palestine, all the regions of Antioch, and all the cities of those provinces, and Tarsus in Cilicia, and the greater part of Armenia, and everything that Heraclius had ever desired'. There is no reference here to any province or city beyond the Euphrates south of the Taurus.

Events then went according to plan. The evacuation of Roman territory as defined in the agreement was completed. Shahrvaraz marched on Ctesiphon, which, after some initial resistance, admitted him, thereby allowing him to take power. He sought out and returned the fragments of the True Cross, which was in Heraclius' hands in time for him to stage its ceremonial reinstallation in Jerusalem on 21 March. A first tranche of reparations may have been handed over at the same time (Sebeos' 'no few presents'). As Flusin argues persuasively, Shahrvaraz must have exercised power initially as regent for the young Artashir, since his execution of the boy and his own ascent onto the throne took place on 27 April 630, after Artashir had reigned one year and six months (Tabari). It was therefore during the regency that he kept his part of his bargain with Heraclius.

Shahrvaraz's assassination 40 days after assuming power is also reported by *Khuz.Chron.*, *Chron.Seert* and Tabari, the last giving a precise date, 9 June 630.

Sources: *Chron.724* 13, 17–18; Nikephoros ch.17; *Khuz.Chron.* 31–2; *Chron.Seert* 540–1, 556; Tabari, tr. Nöldeke 300–303, 386–90; Dionysius 135–7, 141–2; Theophanes 323–4, 329; Strategius xxiv.

Literature: Mango, 'Deux Etudes' 105–12; Flusin, *St Anastase* II, 285–97, 306–9; Howard-Johnston, 'Heraclius' Persian Campaigns'.

46: ch.40, **130**, *Persian succession crisis, 632–634* (cf. T'.A. 97–8). The more precise figure of 16 months for Boran's reign given by *Chron.Seert* and Tabari should probably be preferred to Sebeos' two years. The period of confusion following her death therefore began around October 632. Sebeos mistakenly supposes that her four successors, whom he lists correctly, ruled in sequence. This cannot have been so, since the last-named of them, Yazkert III, dated his accession from the year of Boran's death (*Chron.Seert*, corroborated by the 16 June 632 start of the era of Yazkert used by Zoroastrians after the Arab conquest) and the reigns of both Azarmidukht (*Chron.Seert*) and Ormizd (coins from either side of a Persian new year) lasted a year or so. It follows that Sebeos is listing contemporary, rival claimants to the throne, who, we may infer, were backed by the rival regional armies which he mentions at the end of the notice. Supplementary information on alignments is provided mainly by *Chron.Seert*: the army of Mesopotamia, formerly commanded by Shahrvaraz, installed Azarmidukht, like Boran a daughter of Khosrov, in the capital; she was replaced after a year (so well into the latter half of 633) by Ormizd, a grandson of Khosrov's, whose control of Mesopotamia (as well as north-west Iran) is confirmed by the mints issuing coins in his name. Of the two non-metropolitan candidates, Yazkert was the better placed to move on the capital from his power-base in Persia proper than Mihr-Khosrov, child candidate of the army of Khurasan. The army of Atrpatakan seems to have stood aside, in spite of the execution of its former commander, Khoŕokh Ormizd, who had been Boran's chief minister.

There is more than a passing resemblance between Sebeos' and *Chron.Seert*'s accounts of the prolonged crisis following the death of Boran. The two lists of (rival) rulers tally, save that *Chron.Seert* leaves out Ormizd and Sebeos truncates Mihr-Khosrov's name. Both texts identify regional armies as the principal players in the struggle for power. It may conjectured, hesitantly, that a common source underlies the two accounts, a source which focused on the military and political history of the Sasanian empire as it approached its end. The existence of such a source may also be postulated to account for the presence of similar material, likewise concerned with the military underpinning of political power and major actions in which Sasanian forces were involved, at several places later in Sebeos' text (**137, 139, 141, 163–164**). It will be designated, for convenience, the Persian Source.

Sources: *Chron.Seert* 557, 579–80; *Khuz.Chron.* 32–3; Tabari, tr. Nöldeke 390–9; Dionysius 143; Theophanes 329; Nikephoros ch.16.

Literature: Tabari, tr. Nöldeke 433–4; Christensen, *L'Iran* 498–500; de Blois, 'Calendar' 39; Sellwood, Whitting and Williams 166–74 and ill. 71–73.

47: ch.41, **131**, *reinstallation of the True Cross in Jerusalem, 21 March 630* (cf. T'.A. 96–7 who supplies some details missing from the extant text). Sebeos gives the clearest and most evocative account of the ceremony and its context. He shows a special concern with the fate of Jerusalem's ecclesiastical plate, supplying unique items of information on this and some other matters. Heraclius went, 'with the host of his army' (T'.A.) as well as his retinue, to Hierapolis, on the Roman side of the Euphrates frontier agreed with Shahrvaraz. The True Cross was brought to him there by the delegation sent to fetch it, 'in its original wrapping' (T'.A.) – a reference to the stage-managed unlocking of the sealed container which authenticated the relic after its arrival in Jerusalem (Strategius, Nikephoros). Heraclius was both celebrating the victory of Christendom over Zoroastrian Persia and reimpressing Roman authority on the provinces evacuated by Shahrvaraz a few months earlier (hence the accompanying army). The ceremony itself took place on 21 March 630, on the exact anniversary of the creation of the sun and the moon at the beginning of time (and on the same day of the week, a Wednesday). Cosmic significance was thus added to an occasion already rich in political and religious meaning, and was itself amplified by eschatological expectations triggered by Christendom's spectacular victory. No wonder strong emotions were aroused during the ceremony, no wonder participants and onlookers were overwhelmed and silenced.

Sources: G.P., *In Restitutionem S. Crucis*; Strategius xxiv; Sophronius, *Anacreontica* xviii; Flusin, *St Anastase* I, 98–9; Theophanes 328; Nikephoros ch.18; Dionysius 142.

Literature: Mango, 'Deux Etudes', 112–14, 117; *Chron.Pasch.*, introduction xi–xiii; Mango, 'Temple Mount', 6, 15–16; Flusin, *St Anastase* II, 293–306, 309–19; Beaucamp, 'Temps et Histoire'.

48: ch.41, **131**, *Heraclius in the Near East, 630.* The ceremony at Jerusalem heightened awareness that God had intervened in earthly affairs in spectacular fashion to save the Christian empire, and, with it, the suspicion that the final phase of the war might well have been the first scene in the final act of history. These circumstances may go some way to explaining what looks like a grandiose scheme on Heraclius' part to extend and unify Christendom: (i) with his candidate Shahrvaraz in control of the Sasanian empire and with Shahrvaraz's son and heir a Christian convert, he could dream of an acceleration in the spread of Christianity in Iran; (ii) he inaugurated an empire-wide campaign of coercing Jews into the church on his way to Jerusalem; (iii) the most dramatic development came afterwards, when he received an embassy from the new Persian regime of Boran at Beroea (Aleppo) in northern Syria – he had discussions with the Nestorian Catholicos, Ishoyahb, who was leading the delegation, and agreed a form of words designed to reunite the two churches; (iv) finally (probably after the failure of the Nestorian project, in the face of vociferous opposition in Mesopotamia) Heraclius strove to reconcile the Monophysites of Syria and Armenia with the established Chalcedonian church – the mixture of cajolery and inducement used (together with reasoned argument and doctrinal compromise) is best illustrated by Sebeos' version of how the Catholicos Ezr was persuaded to communicate with Heraclius by the Roman general in Armenia (on which see **131–132** with n.49 below).

The wider political situation was changed by the assassination of Shahrvaraz on 9 June 630. Heraclius' agreement with him now lapsed and the frontier question was reopened. With Heraclius and his army menacingly close to the Euphrates, the new regime of Boran sent the embassy headed by Ishoyahb with the prime, urgent task of negotiating a durable settlement. The Persian position was gravely weakened, since the army which had served Shahrvaraz for so long was alienated, and major concessions had to be offered. The new frontier was to be that imposed on Khosrov by Maurice.

This scenario has been reconstructed from odd pieces of information, some of the most valuable being provided by Sebeos. One point in the text requires clarification: it is likely that Heraclius only crossed the Euphrates into northern Mesopotamia ('Syrian Mesopotamia'), where he is known to have visited Constantina and Edessa (**134** with n.52 below), *after* negotiating the new treaty at Beroea.

Sources: (i) Nikephoros ch.17; (ii) Theophanes 328 and sources cited by Dagron / Déroche (below); (iii) *Chron. Seert* 557–61, *Khuz. Chron.* 32–3, Flusin, *St Anastase* I, 98–101; (iv) Dionysius 138–42, Theophanes 329–30.

Literature: (i) Mango, 'Deux Etudes' 105–106, 112, 115–17; (ii)

Dagron/Déroche, 'Juifs et chrétiens' 28–38; (iii) and (iv) Flusin, *St Anastase* II, 312–13, 319–27.

49: ch.41, **131–132**, *ecclesiastical union imposed on Armenia, 631.* Sebeos' account is selective and slanted. He makes no mention of the council convened by Heraclius at Theodosiopolis and attended by Armenian churchmen and nobles, at which an agreement was hammered out over many sessions. By focusing attention on the Catholicos Ezr and his personal negotiations with the emperor, he distracts attention from the fact that all but a small minority of Armenian churchmen accepted the agreement. This massaging of the facts, which includes the false statement that Ezr met Heraclius in Asorestan (south of the Taurus) rather than in the old Roman sector of Armenia (whither he had been asked to go by Mzhēzh Gnuni, probably to prepare for the council subsequently held there), may well be the work of Sebeos who was an opponent of union.

The date of the council (and preceding negotiations) may be inferred from the context in which it is placed. It post-dated the formal transfer of a large swathe of central Armenia from Persian to Roman control which was agreed, no earlier than summer 630, in negotiations with Boran. The Romans seem to have moved gingerly, first asserting their authority nominally through Mzhēzh Gnuni, military commander of the old Roman sector, then striking a deal with the Catholicosate, and only subsequently setting about establishing a military presence. Sebeos' remark that *shtemarank'* (storehouses, magazines) were to be established in the ceded territory when detachments were stationed there may be an early reference to a type of installation, with a military function, the *apotheke* (storehouse, magazine), which comes into prominence in Asia Minor in the second half of the century. In the context of this cautious, phased take-over, the council of Theodosiopolis should probably be dated to 631, which corresponds to the fourth year after the death of Khosrov (beginning 28 February 631), one of two dates given by the *Narratio de Rebus Armeniae* (the other is the 23rd regnal year of Heraclius, beginning on 5 October 632).

Literature: *PLRE* III, s.v. Mezezius; Garitte, *Narratio* 278–311; Haldon, *Seventh Century* 232–44.

50: ch.41, **132–133**, *career of Varaztirots' I (632/633–636/637).* Like his father Smbat, Varaztirots' features in a number of notices dispersed through Sebeos' text. It is tempting to suppose that they may have been extracted from a second Bagratuni biography. However, in this case, the notices betray a wider interest in expatriate Armenians, in the politics of Constantinople in which they were involved, and in the repercussions of those politics on Armenia. Notices with these broad but Armenian-slanted interests feature later in the text (**133, 137–138, 140–141, 142–145, 162–163**). It may be conjectured that they emanate from the same source of information, and that source may be identified as a record of notable events kept at the Catholicosate in Dvin (possibly by Sebeos himself, since the events in question occurred within 25 years of the time of writing). For convenience, this postulated source will be referred to as the Dvin Source.

The ousting of Varaztirots' from the governorship of Persarmenia, to which he had been appointed by Kawat (**128–129**), is not reported in any other source. If, as seems likely, Mzhēzh Gnuni only made his *démarche* to Ṙostom, commander of the formidable army of Atrpatakan, after securing the Romans' position in their enlarged sector of Armenia, the winter in which Ṙostom sent his brother to arrest Varaztirots' at Dvin and Varaztirots' escaped into the Roman sector, may well be that of 632–633. Varaztirots' probably spent several years in comfortable detention in Constantinople before the next incident in which he was involved, the plot to replace Heraclius with his illegitimate son, Athalarikos. Sebeos' account of this tallies in the main with that of Nikephoros, but is considerably fuller, giving more details about the conspirators' plans and naming more of them. The most likely date is 636 or 637, which allows some four years for the causally connected sequence of events now reported by Sebeos: the seizure of power in Armenia by Dawit' Saharuni, who had been implicated in the plot, the passage of three years before he was discredited and ousted, and the ensuing power-vacuum which is unlikely to have lasted much more than a year and which ended with the appointment of T'ēodoros Ṙshtuni to the Armenian command in winter 640–641 (**139**).

This dating supplies a context which may in turn suggest an explanation for what was evidently a ramified plot against an emperor whose prestige had stood so high but a few years earlier. It may be postulated that confidence in Heraclius plummeted after the rout of the Roman field army in Palestine and Syria (probably in 635, see n.53 below) and that the conspirators' object was to install a more energetic and bellicose regime. The mutilations ordered by Heraclius, which are corroborated by Nikephoros, were an early, if not the first, instance of what was to be a characteristic form of Byzantine punishment.

Source: Nikephoros ch.24.

Literature: *PLRE* III, s.vv. David Saharuni 6, Ioannes Atalarichus 260, Mezezius, Theodorus Rshtuni 167, Varaztiroch; Kaegi, *Military Unrest* 152–3.

51: ch.41, **133–134**, *Dawit' Saharuni, first curopalate of Armenia, 637/638–640*. Dramatic changes occurred in Armenia as the outer world came under increasing military pressure from the Arabs. The greater measure of independence for which different magnates had striven in the past was achieved relatively effortlessly by Dawit' Saharuni, once he had escaped from the soldiers escorting him to Constantinople in 636 or 637. He united local Armenian forces under his command, used them to attack and defeat the Roman commander, Mzhēzh Gnuni, and took command of the regular Roman forces stationed in Armenia. Politically weakened and facing crises elsewhere, Heraclius had no choice but to recognize the *fait accompli* and bow to the expressed wishes of the Armenian nobility. So he made Dawit' 'prince over all the territories [of Armenia]', a phrase which implies that Dawit' had united the two sectors of Armenia under his command. The grant of the grand court title *curopalate* (n.31 above) should be viewed both as an acknowledgement of this unprecedented extension of authority over Persarmenia, and as an inducement offered to retain the loyalty of Dawit' and, through him, of Armenia. By this stage (probably 637, possibly 638), the Persians could do little to oppose this, all available military resources being needed in Mesopotamia (n.54 below).

Dawit' Saharuni reciprocated, demonstrating his attachment to the Roman empire in the church which he sponsored at Mren to commemorate the restoration by Heraclius of the True Cross to Jerusalem. However, the prestige, which, as Sebeos notes, underpinned his authority, leaked away in three years and he was repudiated by the troops who had brought him to power. It should cause little surprise that he was unable to hold the fractious local interests of Armenia together for long, as the pressure from without intensified and the prestige of his Roman backer plummeted.

While the material about Dawit' Saharuni was probably taken from the postulated Dvin Source (because of its connection with the preceding Athalarikos episode), the brief notice which follows about disunity among the nobles was probably tacked on from elsewhere. Since T'ēodoros Ṙshtuni is praised for his defensive measures and later features as the hero of two military episodes which are recounted in considerable detail (**138–139**, **145–147**), it may be conjectured that Sebeos had a second source for this period, which may be dubbed the Ṙshtuni Source.

Literature: *PLRE* III, s.v. David Saharuni 6; Thierry, 'Héraclius'.

III. SECTION III (134–177)

Introduction

Sebeos' account of the rise of Islam is terse, presented in a series of compressed notices. There are more of them and they become somewhat fuller as he approaches the time of writing. A great deal of precise information is given, with a necessary minimum of dating indications. The overriding theme, the ruin of the old world order brought about by the excessive ambition of Khosrov, is followed through to its conclusion. The narrative encompasses the three main thrusts of the Arabs, into Roman and Sasanian territory and into the intermediary zone of Transcaucasia of which Armenia was a part. An overarching strategy is discerned which gives shape to the story. So does a subsidiary theme which is introduced: a partial explanation for the scale of the Arabs' initial success is sought in Jewish guidance and leadership.

So dramatic a transformation of the Near East should have prompted other contemporaries to record what they had witnessed and heard, in the way Sebeos did. The Syriac-speaking population of the Fertile Crescent, which was affected most immediately by the new power of the Arabs and could observe them at closest quarters, had both a greater incentive and a better opportunity than Sebeos to inquire into what had happened and to search for explanations. The need to understand, to scrabble for scraps of hope from the disastrous story of defeat was even greater for the Romans. Shorn of their empire, facing a continuing menace by land and sea from a clearly superior Arab power, massive adjustments had to be made to inherited structures, ideological as well as institutional. The rump of the old empire, conventionally called Byzantium, had to acquire a new rationale in the light of what had happened. It also needed to learn everything which could be learnt from the scrutiny of recent events so as to devise an effective strategy or strategies of survival. Finally the Arabs themselves, for quite different reasons – pride in their extraordinary achievements and concern with the awesome working out of God's will on earth – should have been impelled, with even greater urgency, to write history.

The latter-day historian cannot but be disappointed at the meagre haul of useful information which can be gathered from non-Armenian Christian sources. However devouring the interest of the citizens of Sasanian Mesopotamia and of the Roman Orient in the warfare which transformed their world and the subsequent actions of their Arab masters, all too little of their observations and reflections has survived.

Neither of the principal extant east Syrian chronicles lives up to expectation. The *Khuzistan Chronicle* may cover the same time span as Sebeos but its focus is much narrower and it tails off markedly towards the end. It does, however, present a coherent and plausible account of the conquest of Khuzistan, focused on the fortunes of Susa and Shustar, the cities which held out longest. The *Seert Chronicle*, preoccupied with the careers of great Nestorian churchmen and abbots, contains only two detailed notices about the coming of the Arabs.

Rather more of the west Syrian historical tradition has been preserved. A full and connected history of successive Arab victories and of the gradual dismemberment of the East Roman empire was written by Dionysius of Tel-Mahre, together with an overview of the destruction of the Sasanian empire, but it has to be handled with considerable caution. The demonstrable failings of his account of the Roman-Persian war of 603–630, stemming ultimately from weakness of the critical faculty and carelessness in the arrangement of the material in his principal source (the lost *Chronicle* of Theophilus of Edessa), was compounded, in the case of the Arab conquests, by a laudable decision to draw heavily on Arab traditions both for matter and structure. The resulting amalgam of Arab and Syrian material is both hard to make sense of and hard to square with the evidence provided by other, probably more reliable, sources. Much more trust can be put in the *Chronicle to 724* which has, as has been seen, an impressive record of accuracy in its coverage of the preceding 30 years. The last two notices in that portion of the text which was written around 640 pick out the two stages in the Arab conquest of the Roman Near East which had the greatest impact on civilians: a first devastating invasion of Palestine after a battle fought near Gaza in February 634; and, two years later, the first raid to reach Mardin at a time when the Arabs were taking over Syria and were launching an attack in force on the Sasanian empire.

History is, for the most part, either fragmented or garbled or both in extant Syrian chronicles. Between them they yield only four notices of real value, dealing with specific episodes in a precise way: the conquest of Khuzistan (*Khuz.Chron.*), the battle of Qadisiyya (*Chron.Seert*), and two key stages in the Arab advance into the Roman Near East (*Chron.724*). The track record of Roman sources is even worse. There is a simple explanation in the case of Theophanes, since he drew his material on the Arab conquests almost entirely from the main west Syrian tradition, probably from a Greek translation of the Syriac chronicle of Theophilus of Edessa which was later to be used by Dionysius of Tel-Mahre. His contemporary, Nikephoros, included some material about the fate of Egypt in a selective and impressionistic account of the period. But soon after the accession of Heraclius' grandson Constans II in September 641, his account breaks off entirely, only resuming in 668 with a notice about Constans' unpleasant end in a bath-house in Sicily. Since Theophanes likewise found no usable indigenous source for the secular history of Constans' reign, there is virtually complete silence from the East Roman empire about the most perilous phase in its existence and about the various measures taken to improve its defences and restructure its inherited institutions, which transformed it into a highly militarized and resilient highland power (by convention called Byzantium). The fundamental difficulty confronting Byzantinists is that the formation of the entity with which they are concerned simply cannot be observed. As for the Arab advance over Roman territory, Byzantine sources yield only *one* useful piece of information, about Egypt in the uneasy interlude between the conquest of Palestine and Syria and the attack by 'Amr b. al-'As.

There is no dearth of material in extant Arab sources. Quite the contrary. A new type of historical writing can be observed taking shape in the first century and a half of the Islamic era. It differed radically from the kind of elevated, classicizing history which had evolved in the Graeco-Roman world. Instead of placing a premium on elegance, on stylistic homogeneity, the overriding concern was to capture traditions in circulation and to establish their pedigree and authority. Citations of sources and attention to the particularities of individual versions of events were the hallmarks of Islamic historians. Bulky narratives were assembled out of the voluminous materials gathered by individual scholars. A great deal of hard historiographical labour may be required, but in the end it should be possible to reconstruct a detailed history of the conquests from several Arab points of view, unless appearances are very deceptive.

But it is now the contention of a majority of the Islamicists studying the earliest phase of Islamic history that much of the material preserved in extant texts consists of historical traditions deformed out of all recognition in the course of oral transmission across several generations. They conclude that it is virtually impossible to isolate whatever authentic reports may lurk in a mass of unreliable material in the texts which they analyse. This scepticism is now deep ingrained, and can be justified by several powerful arguments. There is too much that is anecdotal in Arab accounts of the conquests (*futuh*), too much that is obviously serving the sectional interests of a later age (chiefly of family, tribe and confession), too much which appears to be retrojecting phenomena of a later present (e.g. a centralized state, legal norms) into the past or seeking to buttress a case being argued later with largely fabricated historical examples.

There is no evidence, it is argued, that traditions about the conquests were brought together at an early stage in what might be termed a historical clearing-house, a vantage point into which information flowed from many different quarters, whether secular (a military high command, for example, or the Umayyad court at Damascus) or religious (at major Muslim centres, above all Medina). A very different process of evolution is suggested after careful scrutiny of the content of *futuh* accounts. They are characterized as history composed from the bottom up, deriving ultimately from the remembered experiences of a multitude of humble individual combatants, formed by a process of aggregation and lacking the wider view of higher authority. The construction of a coherent general historical narrative, within an articulated chronological framework, is attributed to a second, later, scholarly stage in the development of Islamic historical writing. Since the scholars were working at a distance, temporal and spatial, from events, much guesswork was involved in their reconstructions.

Literary considerations deliver a final blow to those who would nonetheless cling to the view that there is an authentic core with some structure, not entirely denuded of a higher view, in the extant Islamic accounts of the conquests. The basic component of the traditions which have been preserved has been identified as an independent narrative unit (*khabar*, plural *akhbar*), which is more often than not anecdotal in character (the more obviously anecdotal *akhbar* are attributed to beduin tribal traditions and classified as *qisas*). Two key processes are then isolated which transformed these *akhbar* into more or less connected narratives – elaboration as an originally short *khabar* was gradually endowed with much fanciful detail in the course of story-telling across a generation or more, and compilation at the later stage when scholars set to work to collect and edit *akhbar* in circulation. Very little of authentic eyewitness reports was left, it is concluded, by this stage. Hence the latter-day historian should not expect more than a highly distorted view of both the general and the particular in Arab accounts of the conquests.

These conclusions may strike the non-Islamicist as too extreme in their pessimism. They cannot, however, be ignored. The historian determined to try to grasp something of what happened to change the late antique world out of all recognition in the seventh century cannot start from the Islamic sources any more than from the Syrian and Byzantine. A start has to be made elsewhere, in the fourth of the Near East's historical traditions, that of Armenia. This brings us back to Sebeos. No other extant source which touches on the Arab conquests can match his account in its range, coherence, precision and apparent sobriety. A second Armenian chronicle can be used to supplement his material. The *History of the Caucasian Albanians*, put together probably in the tenth century by Movsēs Daskhurants'i, incorporates material on the Arab expansion which is of the same apparently high standard but with a different geographical focus, taken from a lost laudatory biography of Juanshēr, military commander in Albania from 637/638 to his death in 668. There is much less to be learned from a third Armenian text, the chronicle of Łewond written at the end of the eighth century and covering the period 632–789. Łewond seems to have drawn his material on the first half of the seventh century independently from some of Sebeos' sources, but his version is slighter and often garbled (nn.52, 53, 55, 62, 70 below).

Sebeos' account, filled out with Movsēs' material, offers the best hope of reaching back to seventh-century historical reality. By repeated comparisons of Armenian with Islamic versions of individual events and of the connections between them, it may also be possible to determine whether modern Islamicists have taken scepticism too far.

Literature: Haldon, *Seventh Century*; Hoyland, *Seeing Islam as Others Saw It* 182–9, 400–9, 416–19, 428–34, 443–6, 631–71; Robinson, 'Conquest of Khuzistan'; Donner, *Conquests* 143–6; Hoyland, 'Arabic, Syriac and Greek Historiography'; Theophanes, introduction lxxxii–lxxxiv; Nikephoros, introduction 14–15; Humphreys, *Islamic History* 69–91; Conrad, 'Conquest of Arwad'; Leder, '*Khabar*'; Noth/Conrad 1–87; Mahé, 'Łewond'.

Note. So voluminous is the Arabic historical material and so inaccessible for the most part to non-Arabists, that only selective reference
will be made to a very small number of notable works which are available
in convenient translations. These are cited for illustration and to provide
readers with some entry-points into primary material emanating from
Muslim milieux.

52: ch.42, **134–135**, *the origins of Islam* (cf. T'.A. 98–99, 101 with additional information, including two important items [Heraclius' brother
Theodore laid siege to Edessa; the Jews' desert retreat was the ruined
city of Madiam which they restored]). Close attention has rightly been
paid to Sebeos' brief account of Muhammad. For Sebeos was well
placed to gather information (given the Catholicosate's contacts with
other churches of the Near East), and he was writing his chronicle at a
time when memories of the sudden irruption of the Arabs into the Near
East were fresh. Much of what he says about the origins of the new religion conforms to Muslim tradition and probably approximates to the
truth.

He knows Muhammad's name, knows that he was a merchant by
profession, and hints that his life was suddenly changed by a divinely
inspired revelation. He presents a fair summary of key elements of
Muhammad's preaching: advocacy of belief in a single deity; familiarity
with the Old Testament, from which much illustrative material is quarried by the Qur'an; and presentation of Abraham as common ancestor
of Arabs and Jews and as proponent of pure monotheist worship. He
may exaggerate the scale of Muhammad's political success ('they all
came together in unity of religion') – a venial error, given the military
impact of the *umma* on the surrounding world immediately after his
death – but he knows that there was a political dimension to the religious
community formed by Muhammad and that a large number of
previously independent Arabs were drawn into it. He picks out some of
the rules of behaviour imposed on the *umma* (all four prohibitions
feature in the Qur'an), but passes over positive injunctions, such as the
obligation to give alms.

Finally, Sebeos realizes that there was an internal, religious dynamic
directing the attention of Muhammad and his followers to the southern
provinces of the Roman Near East. As descendants of Abraham, they,
like Old Testament Israel, could lay a divinely-sanctioned claim to the
Holy Land. He is also probably right to present Muhammad as author-

izing action to assert that claim. However, this coherent account of how a new monotheist religion superseded a multiplicity of local pagan cults and brought political unity and formidable military power to the Arabs is placed in a context which makes neither logical nor chronological sense. Jews of the Roman Near East become prime movers: first they gather in Edessa during the temporary hiatus between the withdrawal of Shahrvaraz's forces (after his summit meeting with Heraclius in July 629 [n.45 above]) and the arrival of Heraclius with a substantial Roman army in summer 630 (n.48 above); then they withdraw into the interior of Arabia and propose an alliance to which the Arabs cannot respond because of their religious divisions; it is only now (at the earliest autumn 630) that Muhammad comes on stage and begins the process of creating that union on the religious and political planes which is necessary if the Arabs are to be effective allies; finally, when this goal has been achieved, the Arabs march on the Holy Land with the Jews as their guides. An unnecessary second but overarching explanation is thus introduced for the beginning of the Arab conquests, which has the effect of squeezing the whole of Muhammad's religious mission, from his first revelation (conventionally dated around 610) to the opening attack on southern Palestine (in 634 two years after his death), into a mere three years or so.

It was natural for some Christian contemporaries to associate the new with the old non-Christian monotheist religion and to explain the extraordinary success of the Arabs by the action of some familiar agency, the Jews. It was not Sebeos' view, however. He placed these extraordinary events in a far grander context, that of cosmic history: for him the Arabs were the fourth of the successive kingdoms of which the Prophet Daniel spoke; their coming, the great storm from the south, opened the last act in the history of mankind; it was soon to be followed by a final great war between the forces of good and evil (the start of which he may have thought he was witnessing as he wrote in the mid 650s and as internal tensions grew steadily more acute in the new Arab empire) and then by the Day of Judgement with which time would end. It follows that the spurious interpretation and authentic material about the origins of Islam came conjoined into Sebeos' hands. The joinery is indeed neat, only one phrase betraying a momentary unease, at the point when the connection is first made: Muhammad's preaching is placed loosely *around the time* of the flight of the Jews rather than afterwards.

It is plain then that Sebeos is making use of a pre-existing written source in this first section of the final part of his history. A place of composition in Palestine, probably in Jerusalem, may be inferred from the focus of interest. It will therefore be designated the Palestine Source. Sebeos marks the transition to it from the Řshtuni Source with a brief editorial introduction. This also serves to alert the reader to some chronological backtracking (first to 630, then to Arab victories which antedated Dawit' Saharuni's rule in Armenia [637/638-640]). The same story – that Jews were behind the invasion of Palestine (justified likewise by reference to a common descent from Abraham) – appears in Łewond's notice which misdates the attack after Heraclius' death in 641. Łewond seems to have had access, direct or indirect, to the Palestine Source, or something like it.

Sources: Łewond ch.1; Ibn Ishaq.

Literature: Crone/Cook, *Hagarism* 6–8; Millar, 'Hagar'; Hoyland, 'Sebeos'; Hoyland, *Seeing Islam as Others Saw it* 128–31, 532–41; Dagron/Déroche, 'Juifs et chrétiens' 38–43; Rodinson, *Mohammed*; F. Buhl and A.T. Welch, 'Muhammad 1. The Prophet's life and career', *E.I.* VII, 360–376.

53: ch.42, **135–137**, *Arab conquests I (the Roman Near East, 634–636, 639–642)* (cf. T'.A. 101–102 with some additional matter [some of which recurs in Łewond's version] but misdated [as in Łewond] to the beginning of the reign of Constans II [late 641]). Still drawing on the postulated Palestine Source, Sebeos gives a brief account of two Arab victories and the subsequent submission of a large part of Palestine. Then, in a passage which takes a broader view and looks like an editorial interjection, he enumerates the successful campaigns of the following few years. He thus places the conquest of Palestine in the wider context of Arab expansion and picks out the two engagements which were reported in the Palestine Source as the decisive battles which opened the way for the conquest of the Roman Near East. It is his considered view which he is presenting. It therefore deserves close scrutiny.

Sebeos supplies no dates, merely putting events in a sequence. Two chronological fixed points may, however, be obtained from a near-contemporary west Syrian source, embedded in *Chron.724*. This reports a battle between Romans and Arabs 12 miles east of Gaza on Friday 4 February 634. The Romans fled, their commander, a patrician, was captured and killed. So too were four thousand peasants, Christian, Jewish and Samaritan. The Arabs ravaged the whole region (by which a wide swathe of southern Palestine is probably meant). This engagement provides a *terminus post quem* for the first of those recorded by Sebeos which was fought much further north, east of the Dead Sea and just to the south of the Balqa' (Erabovt‘, *er-rabbath*, 'the great city', of Moab [modern Rabba] lay on an important route running north from Kerak towards Dhiban). A *terminus ante quem* for both Sebeos' battles is provided by the next and last notice in the seventh-century text embedded in *Chron.724*: under the year October 635–September 636 it records that 'the Arabs invaded the whole of Syria and went down to Persia and conquered it'; a raid on the Tur Abdin in Roman Mesopotamia is also reported.

Sebeos' two battles should therefore be placed in the intervening period, 634–635. On both occasions the Romans had concentrated relatively large armies. This may be inferred from the presence of the emperor's brother, Theodore (mistakenly called Theodosius), as commander at the battle of Erabovt‘, while a very high figure, doubtless inflated, is put on the second army, commanded by the unnamed eunuch. Nonetheless, on both occasions the Arabs won relatively easy victories, aided by surprise at Erabovt‘ and by 'fear of the Lord' after a Roman attempt to surprise the Arabs in their camp near the Jordan went wrong. The details supplied by Sebeos about the surprise attack suggest: (i) that it was a commando operation relying on stealth (hence it is carried out by infantry), (ii) that the Roman and Arab camps were not far apart, (iii) that the Arabs had good intelligence beforehand and (iv) that there were places of concealment nearby (such as ravines) in which ambushing forces could be stationed. But it was the Arabs' use of their camp both as bait and as killing ground (tents and herds of tethered camels which formed its perimeter trapping and disordering the Roman force) which opened the way for a victorious counter-attack on the main Roman army. There was no effective resistance, the Romans' will having been broken, perhaps at the sight of an unprecedentedly large and well-organized force of Arabs, perhaps on realizing the intensity of their commitment, or perhaps out of a half-conscious acknowledgement that God might indeed be on their side. Łewond's account of the second battle has several features in common with Sebeos': a large Roman army is involved; it leaves its camp on foot to attack the Arabs; the Arabs have numerous camels and horses; exhausted from the weight of their weapons and the heat and the sand, the Romans are surprised and cut to pieces. It looks like a free rendering by Łewond of material taken from the Palestine Source.

Wherever this rout occurred, whether close to the Golan heights or further south along the Jordan's passage to the Dead Sea, it was immediately exploited by the Arabs. They advanced across the river, established a base at Jericho, and, aided again by the dread which they or their divine backing engendered, brought about the rapid submission of 'all the inhabitants of the land', including the people of Jerusalem. There may be some exaggeration of the scale of the Roman collapse (some cities on the coast held out for a while), but Sebeos leaves us in no doubt that there was wholesale surrender within a very short time. It may therefore be fitted into the period of two years or so bracketed by the two notices in *Chron.724*.

An outline history of the Arab conquest of Palestine and Syria may thus be extracted from two near-contemporary Christian sources: a first victory won near Gaza on 4 February 634 (*Chron.724*) which opened Palestine to attack from the south; a second victory over a large Roman army east of the Dead Sea, probably later that year (Sebeos); then a third decisive victory somewhere in the Jordan valley which opened the way for the occupation of Palestine from the east in 635 (Sebeos) and for the invasion of Syria in 636 (*Chron.724*). There ensued, as reported by Sebeos, in the brief strategic overview which he appended to this notice (**136–137**), a first attack on the Sasanian empire in 636 (*Chron.724*), a campaign across the Euphrates into Roman Mesopotamia (Sebeos and other sources – probably in summer 639, after a short truce which the Romans broke), and the conquest of Egypt (Sebeos and other sources – achieved between December 639 and September 642). This is all too skeletal a version of events, but there is no other reliable material in non-Muslim sources which can be safely used to flesh it out. The much fuller west Syrian tradition, which originated with Theophilus of Edessa in the middle of the eighth century and which was recycled by Dionysius of Tel-Mahre, must be discounted, since it makes extensive use of Islamic sources and the value of those sources may be questioned.

Sebeos' version of events does not tally with any of the reconstructions made by Arab scholars in the eighth and ninth centuries. These present different sets of events in different arrangements, but they are all, paradoxically, committed to finding *human* explanations of a conventional sort for Arab success. Hence battles grow in scale and multiply in number. City after city has to be besieged before it capitulates. In the process of expansion and elaboration, real persons (Heraclius' brother

Theodore and the eunuch, described as Sacellarius) and real episodes (an engagement near Gaza, defeat of a Roman force at '*Araba*, defeat of the inhabitants of *Ma'ab*, a Roman surprise attack across the Jordan which is converted into crushing defeat) are pulled into a complicated mêlée of events, presented in different sequences. The rout which followed the failed raid on the Arabs' camp near the Jordan and left 2,000 Roman dead has become the battle of Yarmuk, a conventional battle with huge forces arrayed on both sides. Only the one element common to all the traditions, Khalid b. al-Walid's urgent march across the desert from Sasanian Mesopotamia to reinforce the Arabs confronting the Romans, may be taken as authentic, in spite of Sebeos' silence.

We therefore witness a historiographical failure on the grandest scale imaginable, the failure of Muslims to produce a decent historical record of their conquest of the Holy Land and Syria, the future metropolitan region of the Umayyad caliphate. Whether this failure exemplifies a general weakness in early Islamic historical traditions or may be accounted for, at least in part, by the bewildering speed of the conquest or by some other factor (e.g. an unusual degree of local influence on the formation of historical traditions in a region where Arab settlement was dispersed from the first) is an issue best left to Islamicists to resolve.

Sources: *Chron.724* 18–19; Łewond ch.1; Dionysius 144–50, 154–65; Nikephoros chs23, 26; *Khuz.Chron.* 45; John of Nikiu 178–201; Tabari XI–XIII; Baladhuri I 165–234, 269–83, 335–51.

Literature: A. Legendre, 'Ar, Ar-Moab', *Dictionnaire de la Bible* I, cols814–18; Johns, 'Southern Transjordan' 9; *PLRE* III, s.v. Theodorus 163; Donner, *Conquests* 111–55; Butler, *Arab Conquest of Egypt* 194–367; Hoyland, *Seeing Islam as Others Saw It* 574–90.

54: ch.42, **137**, *Arab conquests II (Sasanian Mesopotamia, 636–640)*. By his reference to the three rival armies which dominated Sasanian politics in the turbulent period following the assassination of Shahrvaraz, Sebeos signals a new transition, in this case back to Persian history and, it may be conjectured, to the Persian Source, which probably supplied the material he used about the succession of rulers from Boran to Yazkert III (**130** with n.46 above). His account of operations in Mesopotamia is clear, though condensed, but lacks all dating indications. Fortunately some are provided by Movsēs Daskhurants'i who had access to a high-grade source. Movsēs, in company with *Chron.Seert*, also provides a fair amount of additional information, which helps to make sense of Sebeos' sometimes elliptical account, and confirms that Sebeos has reported the major operations in their correct sequence. *Khuz.Chron.*, by contrast, has little to say beyond stressing the scale of the fighting and noting the death of Ṙostom and the flight of Yazkert from Ctesiphon.

Sebeos picks out six episodes: (i) a siege of Ctesiphon which was defended by Yazkert; (ii) a Persian counter-thrust in massive force, carried out by the army of Media under the command of its general Ṙostom, which drove the Arabs across the Tigris and back 'to their own borders', beyond the Euphrates in the region of Hira; (iii) a crushing victory in open battle won by the Arabs in which Ṙostom and 'all' (i.e. most) of the senior Persian (and Armenian) commanders were killed; (iv) the withdrawal of the remnants of the Persian army to Atrpatakan, the base of the Median army, where the troops seem to have elected Khoṙokhazat as their general (to be identified with 'the prince of the Medes' who plays an important part in subsequent Transcaucasian and Persian affairs [**143**, **164** with nn.61, 67]); (v) an attempt by Khoṙokhazat to evacuate the government, treasury and population from Ctesiphon, which ended in disaster; (vi) the flight of Yazkert to the 'army of the south', surely that of Persia proper, previously mentioned by Sebeos in association with that of the east (**130**). There is one additional episode described in the later sources which he passes over – a second siege or blockade of Ctesiphon by the Arabs, reported to have lasted either six months (M.D.) or 18 (*Chron.Seert*) and to have taken place between the decisive battle and the failed evacuation attempt. Sebeos' remarks about Khoṙokhazat's haste therefore refer to the speed of his march to Ctesiphon rather than the shortness of the interlude before the Median army returned to the fray.

The two later sources supplement Sebeos' account of Persian mobilization and the counter-attack which drove the Arabs from Ctesiphon (episode [ii]). Movsēs, whose source traced the career of Juanshēr from the 630s to his death in 668, reports that contingents came from Albania (with Juanshēr newly appointed as its commander), Siwnikʻ and Armenia (which explains the presence of the Armenian commanders noted by Sebeos). *Chron.Seert* has Yazkert distribute largesse to the armies before the start of operations (the use of the plural may indicate that the other regional armies also contributed forces). A date for these preparations may be obtained from a later synchronization made by Movsēs (tr. Dowsett 115): he equates Juanshēr's 15th year in the

Albanian military command with Yazkert's 20th and last regnal year
(651/652). It follows that Juanshēr assumed his command in Yazkert's
sixth regnal year (637/638) and that the Persian counter-thrust, which
probably took place immediately after the mobilization, can be dated to
autumn 637. The Persian plan seems to have been to trap the Arabs in
the alluvial land, criss-crossed by canals and irrigation channels,
between the two great rivers, but the Arabs managed to retreat beyond
the Euphrates. Then, according to Movsēs, two battles were fought: in
the first an Arab attack was driven off, but in the second, dated precisely
to 6 January (in 638, as has been established above), the Arabs, who had
evidently received reinforcements, prevailed and drove the Persians
back across the river. *Chron.Seert*, which does not mention the first
engagement, locates the decisive battle near Hira and Qadisiyya (which
has mutated into Movsēs' Katshan).

Neither of the later sources reports the flight and regrouping of the
army of Media, nor the election of Khoṙokhazat as its commander
(episode [iv]). Movsēs follows the fortunes of Juanshēr who was
wounded in the battle. He is nursed back to health in Ctesiphon, is
honoured by Yazkert and wins the esteem of Khoṙokhazat (who thus
makes a sudden, unexplained entrance) by helping to restore peace in
Media. Movsēs then dates the second Arab siege of Ctesiphon and
Khoṙokhazat's evacuation operation, Juanshēr's initial task being to
provide cover on the far side of the Tigris (episode [v]), to Yazkert's
eighth regnal year (June 639–June 640), a date which overlaps with
A.H.19 (2 January–20 December 640) given by *Chron.Seert* (wrongly
correlated with Yazkert's seventh year). Finally, *Chron.Seert* adds that
Yazkert fled to 'the mountain', that is the Zagros range which shielded
both Media and Persia from attack from Mesopotamia.

A coherent and militarily intelligible picture emerges when Sebeos'
evidence is combined with that of the two later sources: the initial Arab
invasion (dated by *Chron.724* to 636) resulted, by 637, in the occupation
of Mesopotamia and a first siege of Ctesiphon; the Persians counter-
attacked in force in the second half of 637, drove the Arabs out of
Mesopotamia, but then suffered a crushing defeat in the vicinity of Hira
and Qadisiyya on 6 January 638; the Arabs subsequently renewed their
attack, reoccupied Mesopotamia and besieged Ctesiphon either for six
or for 18 months in the course of 638 and 639; then, in the first half of
640, the army of Media under its new, elected general, Khoṙokhazat,
marched swiftly down from Atrpatakan, organized the evacuation of

Ctesiphon, but lost its nerve when, in the course of a fighting retreat, it was unexpectedly attacked by a large Arab force and abandoned the people and the state treasures which it was escorting to safety.

This reconstruction of events corresponds in essentials with that of the Islamic sources, which are in general agreement with each other on the course of operations in Mesopotamia. They report: (i) an initial Arab advance into the Mesopotamian alluvium up to al-Mada'in (the conjoined cities of Veh-Artashir and Ctesiphon); (ii) a serious Arab defeat at the Battle of the Bridge followed by an apparently disorderly retreat back to the fringe of the desert near Hira; (iii) some raiding activity while reinforcements were being gathered in Arabia, operations which, according to some accounts, involved one serious engagement, said to have ended in an Arab victory, at Buwayb; (iv) the advance of a large Persian army commanded by Ṙostom across the Euphrates and its crushing defeat in a major battle at Qadisiyya, a short distance south-west of Hira; (v) a second Arab push into the Mesopotamian alluvium which culminated in a long siege of al-Mada'in (said to have lasted from two to 28 months); (vi) the evacuation of Yazkert from the city, swiftly followed by its occupation and the capture of the Sasanian royal treasures (of which much is made by Sayf b. 'Umar, Tabari's source for these events).

Sources: *Chron.724* 19; M.D., tr. Dowsett 109–12; *Chron.Seert* 580–1, 627–8; *Khuz.Chron.* 33; Dionysius 151–4; Tabari XI–XIII; Baladhuri I 387–419, II 51–9.

Literature: Donner, *Conquests* 173–220.

55: ch.42, **137–139**, *death of Heraclius (11 February 641), Arab attack on Dvin (October 640)*. The near-juxtaposition of two notices about Heraclius' death points to use of two sources: the first, fuller notice may be attributed to the postulated Dvin Source, since there is a reference to the *aspet* Varaztirots' in exile; the second to the postulated Ṙshtuni Source, since the initial reference to divisions among Armenian princes picks up a point made in the previous short notice about T'ēodoros Ṙshtuni (**134**) and T'ēodoros himself appears on the scene towards the end of the episode. The Ṙshtuni Source goes into considerable detail (including precise dates) about operations on this and on a later occasion (**145–147** with n.62).

The Arabs were probably in firm control of Roman Mesopotamia before they set off on their northern raid beyond the Armenian Taurus.

They used the easiest of the passes, which debouches at modern Bitlis, and the safest and most direct route across the volcano-studded landscape of south-west Armenia to reach the administrative heartland in Ayrarat. Apart from the mystery of the Metsamawr bridge (destroyed but used), the only puzzling feature concerning the operations themselves is the terminology apparently used of Dvin: when it comes under attack, it is consistently called a *k'alak'* (walled city); but there are two earlier references, in the context of the last-minute warning of attack brought by three named princes, to an *awan* (unwalled town), the first of which explicitly names Dvin as the *awan* in question, and one reference to a *berd* (fortress) apparently at Dvin. Since there was an *awan* near Dvin, namely the town founded across the Azat river from Dvin as the residence of the Chalcedonian Catholicos when the Catholicosate split in 591, it may be suspected that something has gone awry with the text and that the whole district of Dvin was being warned, including the *awan* and an unnamed fortress nearby.

This episode is also reported with much emotional rhetoric by Łewond. He misplaces it in the second year of Constans' reign (642/643). The same basic phenomena are registered (rapid Arab march on Dvin, fall of the city, 35,000 prisoners taken) but Dvin falls because its troops are serving with T'ēodoros Řshtuni and neither T'ēodoros nor any other Armenian noble dares attack the Arabs. If a common source underlies the two accounts, it has been much transmuted by Łewond.

Sources: Nikephoros ch.27; Theophanes 341; Hewsen, *AŠX* 65, 70; Łewond ch.3.

Literature: *PLRE* III, s.v. Theodorus Rshtuni 167, Varaztiroch; Grousset, *Histoire* 296–7; Manandean, 'Invasions' 163–77; M. Canard, 'Arminiya 2. Armenia under Arab domination', *E.I.* I, 635–636; Garitte, *Narratio* 246–67.

56: ch.42, **139**, *Arab conquests III (operations in Arabia and the Gulf, 641)*. This short notice demands careful analysis. (i) The caliph, who is designated *t'agawor* (a general word for king) and *ark'ay* (hitherto applied only to the Sasanian king), is named (correctly) for the first time as 'Umar (634–644). He is presented as directing operations at a distance, as he is in early Islamic historical traditions. (ii) No date is given, but the positioning of the notice in Sebeos' text and the brief editorial recapitulation of previous Arab conquests with which it begins (akin to the cast-forward at **136–137**) point to a date in 641.

(iii) Sebeos gives a cryptic account of the first of the two campaigns conjoined in this notice: it was clearly important since it involved 'royal (i.e. caliphal) armies'; and it was directed into 'the original borders of the territory of Ismael'. The conjunction *apa*, 'then', which prefaces the sentence, dates the campaign after the initial phase of expansion which has just been summarized. It follows that the territory which was attacked was not Palestine, since it had already been conquered, but a region which Sebeos or his source (here probably the Persian Source) regarded as the Arab homeland or part thereof. It appears then that the campaign was an assertion of power by the caliph *within Arabia*, at a stage long after the supposed unification of Arabia in the wars of conquest, misleadingly termed wars of apostasy (*ridda*) in early Islamic historical traditions. It may be conjectured that the targets were secluded by distance and geography from the new Islamic centres in the Hijaz, hence that they probably lay in the south, in the Yemen. The Muslims, it may be surmised, were only ready to confront the Persian authorities who had been governing the southern seaboard of Arabia since the 570s once they had broken Persian power in Mesopotamia. The later reference to prisoners-of-war taken from Arabia (the preposition *i*, 'from', should almost certainly be restored to the text, which makes no sense as it stands) to Khuzistan confirms that there had been military action at this late date in Arabia.

(iv) There is no difficulty in making sense of Sebeos' somewhat fuller report about the second campaign, a new offensive, authorized by the caliph, against the whole length of the Persian coast, from Persia proper to the borders of India. It should probably viewed as the opening phase of a grand assault on the core territory of the Sasanian empire, intended to draw troops away from that sector of the northern Zagros which was going to be assaulted in 642. Sebeos does not diverge from early Islamic historical traditions on this matter, although they date the attack to 640 at the latest.

(v) It is tempting to infer, from the final note about the locality where eyewitness evidence was gathered, that the author of the postulated Persian Source was at work in Khuzistan. If so, he surely included a full account of the hard-fought campaign for Khuzistan (interrupted, according to *Khuz. Chron.*, by a two-year truce [638?–640?], after which the two chief centres of resistance, Susa and Shustar, were captured [the latter after a two-year siege]) and Sebeos must have decided to excise it from his version.

Sources: Tabari X, XIII; *Khuz. Chron.* 41–4; Baladhuri II 105–28.

Literature: Kennedy, *Prophet* 24–5; Donner, *Conquests* 82–90; Hinds, 'The First Arab Conquests'; Robinson, 'Conquest of Khuzistan'.

57: ch.43, **139–140**, *an incident in Jerusalem (641)*. The reference to 'the plots of rebellious Jews' connects this notice with that concerning the Arab conquest of Palestine with its stress on the guiding role of the Jews (**134–136** with n.53 above). It may therefore be attributed to the postulated Palestine Source.

The preamble confirms the dating of the construction of the first Aqsa mosque on the Temple esplanade soon after the Muslims entered the city. This early date is given by contemporary eyewitness testimony, which is to be found in a Georgian translation of an Arabic translation of one of a set of edifying tales written originally in Greek and collected together soon after 668 in the St Sabas lavra near Jerusalem. Sebeos also provides a context: the Muslims reacted swiftly to a pre-emptive move by Jews to rebuild the Temple of Solomon, by appropriating the site and constructing their own place of worship. Arculf, who visited Jerusalem around 670, is derogatory about its architecture but reports that it could accommodate 3,000 people.

The incident reported by Sebeos happened an unspecified amount of time later. The position of the notice would suggest a date in 641. The new Muslim or Muslim-backed authority has redressed the traditional balance between Christians and Jews in the holy city in favour of the latter. Jerusalem, it emerges, has a Jewish governor, and the Jews have been allowed to construct a synagogue very close to the site of the Temple, right at its base. Nonetheless even-handedness was vital if good order was to be maintained. Hence a potentially inflammatory incident, such as the desecration of the mosque by Jewish *agents provocateurs*, was subject to careful, impartial and public investigation. The postulated Palestine Source was well informed but discreet, refraining from naming the Muslim magnate who identified the perpetrators of the sacrilege.

Literature: Mango, 'Temple Mount' 1–3; Flusin, 'L'esplanade du Temple'.

58: ch.44, **140–141**, *succession crisis in Constantinople, 641*. This short notice (taken probably from the postulated Dvin Source) is misleading in certain respects: (i) Constantine III's reign lasted rather more than 'a few days', since he came to the throne on 11 February 641 and died 103 days later (i.e. on 24 May); (ii) the story that Martina had a hand in his death, which also appears in Theophanes, Dionysius and *Chron.Seert*, looks like a *canard* put into circulation by her opponents; neither Nikephoros nor John of Nikiu, the two principal sources for this period of political crisis in Constantinople, breathes a word of it; (iii) according to Nikephoros, Valentinus held no formal military appointment under Constantine III, let alone the supreme command in Asia Minor implied by Sebeos, but was a military officer in the entourage of the treasurer Philagrius, who was entrusted with a large sum in cash for distribution as largesse to secure the support of the army in Asia Minor for the dying Constantine's children.

However, after the sacking and exile of Philagrius which came soon after Constantine's death, Valentinus took over political leadership of the army, brought it to the Bosphorus and put pressure on the new regime of Martina and her young son Heraclius II, known as Heraclonas. He succeeded in extracting a number of concessions from them (first the coronation of Constantine III's son, Constans II, later more largesse for the soldiers and the command of the *Excubitores* for himself [of which a seal provides confirmation]) and, finally, after popular opposition to Heraclonas and Martina (which he helped to foster) burst out into open rebellion in Constantinople, he deposed them and had them mutilated and exiled. Sebeos is right about Martina's punishment (excision of the tongue) but wrong in saying that she and her two sons were executed.

This political turbulence, spread over a few months (from 24 May into September) in 641, was assuredly connected with the grave crisis in the Near East. With the fall in 641 of the last Roman coastal redoubt in Palestine, the provincial capital Caesarea, the only substantial area still under Roman control was the Nile delta, but their position there looked increasingly precarious, as the Arabs, established in the interior of Egypt, pushed north and prepared to lay siege to Alexandria. The burning issue of the day was whether to negotiate the formal surrender of Egypt or to make a final military effort there. Of the three sources, Nikephoros, Theophanes and John of Nikiu, on whose overlapping and largely consistent testimonies the composite account given above is based, it is John of Nikiu who reveals most about the conflict over foreign policy between the hawks (led by Philagrius, and later by

Valentinus) and the doves whom Martina favoured and who included Cyrus, patriarch of Alexandria, and two powerful, if shadowy, figures in the European and Asian provinces of the empire (Kubratos, leader of the Unogundurs or Huns, and a certain David the Matarguem). In the end, the hawks won the political battle at the centre (in September), but by then it was too late to alter the policy of appeasement initiated during the reign of Heraclonas. The patriarch Cyrus returned to Alexandria on 14 September, and before long embarked on negotiations with the Arab commander, 'Amr b. al-'As, which resulted in an agreement, signed probably on 8 November, giving the Romans 11 months to withdraw from Egypt.

Sources: Nikephoros chs22, 28–32 (with commentary 191–93); Theophanes 341–2; Dionysius 166–7; John of Nikiu 184–98; *Chron.Seert* 628–9; Zacos/Veglery nos1087 (Valentinus), 1365 (Philagrius).

Literature: Kaegi, *Military Unrest* 154–7; Herrin, *Formation of Christendom* 215–17; Stratos, *Seventh Century* II, 175–205; Haldon, *Byzantine Praetorians* 174, 178–9; *PLRE* III, s.v. Cyrus 17, Koubratos, Philagrius 3, Valentinus 5; Donner, *Conquests* 152–5; Butler, *Arab Conquest of Egypt* 275–327.

59: ch.44, **141**, *Arab conquests IV (the battle of Nihawand [642] and advance into Iran)*. In this notice Sebeos homes in on what he or his source (almost certainly the postulated Persian Source) viewed as a battle of great strategic importance. He makes it plain that large forces were mobilized on both sides, that the battle was long and hard fought, and that victory, when it came, opened up the Iranian plateau to Arab attack. The synchronized dating by regnal years of Constans and Yazkert places the battle in the first half of 642. By virtue of this date, as well as its military significance and general location in Media, the battle briefly described by Sebeos may be identified with an analogous engagement reported in early Islamic historical traditions and given a precise location at Nihawand. Nihawand was, indeed is of the utmost strategic importance, commanding as it does the point where the main trans-Zagros pass linking Mesopotamia and Media opens out into the large plain of modern Malayer, which acts as a southern ante-chamber to the north-west segment of the Iranian plateau. It was therefore natural that, after the loss of the rich lowland component of their empire, the Persians should mobilize all available military forces for a stand there, so as to prevent the Arabs breaking through the formidable natural bulwark guarding their core highland territories.

Although several *topoi* (most notably a story that Persian soldiers were chained together) have been identified in early Islamic traditions about the battle, Albrecht Noth, one of the foremost revisionists among contemporary Islamicists, clearly goes too far in regarding the traditions as nothing but tissues of fictitious matter. For Sebeos provides independent and solid corroboration for Arab testimony that the battle was important and that Yazkert was still capable of fielding a large army. It may also be inferred that the campaign required caliphal authorization, as claimed by Arab sources, given the size of the forces which were mobilized.

The brittleness of Persian morale, which collapsed at a rumour (a piece of well-timed disinformation?) that Arab reinforcements had arrived, is probably to be explained by the shock induced by the extraordinary recent Arab successes. The dissolution of the Persian field army presented the Arabs with alternative routes of invasion, the easier running over Media towards Ṙeyy and the Elburz mountains, the more difficult leading south-east into the highlands of Persia proper, which could also be approached from Khuzistan by a difficult pass (the Persian Gates). Early Islamic traditions report Arab thrusts in both directions, that into Persia encountering stiffer resistance and taking nearly a decade to achieve success. These campaigns stretching over many years are touched on in Sebeos' last summary sentence. This supplies an important item of information – that 22 fortresses, designated *berd* rather than *kʻalakʻ* (fortified city), were captured in the course of the Arab advance. Most of them were probably small administrative centres (one of which, Qasr-i Abu Nasr, close to Shiraz, has been excavated) which acted as the foci of resistance in the heartland of the Sasanian empire.

After several years of defensive warfare, there was a perceptible weakening in Persian resistance. The naturally fissiparous world of Iran and its dependencies in Transcaucasia began to break apart. Automatic acceptance of membership of a single imperial entity, deep-ingrained by centuries of experience and ideological bombardment, was attenuated as the armed force necessary to sustain imperial pretension visibly failed to meet the Islamic challenge. Movsēs Daskhurantsʻi is the sole witness to this important development, which he dates around 644. For Juanshēr withdrew from the defensive war, after seven years of loyal service beginning with the Qadisiyya campaign. The 'Persian general', probably to be equated with Sebeos' 'prince of the Medes' (identified in n.54 above as Khořokhazat), responded by sending troops to occupy the main centres and lowlands of Albania and took Juanshēr's father and brothers hostage but before long he had no choice but to back down as Iberia came to Juanshēr's aid. The striking power of the army of Media, one of the two major military forces still underpinning Sasanian power, was gravely impaired.

Sources: *Chron.Seert* 581; M.D., tr. Dowsett 112–15; Dionysius 154; Tabari XIII–XV; Baladhuri I 420–33, 469–89, II 3–24, 39–48, 128–38.

Literature: Noth/Conrad 18, 135–6, 142–3, 185–6, 209–11; Spuler, *Iran* 11–18; Whitcomb, *Qasr-i Abu Nasr*.

60: ch.44, **142–143**, *continuing political crisis in Constantinople, 642/643–645/646*. Two distinct episodes have been conjoined in this notice. The date given, Constans II's second regnal year (September 642–September 643), belongs to the first episode. It is confirmed by a fuller notice in John of Nikiu, which places the event loosely in the days following Constans' accession. According to John, Valentinus sought the throne for himself 'in order to contend against the Moslem'. The clear implication of this phrase, which helps clarify Sebeos' obscure reference to his exercising his military command as emperor, is that he was seeking plenipotentiary military and political powers to conduct the war against Islam more effectively. Sebeos adds the important item of information that he gave his attempt to seize supreme power constitutional propriety by involving the Senate. According to John, popular opposition in Constantinople forced him to back down and to reach a compromise with the young, 11-year-old emperor. In return for renouncing his attempt to assume imperial status (presumably as senior co-emperor), he was appointed commander-in-chief of the army (probably *Magister Militum per Orientem*) and obtained an indirect connection with the throne through his daughter, who was married to the emperor and proclaimed Augusta. This was surely the context for Constans' formal address to the Senate in 642/643, reported by Theophanes, in which he thanked the senators for their support against Martina and invited them to advise him in future. It may be surmised that he also announced the terms of the agreement with Valentinus (which had perhaps been brokered by the Senate).

The second episode occurred two years later, in 644/645, and resulted in Valentinus' death. In a curt notice Theophanes reports that Valentinus rebelled against the emperor and was executed, the army's loyalty being transferred to the emperor. Corroboration for the date is to hand in a later notice of Sebeos' (**143** with n.61 below), which places two indirect consequences of Valentinus' fall well after 642–643 – the recall of Varaztirots‘ from exile (dated to 645/646) and the dismissal of T‘ēodoros Ṙshtuni from the Armenian military command (he was taken under armed guard to Constantinople apparently *after* Varaztirots‘ recall, since they met there).

Sebeos gives us a fleeting insight into Roman opinion at a time when the high command and society at large were forced to adjust to the loss of empire and the growing Islamic threat. Two years have passed since Valentinus was granted what may have been near-dictatorial powers. He is directing the war from Constantinople, his authority underpinned by a force of 3,000 soldiers stationed there. 'The burden of subjection', by which is probably meant high taxation, is resented. It is taking time for civilians to accept the scale of financial sacrifice demanded to sustain the war effort from a much reduced resource base. Valentinus and his advisers are impatient and move swiftly to crush the opposition but in so authoritarian a manner, with so little regard for independent authority, as to provoke general outrage.

Sebeos was undoubtedly working from a source which blended together Constantinopolitan and Armenian politics, that which has been termed the Dvin Source. Hence the concluding sentence which reports the appointment of T‘ēodoros, one of the loyal Armenian princes in Roman service, as general (presumably *Magister Militum per Orientem* in succession to Valentinus), referred to in future as 'the Greek general'. This T‘ēodoros, it should be noted, is to be distinguished from T‘ēodoros Ṙshtuni, at the time local Roman commander in Armenia ('the general of the Armenian army', i.e. probably *Magister Militum per Armeniam*). The same Dvin Source then supplies material for the next, long notice about the repercussions in Armenia of what was in effect a new government at the centre, a notice which takes the story on into 645/646. Sebeos, who, here as elsewhere, is compiling his text out of chunks of material quarried from individual, written sources, thus allows his source to take him and his readers on an unadvertised foray of three years into the future from his base point in 642/643.

A final historiographical observation. The episode of Valentinus' downfall is well told. Specific scenes are conjured up. Snatches of direct speech add some fizz. The style is reminiscent of the more anecdotal chapters (chs2, 4, 28) of the first part of the *Short History* of Nikephoros, which reworks and recycles a lost source, probably a continuation of the chronicle of John of Antioch. So too is the focus on metropolitan politics, in particular on the prolonged political crisis following Heraclius' death. The suspicion arises that material from the lost continuation of John of Antioch has made its way into Sebeos' history, perhaps supplying much of the information on Constantinopolitan politics which was then given a strong Armenian spin in the Dvin Source. If so, it may be conjectured that the text circulated widely in eastern Christendom in the years of crisis when the Arabs were carrying all before them – a hypothesis which is lent support by the presence of material similar in style and focus to Nikephoros' and Sebeos' in John of Nikiu, the west Syrian historical tradition represented by Dionysius, and Theophanes.

Sources: John of Nikiu 198–9; Theophanes 342–3; Dionysius 167.

Literature: Kaegi, *Military Unrest* 157–9; Stratos, *Seventh Century* III, 8–15; Nikephoros, introduction 12–14; *PLRE* III, s.v. Theodorus Rshtuni 167, Valentinus 5, Varaztiroch.

61: ch.44, **143–145**, *crisis in Armenia (644/645–645/646)*. Sebeos continues to quarry material from the Dvin Source. Attention turns to a gathering political crisis in Armenia which came to a head a year or more after a second, massive demonstration of Arab military power to the whole of Transcaucasia in 643 (described, out of sequence, in the following notice). Sebeos makes no connection between the episodes, offers no explanation for the actions of his main protagonists. But some tentative suggestions may be made: (i) that the scale of Arab military action in 643 shocked the northern world, making it plain to both the 'prince of the Medes', commander of one of two substantial fighting forces left in Sasanian Iran, and the Roman authorities that their territories were now exposed to attack from Transcaucasia; (ii) that in consequence they negotiated a military alliance, probably in the following winter (an alliance which T'umas was sent out to renew, probably in 644/645); (iii) that the promotion of an Armenian to a senior command in the Roman army had an ulterior purpose, to prepare opinion in Armenia for closer military co-operation between Romans and Armenians under Roman direction; (iv) that the Armenians, or at any rate a faction led by T'ēodoros Ṙshtuni (the last sentence of this notice points to the existence of a substantial faction opposing him), favoured a more defensive stance than either Persians or Romans, preferring, in the light of their experience in 643, to fall back on their natural mountain redoubts rather than take the war to the enemy; (v) that in consequence there were growing strains in relations between Romans and Armenians, which were coming to a head in 644/645–645/646; and finally (vi) that Khoṙokhazat, 'prince of the Medes' (**137** with n.54 above), who was facing growing recalcitrance in his sector of Transcaucasia at this very time (Juanshēr rebelled in 644/645 according to Movsēs Daskhurantsʻi), was anxious to prevent the Armenians from giving support to the refractory elements and pressed for the dismissal of Tʻēodoros Ṙshtuni, of whom he harboured suspicions.

The new Roman general Tʻēodoros, who replaced the murdered Valentinus and who is clearly distinguished from Tʻēodoros Ṙshtuni, army commander in Armenia, cannot but have raised his standing in Armenia by interceding successfully on behalf of Varaztirotsʻ, or being portrayed as doing so in what may have been a stage-managed recall of a number of Armenian princes from exile. The new Roman military regime had to carry Armenian opinion with it if its plans for introducing a more effective command structure or adopting a more offensive strategy in the east were to succeed. Hence the meeting convened by Tʻumas before his discussions with the 'prince of the Medes', to gain support for his negotiating stance. However, Roman plans came to naught despite these efforts. The arrest and deportation of Tʻēodoros Ṙshtuni, at the insistence of the 'prince of the Medes', provoked widespread opposition, forcing the imperial authorities to put on a show trial of Tʻumas outside the palace. Tʻēodoros Ṙshtuni may have been vindicated, but he was nonetheless detained in Constantinople, only later being reinstated in his Armenian command after the death of Varaztirotsʻ. The opposition evidently reached a dangerous level after Varaztirotsʻ slipped out *incognito* from Constantinople – exacerbated first by the security precautions ordered by the high command in Armenia and second by the news that Varaztirotsʻ had reached Taykʻ. At this point the Roman authorities caved in. A second meeting, of army officers and princes, was convened and gave its approval to a compromise which respected Armenian autonomy and took account of the swelling support for Varaztirotsʻ. Varaztirotsʻ was to be recommended for appointment as *curopalate*, probably combining civil and military powers over the whole of Armenia. It was an extraordinary *volte-face* but explicable in the circumstances. For the Romans could not afford to antagonize the Armenians at the time when they were investing their main military effort into a counter-attack intended to raise Egypt against the Arabs.

Several items of incidental information are worthy of note: the number of written documents which feature in this episode, in particular the travel permit issued to Varaztirots's men; the high status of the *proto-spatharios* who commanded the personal bodyguard of the emperor; and the inclusion of Persian-style insignia of office (silver cushions) among the presents sent to Varaztirots'.

Sources: M.D., tr. Dowsett 112–15 (rebellion of Juanshēr); John of Nikiu 199–200 (temporary reoccupation of Alexandria).

Literature: Grousset, *Histoire* 298–9; *PLRE* III, s.v. Symbatius 2, Theodorus Rshtuni 167, Varaztiroch; Butler, *Arab Conquest of Egypt* 465–83; Haldon, *Byzantine Praetorians* 182–90.

62: chs44–45, **145–147**, *Arab invasion of Transcaucasia, 643*. Sebeos has waited for a break in the political story retailed by the Dvin Source before introducing this notice, which, to judge by the prominent role played by Tʿēodoros Ṙshtuni, is taken from the postulated Ṙshtuni Source. In doing so he disregards chronology and backtracks some two years (from 645/646 to 643). His account of operations is remarkably detailed. The campaign is firmly anchored in time by the precise date given for the capture of Artsapʿkʿ by the Arabs – Sunday 10 August 643. There are enough geographical particulars noted for us to follow the movements of the three corps into which the Arab army divided. A great deal of precise information (including two figures for troop strengths and the names of the two Arab commanders killed) is given about the fall of Artsapʿkʿ and Tʿēodoros' deadly counter-attack on the following day. It is the sort of material customarily conveyed in military despatches. In this case it is virtually certain that a despatch was written since Tʿēodoros would not have sent 100 captured Arab horses to the emperor Constans without an accompanying explanatory letter. It may therefore be suggested with reasonable confidence that the Ṙshtuni Source drew its material about the campaign from a copy of a document recording the first Armenian victory over the Arabs.

The Ṙshtuni Source has also left its mark on Łewond's account. He includes a shorter notice about the campaign with many similarities to Sebeos'. The strategic context is sketched before an account is given of

the siege of Artsap'k'. The episode is misdated (to 657) and a fair amount
has been garbled, but, as in Sebeos' version, the invasion army divides
into three, the Arabs enter Artsap'k' under cover of darkness and there
is a body-count of some 3,000 after T'ēodoros' victory. An additional
piece of precise information is supplied: T'ēodoros' force comprised 600
men.

On the basis of Sebeos' notice the following reconstruction of the
campaign may be offered. By their attack through the Bitlis pass in 640
(**138** with n.55 above) and their victory at Nihawand in 642 (**141** with
n.59 above) the Arabs had punched two holes in the mountain defences
of the interlinked northern lands of Transcaucasia and Iran. They were
probably embarking on the piecemeal conquest of Persia in 643 and
may already have been probing the defences of Media, but their main
action was the invasion of Transcaucasia in force. After reaching
Atrpatakan, the army split into three corps which then conducted independent but co-ordinated operations. If the corps were of roughly equal
strength (although that sent directly against Nakhchawan may well
have been larger than the other two), a total of some 10,000 men was
committed to the campaign. One corps marched on Ayrarat, the administrative centre of Armenia, and raided the lands to the north, in a huge
arc from Armenian Tayk' in the west through Iberia to Albania in the
east. A second corps set about the piecemeal conquest of the southern
Armenian highlands between Atrpatakan and the relatively open
country north of Lake Van (*Sephakan gund*). The third invaded
Albania, advanced up the Araxes valley, capturing the fortress of
Khram on the way, and besieged Nakhchawan. Nakhchawan,
commanding the Araxes valley below Dvin, seems to have been the principal objective, an important task of the northern and southern army
corps being to divert attention and mask the initial siege operations,
before converging on the city and themselves joining in the siege.

The second corps had the most difficult assignment. Some of the
population of the southern highlands took refuge in fortresses together
with their livestock (note the large number of cattle found inside
Artsap'k'). Others probably retreated deep into its mountain fastnesses.
Raiding forays were sent ahead, to cause as much damage as possible,
while what was probably the main force advanced west more slowly,
launching assaults against each of the fortresses it passed. Two held out.
The third, Artsap'k', was taken, but a classic guerrilla attack by
T'ēodoros Ṙshtuni's outnumbered force resulted in the annihilation of

its captors. Instead of gaining a large mountainous bridgehead in southern Armenia, flanked by a forward base at Nakhchawan, from which they could have projected their power over much of Transcaucasia and controlled the northern approach to the Bitlis pass, the Arabs were taught a painful lesson – that passive defence, backed by small mobile guerrilla forces, made Armenia extremely difficult to conquer.

This disaster dislocated the whole Arab campaign. Nakhchawan held out against the two army corps which were still unscathed. The only real achievement was the destructive raiding sweep by the northern corps. Nonetheless, this display of Arab striking power must have impressed the peoples of Transcaucasia and deterred them from taking too active a part in the defence of north-western Iran (n.61 above). The Romans gained in two ways from T'ēodoros Řshtuni's victory. First there were the hundred Arab horses which he presented to the emperor. Second it had made it less likely that the Arabs would try to attack Asia Minor from the east, using the relatively easy routes provided by the Euphrates and Aratsani rivers in western Armenia, now that the Armenians had demonstrated their powers of resistance.

Source: Łewond ch.3.

Literature: Grousset, *Histoire* 299; Manandean, 'Invasions' 177–90; M. Canard, 'Arminiya 2. Armenia under Arab domination', *E.I.* I, 635–6; *PLRE* III, s.v. Theodorus Rshtuni 167.

63: ch.45, **147**, *first Arab offensive in the Mediterranean and subsequent negotiations for a cease-fire, 649–650/651.*

(i) *Events as reported by Sebeos.* No reason is given by Sebeos for Muawiya's decision to develop a naval arm, but there was surely a connection with the display of Roman naval power in 645–646, when Alexandria was reoccupied and an attempt made to raise Egypt in revolt. It is not clear whether purpose-built warships were constructed or merchant vessels were converted for naval service. In either case, though, it would have taken time to prepare both ships and crews for action. Muawiya then took personal command and sailed against Constantinople. The expeditionary force was, however, intercepted by the Roman fleet, and an engagement was fought in which Greek fire seems to have been used for the first time. Although Muawiya suffered heavy losses and was clearly forced to halt his advance, his display of naval might shocked the Romans and led them to negotiate a cease-fire.

Terms were agreed, involving payment of an unspecified sum of tribute by the Romans and demarcation of a (temporary) frontier, with Constans' representative (Procopius). The most interesting element in the notice concerns the constitutional arrangements in place during Constans II's minority: the army was directly involved in foreign policy decisions; initiatives required its formal approval, given probably by a military council of senior officers. This happened in the case of the decision to seek an armistice, the army council or, more probably, a delegation thereof then accompanying Procopius to the negotiations in Damascus.

(ii) *Date.* Not much weight should be attached to the position of this episode in Sebeos' text – after the Armenian political crisis of 645/646 (**143–145**) and the Arab attack on Transcaucasia of 643 (**145–147**), and before the Council of Dvin in 649 (**147–161**). For the materials of which it is composed at this point are heterogeneous and the chronological order is disturbed. Firmer indications are provided later: the cease-fire held for three whole years (**164**); the decision to break it was taken and announced by the caliph in Constans' 11th regnal year (September 651–September 652 [**169**]); the order to start operations was issued in Constans' twelfth year (652/653 [**164**]) and resulted in action, on a very grand scale, in his 13th year (653/654 [**170**], with nn.68, 75 below). The cease-fire must have started a minimum of three years before the renewed outbreak of fighting in 654. It follows that the negotiations conducted by Procopius took place at the latest early in 651, but more probably in the latter half of 650. The naval battle should therefore be dated to 650 or 649.

(iii) *The evidence of other sources.* Dionysius retails a lengthy account of naval operations at this time which he found in Theophilus of Edessa's lost chronicle (condensed by Theophanes into two sentences). Muawiya remains the prime mover. Two fleets are raised, one from Syria, his own command, the other from Egypt, 1,700 ships all told. When they combine, their multitudinous masts look like a floating forest. The year is one of the two inferred for Sebeos' battle – Seleucid era 660 (October 648–September 649). The objective, however, is not Constantinople but Cyprus, and operations proceed without a hitch. The island is laid waste. Much booty and many prisoners are taken. The Roman response – to install a defensive force – may revive morale but provokes a second, equally successful attack, carried out by a subordinate of Muawiya's, 'shortly afterwards', probably the next year (650).

Constantinople is the target of a third great naval expedition of Muawiya's, which takes place some years later (of which Theophanes gives a full description). On this occasion, the fleet, again commanded by a subordinate of Muawiya's, is met off Phoinix on the Lycian coast by a Roman fleet commanded by the young emperor Constans. A great battle is fought. Victory goes eventually not to Constans (who escapes *incognito*) but to Muawiya. Nonetheless he does not sail on beyond Rhodes. Dionysius, whose multiple dating is inconsistent, places it five or six years after the first great raid on Cyprus (either 654 or 655). Theophanes puts it six years afterwards.

Theophanes (but not Dionysius) reports the negotiations conducted by Procopius, places them two years after the first attack on Cyprus, and has the cease-fire last for two years. Łewond refers in passing to a three-year cease-fire in the caliphate of 'Uthman (644–656).

(iv) *Provisional reconstruction.* The naval battles reported by Sebeos and the later derivatives of Theophilus of Edessa, Dionysius and Theophanes, have several features in common: both are actions on a grand scale; both involve the emperor himself; both take place apparently far from Constantinople; both are hard fought; although the outcomes are different, in both cases Muawiya's advance is brought to a halt. It seems likely that the battles are one and the same, and that either Sebeos or Theophilus of Edessa has misdated it. So impressive is Sebeos' record as chronographer and historian (and so comparatively weak is that of Theophilus), that Sebeos' dating (before, not after the cease-fire) and account of the outcome (a setback for the Arabs) should be preferred. The following reconstruction of events can then be made:

649: a huge Arab fleet from Syria and Egypt devastates Cyprus, sails on, and encounters a Roman fleet off the coast of Lycia; the Roman fleet wins the engagement and sails on to Cyprus; a large force is left to defend the island.

650: the Syrian fleet returns and devastates the island for the second time, the defending naval force having withdrawn without a fight.

650/651: a cease-fire is negotiated on a Roman initiative.

654: the cease-fire ends when an Arab armada sails for Constantinople and Arab land forces invade Asia Minor.

Confirmation that there were two Arab raids on Cyprus, dated to the seventh indiction (the Roman financial year running from 1 September 648 to 31 August 649) and the next year, and that they caused extensive damage and captured a very large number of prisoners is provided by a two-part inscription commemorating the completion of repairs to the episcopal church of Soloi in 655. There is also an incidental reference to 'the first conquest of the island of Cyprus' in the *Life* of St Spyridon, which was first declaimed by its author, Theodore Bishop of Paphos, on 14 December 655 (but the date given, the eighth indiction [September 649–August 650], is that of the second attack).

Sources: Dionysius 173–7 (Cyprus), 179–80 (naval battle); Theophanes 343–4 (Cyprus), 344 (cease-fire), 345–6 (naval battle); Łewond ch.2; Feissel, 'Inscriptions'; Spyridon, introduction 86–88, 101–8, text 88–91.

Literature: Butler, *Arab Conquest of Egypt* 465–83; Canard, 'Expéditions' 62–7; Ahrweiler, *Byzance et la mer* 17–25; Stratos, *Seventh Century* III, 38–55; *ODB*, s.v. 'Greek Fire'.

64: ch.45, **147**, *the building of the church of the Heavenly Angels (644–after 659/660)*. The church of the Heavenly Angels (Zuart'nots'), of which the foundations and various architectural fragments remain visible, was one of the masterpieces of the first great period of Armenian architecture (*ca*.610–*ca*.670). In plan it was a double-shell quatrefoil, an inner space with four large semi-circular recesses being surrounded by an outer ambulatory, measuring 123 feet in diameter. In elevation it comprised three superimposed cylinders which diminished in diameter and rose to a masonry dome, set on squinches. Inspiration from outside Armenia, mainly from Syria, is attested by the use of columns (normally absent from Armenian churches) and basketwork capitals. Carved monograms in Greek of the Catholicos Nersēs have left his signature on the building. The church was only completed after his return to Dvin in 659/660, following six years' exile in Tayk' (**174–175** with n.81 below).

Literature: Khatchatrian, *L'Architecture Arménienne* (1949), 25–7; Mango, *Byzantine Architecture* 98–107.

65: chs45–46, **147–161**, *Council of Dvin, 649*. The council, convened at the request of Constans, was attended by nobles as well as bishops. It was held four years before Constans' visit to Dvin in 653 (**168** with n.71 below). The Catholicos Nersēs and 'the pious Armenian general' T'ēodoros Ṙshtuni (reinstated in his command after the death of Varaztirots' in 645/646 [**145** with n.61 above]) presided. Although it must have been torn between the commitment of a majority of

Armenian churchmen to the Monophysite confession and the need to maintain good relations with the court at Constantinople in the face of the threat from Islam, it adhered to the beliefs of the majority. RWT discusses (Part I, Introduction II., The Armenian Text, above) whether or not the long defence of its doctrinal position, which Sebeos includes in his text, is an authentic document. A detailed commentary on the text is given in the footnotes to the translation. As Flusin has shown, there has been some tampering with the historical record in the first part where an anti-Chalcedonian spin has been put on an account of a meeting convened by Khosrov between 605 and 609 to provide public justification for his switch of favour from Nestorians to Monophysites. But this is as likely as not to have been the work of the council (certainly it served its interest) and may well have featured in the original document. It is hard to withhold assent from RWT's conclusion that the text is not a later medieval concoction but represents, for the most part, the majority view of the council, given its anomalous features and, above all, its studious avoidance of the divisive issue of differences in ritual practice. The deferential tone in which Constans is addressed and the respect shown towards Roman imperial authority (**148–149, 151–152, 161**) provide additional authentic touches.

Literature: Grousset, *Histoire* 300; Flusin, *St Anastase* II, 114–18; Thomson, 'The Defence'.

66: ch.47, **161–163**, *purge in Constantinople (651)*. Sebeos marks the transition from the lengthy exposition of the Armenian church's doctrinal position back to his main subject of Near Eastern political and military history with an emotive passage of his own composition. He touches on the apocalyptic theme which he has developed earlier (**141–142** above): the Arabs are the fourth beast of Daniel; they have emerged from the desert like a tempest of burning wind to punish Christians for their sins. Then he returns to his principal source on Constantinopolitan politics, the postulated Dvin Source, but does not immediately alter his tone.

He writes of disorder, disasters, civil war, wholesale slaughter of leading figures in the government (all *exterminated*). He takes time to wind down and to resume his customary practice of purveying material from his sources to his readers in a neutral manner. Once he begins giving details about the course of events and the parties involved in the crisis, it becomes plain that there is a great deal of exaggeration in his opening remarks. If due allowance is made for his highly-charged language, the following picture emerges. The emperor Constans gets wind of a conspiracy involving a senior general stationed close to Constantinople (Gēorg) and a leading minister in the city (Manuēl, an Armenian with Arsacid blood in his veins [144–145]). He then sends Smbat Bagratuni (who is Manuēl's son-in-law and probably one of Gēorg's subordinate commanders) to bring Gēorg, by devious or open means, to Constantinople. As soon as Gēorg has been isolated from the troops devoted to him, a pre-emptive strike is made against the conspirators, all apparently in Constantinople. It is now that the blood flows, as the executions mount up. Smbat, discredited with the troops under his command, is implicated by them in the conspiracy. The emperor does not dismiss the charge nor does he spare him entirely from punishment (exile), perhaps in the hope of improving his standing in army circles.

Roman domestic sources have fallen silent well before this episode. It can only be dated by its position in Sebeos' text, after the naval battle of 649 and the Roman-Arab negotiations which followed in 650/651 (**147** with n.63) and before the Arab advance into eastern Iran in the first half of 652 (described at **163–164**, in a notice taken from the Persian Source). This points to a date in 651, one close enough to the time of writing to have been remembered by Sebeos. Kaegi is probably wrong to put it in 652, but makes the attractive suggestion that Constans II (now 20 years old) launched the purge to free himself from the tutelage of the military and civilian elite. It also looks as if the reorganization of the field armies and their collective renaming as themes (commanded by *strategoi*) has not yet been completed. For Gēorg was a *Magister*, presumably *Magister Militum Praesentalis*, since he was stationed 'in that region', i.e. the region of Constantinople. Smbat's command is harder to identify: Kaegi suggests the regular army of Thrace, but Sebeos' phrasing ('leader of the army of the Thracian princes') may point rather to a force raised from descendants of Armenians settled in Thrace.

Literature: Kaegi, *Military Unrest* 160–1; *PLRE* III, s.v. Symbatius 2; Haldon, *Seventh Century* 208–20.

67: ch.48, **163–164**, *Arab conquests V, the end of the Sasanian dynasty, 652* (cf. T'.A. 104). Curt notices in Movsēs Daskhurants'i's chronicle (simply noting the date of the death of the last Sasanian king, Yazkert III) and *Khuz.Chron.* (merely noting the place of his death, Marv), together with a somewhat more informative one in *Chron.Seert* (reporting his failure to assemble an army, his flight, concealment, discovery and execution) bid farewell to the Iranian power which had dominated the continental hinterland of the Near East throughout late antiquity. Early Islamic traditions devote much more space to the event, thereby underlining its significance, but treat it in a tabloid manner: attention is focused on Yazkert, antagonisms and intrigues in high places at Marv, and the precise details of his death. For example, five different but related versions of his death are presented side by side by Tabari, three of which involve the Turks, Yazkert's last hope, turning against him, and all five of which end with him caught and killed in the house of a miller. Another variant of this story turns up in Dionysius. Considerable effort is required to extract the barest outline of Arab strategy: the attack on Khurasan, bastion of Iranian power facing the steppes, came from the south; Yazkert was unable to assemble an effective fighting force and withdrew east to Marv, placing his hopes in the Turks. No explanation is given for the failure of the two functioning Persian armies in the field to unite, that directly under Yazkert's command (from Persia proper and Khurasan) and that serving under Khoṙokhazat, Sebeos' 'prince of the Medes'. In combination they would have become a formidable adversary.

Sebeos, by contrast, presents a clear, intelligible account of the strategic circumstances which led to the death of Yazkert. He had summoned the army of north-western Iran to join that under his own command in the east, in Khurasan. He had also called on the Turks (referred to as T'etalk') for aid. An Arab army, evidently mobilized from troops across the whole of Khuzistan and Iran, advanced across the Iranian plateau in the first half of 652 (the importance of the episode being underlined by the triple dating used by Sebeos). The Arabs managed to prevent the three armies facing them from coalescing. They surely had a hand in the rebellion of the 'prince of the Medes', to which there is a cryptic reference (either a passage has dropped out of Sebeos' text in its long transmission and the cross-reference is his, or, possibly, the cross-reference was lifted together with the notice in which it was embedded, from Sebeos' source, probably the Persian Source). Meanwhile the Turkish army, careful not to cross the frontier with Persian territory, was a spectator as Yazkert's army was caught as it retreated towards the frontier and was annihilated. Yazkert himself sought asylum with the Turks but was put to death by them, while the 'prince of the Medes' came out of the stronghold to which he had withdrawn and formally submitted to the Arabs in the desert. It is a coherent and plausible account, which, unlike the other extant sources, explains the sudden, apparently painless snuffing out of Sasanian power.

Sources: M.D., tr. Dowsett 115; *Khuz.Chron.* 33; *Chron.Seert* 581; Dionysius 178; Łewond ch.2; Tabari XV; Baldhuri I 490–3.

Literature: Spuler, *Iran* 18–21.

68: ch.48, **164**, *end of cease-fire, 652/654* (cf. n.63 above). There appears to be a contradiction between the date given in this notice, the 12th regnal year of Constans (652/653), for the caliph's ending of the cease-fire, and the preceding 11th regnal year reported in a later, apparent doublet of this notice (at ch.49, **169**). Tempting though it may be to amend the second date, it is more prudent to refrain from tampering with the text, especially since both dates are written out in full. There are significant differences in the substance of the two notices which should not be overlooked. That dated to 651/652 records that this was the year when 'the treaty between Constans and Muawiya, prince of Ismael, was broken' (i.e. when the intention to break it was formulated) and the caliph ordered a general redirection of Arab forces to the west for war against the Romans, defining Constantinople as the objective. That dated to 652/653 gives a context (news of victory in the east [in summer 652] and the [consequent] destruction of Persian power has reached the caliph), defines the length of the cease-fire as three full years, and has the caliph order operations against the Romans to begin by sea and land. There is nothing implausible about this sequence of events: the decision in principle to break the cease-fire was taken and mobilization in the west was ordered, as soon as the Arabs' position was secure in Iran (mid or late summer 652); this was followed in 653 by the order to begin operations; the main attack on Constantinople then took place in 654 (ch.50, **169–171** with n.75).

The caliph (*ark'ay*, 'king') is portrayed as exercising effective authority over Arab armies in the field. Sebeos views the caliphate at this early stage in its evolution as a cohesive political entity which is capable of concentrating resources dispersed over vast areas against a single principal adversary, or, as was the case in 642, of co-ordinating separate operations in separate theatres to maximize the effect of each (**139** with n.56 above). How much initiative in strategic matters was exercised by the centre as opposed to the commanders in the field must remain a matter of speculation, but major operations are presented as requiring authorization from the caliph. This accords with the picture presented by early Islamic historical traditions, a picture which has been rejected recently as the product of later reworkings of an original core of early traditions.

Literature: Noth/Conrad 11–12, 55–7, 80–1.

69: ch.48, **164**, *T῾ēodoros Ṙshtuni's submission to the Arabs, 652/653*. This important event is dated to Constans' 12th regnal year (652/653). The contracting parties were T῾ēodoros Ṙshtuni, representing all the princes of Armenia in his capacity as an influential prince as well as general commanding the Roman field army in Armenia (**145** for his reinstatement in 645/646), and the 'prince of Ismael', identifiable as Muawiya. The precision and coherence of Sebeos' summary of the terms suggest that he had access to a copy of the original agreement.

The terms offered by Muawiya were not unattractive in the circumstances. The main burden falling on the Armenians was military. They were to maintain a large standing army of 15,000 cavalry, for deployment by the Arab authorities as they saw fit, but north of the Taurus. In return the Arabs undertook to provide military aid on request, but otherwise to refrain from establishing a political or military presence in Armenia. Of the fiscal terms, the following conjectural interpretation may be offered: after an initial period of three tribute-free years, the amount of tribute was to be subject to negotiation, based upon some sworn declaration by the Armenians (perhaps concerning the size of the harvest, if a particular proportion was to be paid over, or concerning their assets in general). The annual tribute was expected to be substantial, since the cost of provisioning the 15,000 cavalry which the Armenians undertook to field would be offset against the total 'royal tax'.

It is made plain, from subsequent events reported in this chapter (**165**), that T῾ēodoros Ṙshtuni had not obtained the agreement of all the princes of Armenia before negotiating purportedly on their behalf. The making of the agreement looks like a political act intended to bring about a general shift of allegiance in Armenia. It was not kept secret. The news may indeed have been allowed deliberately to leak out. Many princes, who were opposed to it, were aware of T῾ēodoros' plan, and had observed the coming and going of Arab emissaries. News of what was afoot soon reached Constans, who made a counter-proposal to shore up his position in Armenia and announced that he was coming to Karin (Theodosiopolis). There he would be met by the princes of western and central Armenia, who had not defected (**165**).

It is surprising that Muawiya was not called on to provide the military aid which he promised, in anticipation of opposition within Armenia or from the Romans. There was every prospect of Roman intervention in force, since the treaty included a provocative statement barring an enemy (immediately afterwards defined as Roman) from entering Armenia.

Theophanes reports the defection of the patrician of Armenia, whom he calls Pasagnathes, and the treaty which he made with Muawiya, and dates it a year earlier (651/652).

Source: Theophanes 344.

Literature: Grousset, *Histoire* 300–1; Laurent/Canard 55–6, 195–7.

70: ch.48, **165**, *Roman defeat in Mardastan, 652*. Sebeos' elliptical account must be read with care to discern what happened. T'ēodoros Ṙshtuni, general in command of the local field army of Armenia ('the pious Armenian general' [**148**]), was accused of having colluded with the Arabs when they attacked and defeated Roman troops serving in a separate command. Mardastan, where the encounter took place and the Romans lost all their equipment, lay north-east of Lake Van. Together with the districts of Gaṙni to the west and Artaz to the east, it formed the northern rim of the highlands of Vaspurakan. The plain of Gogovit, commanded by the Bagratuni fortress of Dariwnkʻ (modern Doğubayazit) (**104, 144**), lay immediately north of Mardastan. Since the aggrieved Roman troops are unlikely to have been slow about lodging their complaint and Constans, who went to Armenia in his 12th regnal year (September 652– September 653), is presented as responding swiftly, the engagement should be dated to the second half of 652.

The same incident is described in greater detail by Łewond. Again a Roman army serving under a Roman general, named as Procopius, is surprised and defeated by an Arab force. The Arabs are returning west after the defeat and death of Yazkert and the completion of the conquest of Iran (so the date is the same, the second half of 652). They are a part of the returning force which has taken a northern route and conducts a sweeping raid through Media and up the valley of the Araxes (past Gołtʻn and Nakhchawan). The raiders then divide, some taking the prisoners 'to their own country', others advancing and raiding Artaz (and thus approaching the neighbouring district of Mardastan). 'The Greek general Procopius', stationed with a large army in southern Gogovit, close to the boundary with Mardastan, prepares to attack the raiders but the Arabs act more swiftly, launch a surprise attack and inflict a serious defeat. As in Sebeos' notice, T'ēodoros Ṙshtuni stands aside, although the charge of active collusion is rebutted, the blame being transferred to Procopius who is accused of indolence (ignoring repeated warnings from T'ēodoros), of irascibility (provoking reciprocal anger in T'ēodoros, who then 'stayed away from him') and, implicitly, of incompetence. T'ēodoros himself is presented as taking effective action to bar the Arabs' way into Vaspurakan.

It is evidently the same incident which is viewed from different angles. Łewond, it may be conjectured, drew his version, which amounts to an apologia for T'ēodoros' admitted inaction, from the Ṙshtuni Source which, as we have seen, supplied him, as also Sebeos, with information about the Arab raids of 640 and 643. Sebeos, who, it is clear from his language, was outraged at T'ēodoros' agreement with Muawiya ('a pact with death', 'an alliance with hell' [**164**]), has chosen to disregard the Ṙshtuni Source and to give the Roman view instead. When the information from the two sources is combined, three tentative observations can be made:

(i) Procopius, described as 'the Greek general' by Łewond, held a command separate from that of T'ēodoros Ṙshtuni, 'the Armenian general' (Sebeos, **148** above). If Procopius' command was the same as that of the other T'ēodoros, who succeeded Valentinus in the supreme military command in 644/645 and then took personal charge of affairs in Armenia in 645/646 (where he too was called 'the Greek general' [**144**]), Procopius was probably *Magister Militum per Orientem*. It was perhaps in this capacity that he had earlier acted as Constans' and the army's representative and had negotiated a ceasefire in 650/651 (**147** with n.63 above). T'ēodoros Ṙshtuni was probably *Magister Militum per Armeniam* (as suggested in n.69 above).

(ii) A further inference may now, hesitantly, be made. The East Roman empire attached a very high priority to the defence of Armenia, so high that it was ready to deploy a second high-ranking general there and, presumably, a substantial field army serving under his command on at least two critical occasions in the 640s and early 650s. It is possible, indeed, that the assignment was more permanent, that the *Magister Militum per Orientem* was stationed in Armenia continuously in this period.

(iii) Such a forward concentration of Roman troops would have served three purposes. First, by consolidating Roman control of

Armenia and reinforcing the regional field army under the command of the *Magister Militum per Armeniam*, the Anatolian heartland of the reduced empire was secured from attack along the relatively easy eastern approaches. Second, Roman forces were well placed to intervene in Atrpatakan and Media, if the opportunity presented itself. Third, the presence of a formidable Roman fighting force, firmly entrenched in Armenia and holding its natural south-eastern bastion (the mountains of Vaspurakan), was a standing threat to Arab control of the plains of northern Mesopotamia to the south.

Source: Łewond ch.2.

Literature: Grousset, *Histoire* 296 (summary, misdated); Hewsen, *AŠX* 66 (map xviii), 187 (Mardastan and Artaz), 218 (Gogovit and Dariwnkʻ); Haldon, *Seventh Century* 208–20 (Roman command structure).

71: chs48–49, **165–168**, *Constans' intervention in Armenia, 653*. The narrative is in the main self-explanatory. Constans' arrival at Karin (Theodosiopolis), dated to his 12th regnal year (652/653), probably took place towards the end of summer 653, not long before the start of the next regnal year in September. If Sebeos' figures are to be trusted here, Constans was bringing an army as large as any ever fielded by the Roman empire in late antiquity (amounting to 100,000 men), which he then reduced to a more manageable force (20,000 strong) before marching on to Dvin. For he had decided to undertake limited operations over the winter months. There were five of these, designed to isolate Tʻēodoros Ṙshtuni and to bring Persarmenia and the rest of Transcaucasia under Roman control. It is not clear whether Musheł Mamikonean, who was made commander of the Armenian cavalry and led them on one of these forays, held a senior command in the Roman army of Armenia or the position of *aspet* traditionally held by a Bagratuni.

Sebeos' personal interest in church affairs (and possibly his personal involvement) may account for the length and detail of the account of the celebration of the Chalcedonian liturgy in the cathedral at Dvin. It should not be inferred that Constans' hurried return to Constantinople which is reported in the next notice came immediately after the ceremony. Juxtapositions of notices in the text do not necessarily reflect juxtapositions in reality. The ceremony probably took place earlier rather than later during Constans' stay in Dvin, if, as seems likely, it was staged not only to impart more ideological cohesion to the Roman-Armenian partnership but also to influence opinion in the Romans' favour elsewhere in Transcaucasia and thereby to reinforce the military operations undertaken that winter.

Before he left, Constans gave the command of the Armenian army to Maurianus, and gave him authority over civil government as 'prince of Armenia'. This was the first occasion, in this period, that both powers were vested in a Roman.

Literature: Grousset, *Histoire* 301–2; M. Canard, 'Arminiya 2. Armenia under Arab domination', *E.I.* I, 636; Howard-Johnston, 'The Great Powers' 165–9; Garitte, *Narratio* 337–43.

72: ch.49, **168**, *Constans' return in haste to Constantinople, 653/654*. The pressing summons came well before the end of winter, which is reported later (**169**) in connection with the start of Tʿēodoros Ṙshtuni's offensive (with Arab backing) against the forces which Constans had left behind under the command of Maurianus. The reason for the summons and Constans' instant departure is made plain in the next chapter: the authorities at Constantinople had realized that a massive Arab offensive was being prepared against what remained of the empire; the presence of the emperor and the crack troops under his command was urgently needed.

Things had worked out extraordinarily conveniently for the Arabs. News, perhaps deliberately leaked, of Tʿēodoros Ṙshtuni's defection, and the consequent fear that the whole of Armenia might follow suit had drawn Constans and the largest field army which he could muster away from his capital in 653. The warning not to enter Armenia delivered by an Arab delegation when he had reached Derjan (on the upper Euphrates below Karin) had acted (predictably) as an additional spur (**165**). It was not followed up. No attempt was made by Tʿēodoros Ṙshtuni with the backing of Arab forces to take over Armenia. None of the promised Arab military aid materialized. Tʿēodoros and his local supporters simply withdrew to their strongholds, placing their treasures (perhaps by a pre-arranged plan) in the strongest of them. There was no active resistance to the Romans, no apparent attempt to call on the support of the princes of Armenia whom Tʿēodoros claimed to be representing. The prospect of achieving real success in the winter months was alluring, and Constans was drawn deeper into Armenia to Dvin, and yet further from his capital.

Meanwhile Muawiya, so inactive in Armenia, was preparing for a land and sea assault on the core territories still retained by the Roman empire. These had been denuded of troops in summer 653, and, although many were able to return home for the winter, the best were engaged in operations in Transcaucasia. When at last the Roman authorities realized what was afoot, there was inevitably disruption to their defensive preparations and a significant weakening in available fighting strength, not to mention the depressing effect on morale of the emperor's absence until shortly before the Arabs closed in on Constantinople.

Sebeos' narrative presents cumulatively convincing evidence that Constans was the victim of strategic deception on a grand scale. The prime function of Muawiya's agreement with Tʻēodoros Ṙshtuni, it may be conjectured, was not to establish a permanent framework for Armenian-Arab relations (although it may have done so), nor to multiply the number of Arab clients among the princes, but to lure and entangle Roman forces in Armenia, thereby weakening the defences of the capital and Anatolia. The scheme was remarkably successful, almost bringing about a replay of the 626 siege, with emperor and field army cut off from the capital, but this time with all the additional dangers posed by a large enemy armada.

73: ch.49, **169**, *Arab occupation of Armenia, 654*. A short notice summarizes the sudden reversal in military and political fortunes which followed Constans' departure and the arrival of a 7,000 strong Arab force to help Tʻēodoros Ṙshtuni. The ease with which the Arabs took over the whole of Armenia in 654 should probably be attributed mainly to a swift and general change in Armenian attitudes at the news from the west. Maurianus, the Roman commander, probably had little choice but to retreat in the circumstances, especially as the news must have harmed the morale of his men.

Several detached and misplaced notices, which appear later in the text, fill in the missing parts of the story. (i) A second notice about Tʻēodoros Ṙshtuni's formal request for Arab military aid defines his objectives as the expulsion of the Roman army of Armenia and the devastation of Iberia (the last sentence of chapter 50 [**172**]). Both objectives were pursued by Arab forces in 654 but only the first was achieved. (ii) The Arab general, described as a merciless executioner, is identified as Habib (probably Habib b. Maslama, for whom see below), on the occasion of the betrayal and execution of Artavazd Dimakʻsean (**173–174**). (iii) Some information about Armenian reactions to the arrival of the Arab army is supplied at the beginning of chapter 52 (**173**). Musheł Mamikonean, who had been appointed to a senior command by Constans (**166**), took the lead in changing sides. After the Arabs had secured control of the whole of Armenia, all the princes submitted to Arab authority with Tʿēodoros Ṙshtuni at their head, perhaps in a public ceremony. This event provides a context for Tʿēodoros Ṙshtuni's later visit to Damascus, where Muawiya invested him as client-ruler of Transcaucasia (**169**). (iv) A notice, placed immediately after the account of the attack on Constantinople in 654, reports that the Arabs tried to invade Iberia, the second of Tʿēodoros Ṙshtuni's two aims, as winter was approaching, but were thwarted by the weather (ch.50, **171**).

Theophanes reports the Arab take-over under the right year (653/654), names the Arab commander correctly (Abibos), but has him pursue Maurianus north to the Caucasus rather than west-north-west to the Black Sea coast. Arab historians also take note of it but envisage heavy fighting (with Khazars and Alans aiding the Romans). The general is identified as Habib b. Maslama, who had distinguished himself in earlier campaigns in Syria and Mesopotamia. His army moves in a sinuous way, first to Karin, then a short distance down the upper Euphrates, then south-east to the north shore of Lake Van, then north-east to Dvin and finally north to Tpʿkhis. The campaign is dated much earlier, towards the end of A.H.24 (645/646).

Source: Theophanes 345.

Literature: Grousset, *Histoire* 302–3; M. Canard, 'Arminiya 2. Armenia under Arab domination', *E.I.* I, 636.

74: ch.50, **169–170**, *caliph's ultimatum to Constans, 654.* An introductory sentence along the lines of 'the king of Ismael wrote a letter to Constans king of the Greeks' probably dropped out when the chapter heading, which now provides the necessary introduction to the quoted letter, was inserted. There is nothing in the letter's contents or in what is stated about the circumstances of its composition and delivery to occasion doubt about its authenticity. As in the case of Muawiya's agreement with Tʿēodoros Ṙshtuni, it is presented in summary form. The caliph issued Constans with an invitation to convert to Islam, demanded the disbandment of the bloated armed forces of the empire which alone could offer serious resistance to his armies, and proposed to leave Constans in charge of his territories, as a client-ruler of a grand sort ('a great prince').

Noth and Conrad believe that the *da'wa* or invitation to accept Islam was not issued in the course of the conquests, because it would have had no effect on peoples with deep attachments to long-established religions (in contrast to the first phase of Islamic history when small groups in the fractious world of Arabia could be drawn into the Muslim community). They therefore view it as a secondary, fictitious feature introduced later in the process of remoulding traditions, when *mawali*, non-Arab converts, were becoming a significant component of the Islamic community. They recognize the difficulty posed by Sebeos' version of the 654 ultimatum, but dismiss it as a confection of his. Their rejection of his testimony is unjustified.

A well-thought-out plan for the peaceful take-over of the East Roman empire was outlined in the caliph's letter. Arab troops would be deployed with the emperor's (nominal) agreement in place of his own disbanded forces; governors would be appointed to Roman cities; the emperor would be consulted on the amount to be raised in tribute; and the reserves in the treasury would first be inventoried and then apportioned, the emperor being allowed to retain a quarter. It is hard to conceive of such a scheme being devised unless the Arabs had by this stage developed an organized state of their own with effective managerial capacity.

Literature: Noth/Conrad 146–67.

75: ch.50, **170–171**, *Arab attack on Constantinople, 654*. Sebeos dates the Arab offensive, which had long been in preparation, to Constans' 13th regnal year, 653/654, a date which squares with that of the previous regnal year given in the previous chapter (**165**) for Constans' march into Armenia. Operations probably began in early summer 654 when there should have been little danger of storms. The notice, although brief and stressing religious factors, provides a great deal of detailed information, some of it partially but not entirely obscured in the editing process (or subsequent transmission by copyists). It is therefore possible to produce a reconstruction on the following lines (a number of hypotheses, italicized, are included).

A huge effort, itself bespeaking impressive organizational capacity, was made to assemble land and sea forces so large as to assure the Arabs of success in their campaign of conquest. Troops were summoned from far-flung reaches of the nascent empire, from the interior of former Sasanian territories (Khuzistan, Persia and the *south-east marches facing* India), from northern Mesopotamia (Aruastan) and from Egypt, to reinforce the army of Palestine and Syria under Muawiya's command. The cities of the eastern Mediterranean littoral, chief among them Alexandria, were put to work *building* and equipping a huge invasion fleet, including large transport vessels and small, swift fighting ships. There is evident exaggeration both of numbers of ships and of their carrying capacity in the story as retailed by Sebeos. Siege-engines of various sorts were prepared, including fire-throwing machines, artillery and *ship-borne towers* from which to assault the sea-walls (the towers are not mentioned in the list of war-machines, but are mentioned *à propos* of the assault plan and were among the equipment destroyed at sea by the storm).

When the forces, ships and equipment were assembled after a year and a half of preparations (if, as argued in n.68 above, the caliph ordered preparations to be made in the second half of 652), they were organized into four independent fighting forces: an army under Muawiya's personal command which advanced across Anatolia to Chalcedon, opposite Constantinople; a second reserve army, which took up a position in Cappadocia, from where it could secure the advance force's communications and keep control of Anatolia; a first fleet, consisting entirely of light vessels *which probably set off from the coast of Palestine and Syria* (i.e. from within the area of Muawiya's command) and arrived at Chalcedon at roughly the same time as Muawiya where they were kept inshore until the arrival of the great ships; and a second fleet, stated to have come from Alexandria, which arrived later and included all the great ships.

If ever the hand of God played a part in human affairs, Sebeos is right to suppose that it did so on this occasion. There is much rhetoric and some Old Testament reminiscence in his descriptions of the armada and the storm which destroyed it, but there is no reason to doubt the bald statement of its effect – 'their hearts broke'. There was nothing surprising if Arab morale suddenly plummeted when Allah seemed to have turned against them, nothing surprising if Muawiya set off soon, under cover of darkness, for home.

There is one particularly arresting sentence in this chapter: when Muawiya crossed Anatolia, 'all the inhabitants of the country submitted (literally, here as elsewhere, 'subjected themselves to servitude'), those on the coast and in the mountains and on the plains' (**170**). The whole people who would later show obstinate determination in resisting the

Arabs decade after decade, who would commit themselves whole-heartedly to a guerrilla war of defence, surrendered without a fight. All three geographical zones of Anatolia were involved, coastlands, high-lands and interior plateau. There could be no more telling evidence of the shock of the initial, ultra-dynamic phase of Arab expansion, when it had carried all before it and resistance had indeed been useless.

Other extant sources do not mention this episode, save for glancing references by Dionysius (179) and Theophanes (345) to a planned attack on Constantinople, apparently not executed, *à propos* of the Battle of Phoinix (n.63 above). It is overlooked in the standard authorities, apart from a fleeting and dismissive reference in Canard, 'Expéditions' 63, n.4.

Some standard authorities: Ahrweiler, *Byzance et la mer*; Ostrogorsky, *History of the Byzantine State*; Stratos, *Seventh Century*; Kennedy, *Prophet*; Herrin, *Formation of Christendom*; Haldon, *Seventh Century*; Whittow, *Orthodox Byzantium*; Treadgold, *History*.

76: ch.50, **171–172**, *events in Armenia after the Arabs' failures in the west I 654–655*. Before launching their abortive attack on Iberia (placed in context in n.73 above), the Arabs established their base for the winter at Dvin and set about negotiating the surrender of the Iberians. They encountered unexpected diplomatic resistance, and then, after winter weather impeded their attack on Iberia, withdrew not to Dvin but south to Asorestan (Syria, as at **176** below) at high speed. News of the scale of the disaster which they had suffered in the west, massive storm damage to the fleets and the defeat of the reserve army in Cappadocia, were prob-ably responsible for both of these developments.

The Armenian princes were more cautious than the Iberians. In the absence of T'ēodoros Ṙshtuni who was ill (he was to die in 655 [**174**]), his chief ally and son-in-law Hamazasp Mamikonean (**169**) joined with Musheł Mamikonean who had remained loyal to the Romans until early 654 (**173**), to convene a general assembly of the princes of Armenia. Prefaced with some sort of ringing declaration about their concern for the peasantry, the princes agreed to refrain from fighting that winter (654–655) and to raise taxes, probably those owed to the Arabs. The method of apportionment, according to the size of each prince's cavalry contingent, was the fairest, since the moneys raised were probably to be spent on provisioning the army which they had undertaken to provide, according to the terms of T'ēodoros' agreement with Muawiya.

Literature: Grousset, *Histoire* 303; Toumanoff, *Studies* 394–5.

77: ch.51, **172–173**, *rebellion in Media, 654–655*. Sebeos leaves his readers in no doubt about the crucial role played by Media during the Arab conquests (nn.54, 59, 61, 67 above). The regional army, with its own elected leader (the 'prince of Media'), had been one of two formidable Sasanian fighting forces left after the loss of Mesopotamia. Its defection had opened the way for the decisive victory over Yazkert in Khurasan in 652. This successful cultivation of Media had evidently required considerable diplomatic skill on the part of the Arabs.

There was a marked change in their approach after the defeat and death of Yazkert, as this chapter makes plain. Media was subjected to a tough regime, analogous to that proposed for the rump Roman empire in 654. Its army was disbanded and the rate of taxation was determined by the Arabs. Whether or not the rate was exorbitant and a prime cause of discontent, as Sebeos reports, it is impossible to decide, but we may suspect that a strong sense of regional identity and pride in the imperial past of Iran were more important factors.

Sebeos dates the start of the rebellion to the same year as the events of the previous chapters, the occupation of Armenia, the attack on Constantinople and the abortive invasion of Iberia (**169–171**). This yields a secure date of 654. The murder of the chief tax-collector was the signal for a general rising. The rebels began to reconstitute the regional army and gained the backing of the highlanders of Gełum and Delum in the western Elburz. They were then able to exploit the natural defences offered by fissured and forested mountains and by equally impenetrable fens to harass the Arabs as they sought to re-impose their authority.

It may be inferred, both from the dating indications supplied by Sebeos and from his evocation of the fighting, that Arab counter-insurgency operations, which were wearing and achieved little, lasted for several months. If the rebellion began in late summer 654, triggered perhaps by the news of Arab failures in the west, the campaign is likely to have dragged on through the following autumn and winter. Eventually, probably in spring 655, the decision was taken to change strategy and to seek elsewhere a notable success which might shake the resolution of the rebels, or, at any rate, might recoup some of the prestige lost in the mountains of Media.

Literature (Gełum and Delum): Hewsen, *AŠX* 87–8; Gyselen, *Géographie* 45, 49–50, 81–8.

78: ch.51, **173**, *Arab defeat in the Caucasus, 655*. The new strategy was to march to the Caucasus and take firm control of the easiest route north, which runs between the east end of the mountains and the Caspian Sea. This long narrow coastal passage extends from modern Sumgait in the south to Makhachkala in the north, and includes a number of pinch-points, of which the narrowest is at Darband. The Sasanians had constructed four or five defensive lines, the strongest of which barred the Darband pass. On the assumption that Sebeos meant to distinguish between the places which he named, the following reconstruction may be suggested. The Arabs advanced unopposed up the southern half of the coastal passage (the whole of which appears to be designated the Caspian Gates) and passed Darband and its associated defences (the Pass of Chor). They then set about ravaging the foothills of modern Dagestan, presumably with the intention of imposing their authority on the local tribesmen. They had, however, marched into a natural trap. A small force attacked them from the Gate of the Huns, perhaps to be iden-tified with the northern outlet of the coastal passage. This was then backed up by a large nomad army which came down from the steppes beyond. The Arabs were decisively defeated in a close engagement. Meanwhile another army appeared in their rear and cut off their retreat. The only hope of escape was to take to the hills. Only a small number managed to do so and eventually made their way back to Ctesiphon.

Taking account of the considerations discussed in the previous note, this defeat should probably be placed in late spring or early summer 655. The identity of the Arabs' adversaries is left obscure, since the name they are given, T'etalk', is used generically for nomads. The most likely candidates are the Khazars, who were building up their power in the steppes to the north of the Caucasus at this time.

The defeat has left its mark on Arab sources. The episode has been remoulded and redated (to A.H.32 [652]), but nonetheless remains recog-nizable: the expeditionary force made its way through the pass and laid siege to the town of Balanjar, probably a short distance from its northern outlet; there it was caught between a sortie from the town and a relieving force, and was cut to pieces.

Literature: (i) (Caspian Gates) Hewsen, *AŠX* 56A (map vii), 122–3; Howard-Johnston, 'The Great Powers' 191–2; E. Kettenhofen, 'Darband', *E.Ir.* VII, 13–19; (ii) (Khazars) Dunlop, *Khazars* 41–57; W. Barthold and P.B. Golden, 'Khazar', *E.I.* IV, 1172–3.

79: ch.52, **174**, *events in Armenia after the Arabs' failures in the west II*
655. The winter of 654–655 was severe. The Arabs had called off their
invasion of Iberia because of the cold and snow (**171**). 'The days of pier-
cing winter cold', to which Sebeos now refers, probably came somewhat
later. For a Roman army had had time to return to Armenia.
Maurianus was in command, so the army was probably that which had
fled ignominiously to the Pontic coast in 654. The Arabs now made a strategic withdrawal to Zarehawan, a plain immediately to the west of the
head of Lake Urmia. Maurianus, who had clearly recovered western
Armenia, including Karin, launched an offensive aimed at the chief
towns of what used to be Persarmenia, Dvin which fell and
Nakhchawan which held out. An Arab counter-attack brought about a
sudden reversal of fortunes in spring 655. Once again Maurianus took
to his heels, this time fleeing north to Iberia. Theophanes' notice (345 –
cited in n.73 above) may well refer to this second defeat of Maurianus,
since this time his flight did take him towards the Caucasus.

Time-honoured methods were now used by the Arabs to reimpose
their authority: (i) shows of force (probably exaggerated in their effects
by Sebeos) in Armenia, Albania and Siwnik'; (ii) punitive exactions (to
judge by the case of Karin); and (iii) deportation of a large number of
hostages, amounting to some 1,797 in all (**175**). These measures were
probably taken in early summer 655. Together they constituted a well-
judged response to the recent fickle behaviour of the Armenians, and
testify to a well-developed Arab statecraft, able and ready to learn from
the practice of the great powers in late antiquity.

Literature: Grousset, *Histoire* 303–4.

80: *general remarks on the events of 654–655*. With this second notice
about Armenian affairs in the changed climate following Arab failures
in the west, Sebeos brings the main body of his history to a close. His
coverage of contemporary events is considerably fuller than that of the
first Arab conquests or the campaigns of the 640s. Although there is
some disarrangement of the material, as he acknowledges (**176**), it is not
so serious as to prevent us from piecing together a connected history of
Arab actions in the year and a half between the end of the three-year
cease-fire and the time when Sebeos laid down his pen for several years
(early summer 655, after recording the tough regime imposed on
Armenia). It is worth pausing for a moment and taking stock of what
Sebeos has enabled us to see.

The expansion of the small religio-political community established by Muhammad to the status of a world power within 20 years of the *Hijra* is the most spectacular, observable example of dynamic growth of political power in history. Success in the defensive war against Mecca created an initial momentum. Each subsequent victorious campaign added to the momentum. Islam's fighting forces increased in size, its managerial skills were improved, and confidence grew that the Arabs were indeed the earthly shock-troops of a single, awesome, truly omnipotent deity. The converse was true of the established great powers as defeat came hard on the heels of defeat. Their material and, much more important, their immaterial resources haemorrhaged away. This was compounded in the case of Iran by a tendency towards regionalism and division programmed in by geography and history.

One of Sebeos' great services is to cast light on the first serious faltering of this dynamic process. Failures, if they were serious and if there were several of them, could put the dynamic process into reverse – draining the Arabs of some of their confidence, raising new hope and encouraging resistance among the occupied peoples, especially traditionally refractory highlanders, inflicting losses and forcing the Arabs to fight on several fronts at once. Something of this sort happened in 654 and 655. First came the destruction of the great armada assembled before Constantinople in summer 654. The news of this had important repercussions as it spread. The defeat suffered by the field army quartered in Cappadocia is surely partly attributable to shaken morale. Further east, two peoples, both endowed with formidable natural defences, took heart: the Medes rebelled and began reconstituting their formidable army; the Iberians refused to negotiate terms when threatened with attack at the end of the year.

The defeat (in Cappadocia), failure against Iberia and the increasing danger posed by the rebellion in Media between them dealt Arab prestige and morale a second serious blow. Their position now began to crumble in Armenia. The army which had set off against Iberia did not withdraw to its designated winter-quarters at Dvin but scurried south, beyond the line of Zagros and Taurus mountains. The other Arab troops in Armenia withdrew to a safer position in Atrpatakan, by Lake Urmia. Maurianus, *Magister Militum per Armeniam*, was now emboldened to march into the heart of Armenia and to bring it back under Roman control, continuing operations through the worst of winter, early in 655.

Further east, the rebels in Media had no difficulty in holding out against the Arab army sent against them.

By spring 655, there was an evident confidence (over-confidence, it later transpired) on the part of the Roman forces in Armenia as they pressed their siege of Nakhchawan, while the Arab army in Media was disheartened by a wearisome and fruitless counter-insurgency campaign. The prestige of the new imperial power was dropping fast in the north. This spurred the Arabs to two bold but risky counter-strokes. They launched a surprise attack on the Roman field army in Armenia in spring 655 outside Nakhchawan, won a decisive victory and recovered the ground lost in winter. Meanwhile their forces extricated themselves from their entanglement in Media and sought to re-establish their invincibility by exploits in the Caucasus region. But if the first gamble in Armenia had come off, this one went disastrously wrong, resulting in a defeat almost as damaging to Arab prestige and confidence as the loss of their fleet before Constantinople. The arrival of the ragged remnants of the expeditionary force in Ctesiphon surely made a considerable impression on opinion throughout the central lands of the nascent empire.

At this point Sebeos broke off writing. The immediate political and military consequences of these successive reverses suffered by the Arabs were covered cursorily in postscripts added several years later. It is tempting to suppose that he stopped writing and concealed his manuscript for fear of what would happen were it to fall into Arab hands. If so, the new repressive regime may have been sustained for a year or so in Armenia, while the troubles elsewhere grew more serious. But it is impossible to follow, in any detail, the chain of actions and reactions within and beyond the territories controlled by the Arabs after early summer 655. It is, however, clear that whatever the exact course of subsequent events, the defeats and difficulties of 654 and 655 were inducing increasing stress within the ruling elite of the caliphate, probably prompting recriminations and anxious reflection seeking to identify the causes of Allah's evident displeasure. Within a year the crisis intensified. The caliph 'Uthman was assassinated and the hitherto cohesive caliphate broke up into four antagonistic regional powers. A civil war began which would last five years.

81: ch.52, **174–175**, *Catholicos Nersēs in exile, 654–659/660*. Nersēs, whose support for the Chalcedonian position had been made manifest during Constans' visit to Dvin, prudently left at the same time as the emperor, probably early in 654 (**168** with n.72 above). Sebeos adds, in the first part of this notice, that, after leaving Dvin for his home region of Tayk', Nersēs paid a visit to Constantinople and was received with great honour – a visit which surely took place after the great Arab attack of 654 (rather than before, as implied by the phrasing). These were probably the last words he wrote before penning the final peroration (**176–177**) which brings the main body of the chronicle to a close (in late spring or early summer 655). Six years later he returned to the text and added three *scholia* to bring it up to date. The first was squeezed in before the final peroration (there was presumably a small blank space in his original manuscript between the last notice and the peroration). He notes that Nersēs spent six years in exile in Tayk', his former episcopal see (**166–167**), at the north-western extremity of Armenia. Tayk', it may be inferred, was of Chalcedonian inclination, doubtless influenced by its proximity to areas where Chalcedonianism was entrenched, Iberia and Roman territory along the Black Sea coast. The occasion of his return was almost certainly the second visit of Constans to Transcaucasia six years after he left Dvin, in his 19th regnal year (September 659–September 660), when he consolidated Roman authority throughout Transcaucasia (n.82 below). The completion of Nersēs' great church of Zuart'nots' (**147** with n.64 above) can then be dated to the early 660s.

Source: M.D., tr. Dowsett 118.

Literature: Garitte, *Narratio* 339; Hewsen, *AŠX* 204–10.

82: ch.52, **175**, *secession of Armenia from Arab rule, 656 (?)*. This notice concerns a grim episode in which the new great power showed that it was prepared to act ruthlessly to maintain its authority. The date cannot be fixed exactly, but the year mentioned at the start is probably best taken as the year of the outbreak of civil war in the caliphate, i.e. 656, intimations of which run through Sebeos' peroration. This would explain both why the Armenian princes were prepared to secede and why there were no Arab forces to hand to take direct punitive action against them. The army, which had reimposed Arab authority and had removed some 1,797 hostages in 655, had probably been drawn south when the political crisis broke.

Hamazasp Mamikonean, a bookish prince without experience of warfare, seems to have been inspired by his reading to emulate the exploits of his ancestors (**174**). To judge by the position of *curopalate* of Armenia granted to him afterwards, he took a leading part in the defection of a large number of princes (probably those of western and central Armenia, who had sided with Constans against T'ēodoros Ṙshtuni in 653 [**165** above]), which Sebeos reports in his second postscript. There were other princes, though, led by Musheł Mamikonean (so probably from the rump of the former Persarmenia, now described as the Arab sector [**171**]), who were deterred from following suit for fear of what might befall their relatives held hostage by the Arabs but were equally nervous of obeying a summons to go south with their wives. The Arab response – indiscriminate slaughter of all the hostages to hand (all but twenty-two of them) – drove Musheł and his allies, together with the army of Albania under its commander, the prince of Albania (Juanshēr who, Movsēs Daskhurants'i confirms, submitted to Constans at roughly this time) and the princes of Siwnik' into the arms of the Romans. Although they were taken into custody, the princes with Musheł were soon released on the emperor's orders while Musheł himself was summoned to Constantinople. The ill-judged brutality of the Arabs had placed the Romans in firm control of the whole of Transcaucasia.

This notice provides a context for a detailed account, taken by Movsēs from the laudatory biography of Juanshēr which he was using, of Juanshēr's dealings with Constans. Juanshēr first concluded a treaty with 'the Armenian general' (Hamazasp, who is later named) and then forwarded an offer of submission by letter to Constans. Constans replied with fine presents, a large number of titles for redistribution by Juanshēr in Albania and, the most precious gift, a fragment of the True Cross, which sealed this new alliance of senior with junior Christian ruler. Juanshēr was designated, in Constans' reply, 'lord of Gardman and prince of Albania, ex-consul and first patrician and governor of the east'. Movsēs then continues the story. Constans made a second journey to Transcaucasia in his 19th regnal year (659/660), when the Arab civil war was probably reaching a crescendo of violence (n.83 below). This was a grand imperial progress which took him into Media in the autumn of 659, then back to central Armenia where he was in the following spring. To judge by the case of Juanshēr, local client-rulers were given audiences and formally invested with the insignia of their offices, and largesse, comprising presents, titles and land, was distributed. The aim was clearly to consolidate Roman authority throughout Transcaucasia and to transform the region into a Christian highland redoubt which would act in unison against the Muslim forces in the south, whenever the civil war came to an end. Constans may even have sought to draw Media with its formidable highland forces into an alliance. This would explain his visit to Media, where Juanshēr had the first of this two audiences (in the presence of Armenian nobles and 'the general Hamazasp').

Constans left Transcaucasia in 660 and, before long (by 663), was at the opposite end of his realms, apparently trying to organize a trans-Mediterranean maritime front against Islam, with Sicily and North Africa as its outer bastions, as distant western analogues to Armenia and Albania.

Source: M.D., tr. Dowsett 115–20.

Literature: Grousset, *Histoire* 304; Herrin, *Formation of Christendom* 263–7; Haldon, *Seventh Century* 59–61.

83: ch.52, 175–176, *first Arab civil war, 656–661.* Sebeos' account of the first great crisis of the nascent Islamic empire differs fundamentally from that of the main strands of extant early Islamic tradition. Such, however, is the authority of Sebeos, a well-placed contemporary who has been seen at work gathering and arranging primary material of high quality on the complex events of the preceding 80 years or more, that his version cannot simply be pushed aside and ignored. Rather attention should be focused on the grave doubts which it arouses about the truth of the main thrust of extant Islamic accounts.

Political dissension at the apex of the Muslim community preoccupies Islamic tradition. There is no hint that serious reverses suffered by Islamic forces in distant theatres of war (as reported by Sebeos) played a part in rousing opposition to the Caliph 'Uthman's rule. Instead it is domestic grievances, above all 'Uthman's alleged nepotism, which led a deputation of Arabs from Egypt and their allies to assassinate him in summer 656, when their demands were not met. 'Ali, Muhammad's cousin and son-in-law then assumed power, *qua* leading member of the Prophet's family, only to encounter growing opposition from the established Meccan elite, and in particular from the Umayyad relations of 'Uthman, who claimed that a caliph should be chosen by consultation (*shura*) among the leaders of the Muslim community. For Sebeos, by contrast, the civil war was a struggle for military and political hegemony between a number of competing regional military forces. He therefore begins by sketching the composition of the rival groupings, of which there are four rather than the two of Islamic historical tradition.

It is not easy to identify all the regional armies named by Sebeos. A start can be made by noting that Asorestan here designates not the whole of the Fertile Crescent south of the Taurus and Zagros, but its western, Syrian component which had been governed by Muawiya since 639 and had been enlarged with the addition of Jazira (northern Mesopotamia) late in 646 or early in 647. It follows that the great Arab garrison cities of Iraq, Kufa and Basra, where much of the political and military action after 'Ali's assumption of power takes place according to early Islamic tradition, are not mentioned by name in Sebeos' account. It may therefore be postulated that they lurk concealed in Sebeos' fourth part, which he locates 'in the territory of the Arabs and the place called Askarawn'. Hewsen notes that, for Armenian authors, Arabs normally meant the Arabs of Mesopotamia, while the mysterious place-name 'Askarawn' surely has something to do with Arabic *askar*, 'army'. The disposition of Arab military forces on the eve of the civil war may then be reconstructed with a reasonable degree of probability as follows: (i) an army in southern Iran targeted on the Indus valley, with elements probably stationed in Persia, the old heartland of the Sasanian empire; (ii) the army of Syria, commanded by Muawiya, and an army in the north, presumably the force which had reoccupied Armenia in spring 655, together with such troops as had been left to hold Media after the end of the counter-insurgency campaign there; (iii) the army of Egypt and, aligned with it, the army which had driven Yazkert from Khurasan and now faced the (former) territory of the Hephthalites; (iv) the army of the Arabs garrisoned at Kufa and Basra on the edge of Iraq. The picture presented by Sebeos is one of a single Arab-controlled world, in which political alliances can be formed between widely separated forces and in which the competition is for a central unitary authority.

The picture presented by early Islamic tradition is very different, above all because it is parochial. Attention is focused on Iraq, in particular on Kufa and its fractious politics. The rival political parties of the Hijaz look to Iraq for support, the opposition to Basra, 'Ali to Kufa. A battle takes place outside Basra in December 656 which is remembered as the Battle of the Camel, because the fighting revolves around the camel ridden by 'A'isha, widow of Muhammad. 'Ali wins a decisive victory, only to face a new adversary in Muawiya who launches a propaganda war from Syria. In spring 657 'Ali and Muawiya mobilize their forces and confront each other at Siffin, on the right bank of the

Euphrates, not far from the old Roman-Persian frontier. The confrontation ends in an inconclusive engagement and an agreement by both sides to go to arbitration. The arbitration is equally inconclusive and the two parties remain openly antagonistic but keep their distance from each other. The political and military balance shifts in Muawiya's favour in 658. While 'Ali is distracted by political dissidence in Iraq, Muawiya takes control of Egypt which has hitherto obstinately resisted overtures from him and 'Amr. b. al-'As, its original conqueror and first governor. At some stage, perhaps before the acquisition of Egypt but more likely after it, Muawiya is formally declared caliph by his Syrian supporters. The stand-off continues until, in January 661, 'Ali is assassinated by an Iraqi dissident at Kufa. Thereafter Muawiya has little difficulty in imposing his authority on Kufa and the whole of the caliphate.

Sebeos' version is initially compatible with early Islamic tradition. The king killed by an alliance of the army of Iraq (the suggestion made above) and the Egyptian army was the Caliph 'Uthman. The king whom they installed in his place was 'Ali. The allied forces then parted, allowing Muawiya, governor of Syria and second-ranking ruler in the caliphate (probably by virtue of his command of the war against the Christians in the north and the north-west), to deal with them separately. So far so good, but from this point it becomes impossible to reconcile the two accounts. For in the second phase Sebeos has Muawiya march into the desert, kill 'Ali and then inflict a heavy defeat on the army of Iraq. 'Ali's death is thus dated long before the end of the civil war and takes place in the desert, rather than at Kufa. Muawiya is made directly responsible for it. The battle fought between Syrian and Iraqi forces (which may have mutated into the Battle of Siffin) ends in a decisive victory for the former.

Some corroboration for Sebeos' version can be obtained from a probably late seventh-century Syrian Maronite chronicle, which dates 'Ali's assassination to 658 rather than 661, locates it at Hira and does not name those responsible (who could therefore have been acting or thought to be acting on orders from Muawiya). This was followed by Muawiya's arrival at Hira and the submission to him of all the Arab forces there (which could have followed an engagement).

One crucial point is firmly established by the Maronite chronicle. Muawiya became caliph in 660, well after 'Ali's death. The opening ceremony took place in Jerusalem, in the course of which Muawiya visited Golgotha and Gethsemane. It was followed by an assembly of emirs and Arabs in July (evidently held outside the city) which proclaimed him caliph. Sebeos, who was concerned with underlying military realities, turns rather to the third phase of the conflict, between the army of Egypt and Muawiya's forces. Perhaps the most startling single piece of information which he supplies is his notice that the army of Egypt sought to strengthen its position by making a treaty with the emperor (Constans) and that the whole host, some 15,000 men, converted to Christianity. A stray reference in early Islamic tradition to Muslims reverting to Christianity in a quite other part of the caliphate at this time because of the deadly strife within the congregation of Muhammad (in Bahrain) may ease some of the incredulity which Sebeos' statement is likely to arouse in Islamicists. As regards other events of the third phase, lasting, we may guess, from 658 to 661, Sebeos, alas, supplies no details but gives the clear impression that all the armies which he enumerated were involved, that the fighting was widespread and the casualties heavy. The outcome had become all too clear by the time he completed the last postscript to his history. Muawiya was the victor and had pacified the whole Muslim-controlled world.

A postscript to these postscripts of Sebeos will bring this commentary to an end. It is based on Movsēs' version of the life of Juanshēr, prince of Albania, who ruled (and naturally prayed for) 'those who dwell on the shores of the sea in the east'. Five years after Constans' second visit to Transcaucasia, in Juanshēr's 28th year as military commander in Albania (664/665 – the dating is precise and faultless, with a single exception noted below), the extended eastern front against Islam which he had created along the Taurus and northern Zagros mountains collapsed without a fight. The seat of Arab government had been transferred to Damascus six years before (a remark which corroborates the Maronite chronicle's date of 658 for the death of 'Ali). Muawiya, who is not named, 'began to suck the marrow of the land around him'. He is described as ruling 'the four corners of the earth'. Juanshēr recognized brute reality (so too probably did 'the Armenian general' and nobles who met him and honoured him on his way south) and went to do obeisance to 'the conqueror of the world' at 'the universal court'. There he was honoured, says his biographer, was given presents, and made a treaty to which he remained faithful. Three years later (so in 667/668, mistakenly equated with an impossible 30th regnal year of Constans

[670/671]), he was summoned again to Muawiya's court, his advice being sought on a scheme to assassinate Constans. He was rewarded with the extension of his authority to cover Siwnik' and a reduction of a third in Albania's tribute. He then returned home by winter 667–668, with many presents – horses, robes, a sword, an elephant and a parrot (the last two described in rich, evocative prose by his biographer who saw them at the assembly which he held on his return). Within a year he, like Constans, was assassinated.

A new Arab and Islamic world-order was firmly established in the 660s, as Sebeos foresaw when he laid down his pen. Muawiya, victorious in the civil war, did indeed rule the four corners of the earth from a universal court at Damascus.

Sources: (i) (civil war) *West-Syrian Chronicles* 29–32; Tabari XVI–XVII; (ii) (postscript) M.D., tr. Dowsett 120–30, 142–5.

Literature: Hewsen, *AŠX* 229; Wellhausen, *The Arab Kingdom* 75–112; Hawting, *The First Dynasty* 24–33; M. Hinds, 'Mu'awiya I', *E.I.* VII, 263–5; Noth/Conrad, 33–5; Madelung, *Succession* 113–326.

BIBLIOGRAPHY

I. TEXTS

Agat'angełos. Critical Armenian text: *Patmut'iwn Hayots'*, ed. G. Tēr-Mkrtch'ean and S. Kanayeants' (Tiflis, 1909; repr. Delmar, NY, 1980). English translation with facing Armenian text in R.W. Thomson, *Agathangelos: History of the Armenians* (Albany, 1976). Italian version by N. Tommaséo, *Agatangelo, Storia dell'Armenia* (Venice, 1843). These omit the section known as 'The Teaching', for which see R.W. Thomson, *The Teaching of Saint Gregory: an early Armenian catechism* [HATS 3] (Cambridge, MA, 1970). The Armenian text is abbreviated to Aa. There is a Greek rendering of this version in G. Lafontaine, *La Version grecque du livre arménien d'Agathange* [Publications de l'Institut orientaliste de Louvain 7] (Louvain, 1973). For an earlier recension of the text, in Greek, abbreviated to Vg, see Garitte, *Agathange*, s.v. Secondary Literature.

Alexander Romance. Patmut'iwn Alek'sandri Makedonts'woy, ed. H. Simonyan (Erevan, 1989). English translation: A. Wolohojian, *The Romance of Alexander the Great by Pseudo-Callisthenes translated from the Armenian Version* [Records of Civilization: Sources and Studies 82] (New York, 1969).

Anastasius the Persian. See Secondary Literature, s.v. Flusin, *St Anastase* I 40–91, 98–107.

Ankanon Girk', vol. 1, ed. S. Yovsep'eants' (Venice, 1896).

Anonymous Chronicle. Ananun Zhamanakagrut'iwn, ed. B. Sargisean (Venice, 1904).

The Anonymous Story-teller. Patmut'iwn Ananun Zruts'agri, ed. M.H. Darbinyan-Melik'yan (Erevan, 1971); identified as Shapuh Bagratuni by G. Tēr-Mkrtch'ean and M. Tēr-Movsēsean, *Patmut'iwn Shaphoy Bagratunwoy* (Ejmiatsin, 1921). English translation in R.W. Thomson, 'The Anonymous Story-Teller (also known as Pseudo-Shapuh)', *REA* 21, 1988–89, 171–232.

Antiochus Monachus. *Epistula ad Eustathium*, *PG* 89, col.1421–1428.

Antiochus Strategius. *La Prise de Jérusalem par les Perses en 614*, ed. and trans. G. Garitte [*CSCO* 202, 203, *Scriptores Iberici* 11, 12] (Louvain,

1960) and *Expugnationis Hierosolymae AD 614 Recensiones Arabicae* [*CSCO* 340–1, 347–8, *Scriptores Arabici* 26–9] (Louvain, 1973 and 1974).

Armenian Bible. *Astuatsashunch' Matean Hin ew Nor Ktakaranats'*, ed. Y. Zohrapean (Venice, 1805; repr. Delmar, NY, 1984).

Asołik. See Step'anos Taronets'i.

Ashkharhats'oyts'. A. Soukry, *Géographie de Mose de Chorène* (Venice, 1881). See also *Eranšahr* and Hewsen, *AŠX*.

Baladhuri. *The Origins of the Islamic State* I, P.K. Hitti (New York, 1916) = 'Baladhuri I'; *The Origins of the Islamic State* II, F.C. Murgotten (New York, 1924) = 'Baladhuri II'.

Book of Letters. See s.v. *Girk' T'łt'ots'*.

Buzandaran. [Attributed to P'awstos]. *Patmut'iwn Hayots'* (Venice, 1933).

EH = English translation and commentary by N.G. Garsoïan, *The Epic Histories (Buzandaran Patmut'iwnk')* [HATS 8] (Cambridge, MA, 1989).

Chronicle to 724. See s.v. *West-Syrian Chronicles*, 13–24.

Chronicon Anonymum, ed. I. Guidi, in *Chronica Minora* (Paris, 1903).

Chronicon Paschale 284–628 AD, trans. M. and M. Whitby [*TTH* 7] (Liverpool, 1989).

Dawit' Anyalt'. *Sahmank' Imastasirut'ean*, ed. S.S. Arevshatyan (Erevan, 1960). English translation and commentary by B. Kendall and R.W. Thomson, *Definitions and Divisions of Philosophy by David the Invincible Philosopher* [PATS 5] (Chico, CA, 1983).

Dionysius of Tel-Mahre. See s.v. *West-Syrian Chronicles*, 111–221.

Ełishē. *Ełishēi vasn Vardanay ew Hayots' Paterazmin*, ed. E. Tēr Minasyan (Erevan, 1957). English translation and commentary by R.W. Thomson, *Ełishē: History of Vardan and the Armenian War* [HATS 5] (Cambridge, MA, 1982).

Eranšahr. See Secondary Literature, s.v. Marquart.

Eusebius. *Chronicle* = *Eusebii Pamphili Caesarensis Episcopi, Chronicon Bipartitum*, ed. J. Aucher, 2 vols., (Venice, 1818) [Armenian text with Latin translation]. German translation: J. Karst, *Die Chronik des Eusebius aus dem armenischen übersetzt* [*GCS* 20] (Leipzig, 1911).

Eusebius. *Ecclesiastical History* = *Patmut'iwn ekełets'woy Eusebiosi Kesarats'woy*, ed. A. Charean (Venice, 1877).

Evagrius. *The Ecclesiastical History of Evagrius*, ed. J. Bidez and L. Parmentier (London, 1898).

Eznik. *Eznik, De Deo. Edition critique du texte arménien, traduction française, notes et tables*, L. Mariès and C. Mercier [*PO* 28.3–4] (Paris, 1959).

George of Pisidia. *Giorgio di Pisidia Poemi I. Panegirici epici* [*Studia Patristica et Byzantina* 7], ed. and trans. A. Pertusi (Ettal, 1960).

Georgian Chronicles. See s.v. K'art'lis Ts'khovreba.

Girk' Pitoyits', ed. G. Muradyan (Erevan, 1993).

Girk' T'łt'ots' (Tiflis, 1901).

Histoire nestorienne, ed. A. Scher [*PO* 7] (Paris, 1911).

History of Taron. See s.v. Zenob.

Ibn Ishaq. *The Life of Muhammad. A translation of Ibn Ishaq's 'Sirat Rasul Allah'*, A. Guillaume (Oxford, 1955).

Joannes Antiochenus. *Chronica*, ed. C. Müller and V. Langlois in *Fragmenta Historicorum Graecorum* V (Paris, 1870), 27–38.

John Catholicos. See s.v. Yovhannēs Draskhanakertts'i.

John of Ephesus. *Iohannis Ephesini Historiae Ecclesiasticae pars tertia* (*Ecclesiastical History*), trans. E.W. Brooks [*CSCO* 106, *Scriptores Syri* 55] (Louvain, 1952).

John of Nikiu. English translation in R.H. Charles, *The Chronicle of John, Bishop of Nikiu* (London, 1916).

John Mandakuni, *Démonstration*, M. Tallon, *Livre des Lettres. 1er Groupe: documents concernant les relations avec les Grecs* [Mélanges de l'Université Saint Joseph XXXII, fasc. 1] (Beirut, 1955), 78–138.

Kanonagirk' Hayots', ed. V. Hakobyan, 2 vols. (Erevan, 1964, 1971).

K'art'lis Ts'khovreba, ed. S. Qaukhch'ishvili, 2 vols. (Tbilisi, 1955, 1959). English translation of the Armenian [=V] and Georgian [=Q] texts in R.W. Thomson, *Rewriting Caucasian History. The Medieval Armenian Adaptation of the Georgian Chronicles* (Oxford, 1996).

Khuzistan Chronicle. Translated by Th. Nöldeke, 'Die von Guidi herausgegebene syrische Chronik übersetzt und commentiert', in *Sitzungsberichte der kaiserlichen Akademie der Wissenschaften*, Phil.-Hist. Classe 128.9 (Vienna, 1893).

Kirakos Gandzakets'i. *Patmut'iwn Hayots'*, ed. K. Melik'-Ōhanjanyan (Erevan, 1961).

Knik' Hawatoy, ed. K. Tēr-Mkrtch'ean (Ejmiatsin, 1914); repr. as *Sceau de le Foi* (Louvain, 1974).

Koriwn. *Vark' Mashtots'i*, ed. M. Abełyan (Erevan, 1941; repr. Delmar, NY, 1985). German translation and commentary by G. Winkler, *Koriwns Biographie des Mesrop Maštoc'* [*OCA* 245] (Rome, 1994).

Łazar Pʻarpetsʻi. *Patmutʻiwn Hayotsʻ*, ed. G. Tēr-Mkrtchʻean and S. Malkhasean (Tiflis, 1904; repr. Delmar, NY, 1985). English translation and commentary by R.W. Thomson, *The History of Łazar Pʻarpecʻi* [OPP 4] (Atlanta, GA, 1991).

Łewond. *Patmutʻiwn*, ed. K. Ezean (St Petersburg, 1887). English translation by Z. Arzoumanian, *History of Lewond* (Philadelphia, 1982).

Life of Nersēs. *Patmutʻiwn srboyn Nersisi Partʻewi* (Venice, 1853).

Liu Mau-tsai. *Die chinesischen Nachrichten zur Geschichte der Ost-Türken (Tʻu-Küe)*, *Göttinger Asiatische Forschungen* 10, 2 vols. (Wiesbaden, 1958).

Matthew of Edessa. Mattʻēos Urhayetsʻi, *Patmutʻiwn* (Jerusalem, 1869). English translation by A.E. Dostourian, *Armenia and the Crusades. The Chronicle of Matthew of Edessa* (Lanham, MD, 1993).

Menander. *The History of Menander the Guardsman*, ed. and trans. R.C. Blockley (Liverpool, 1985).

Michael the Syrian. *Zhamanakagrutʻiwn Tearn Mikhayeli Asorwotsʻ Patriarkʻin* (Jerusalem, 1871). French translation in V. Langlois, *Chronique de Michel le Grand*, (Venice, 1868).

Mkhitʻar Anetsʻi. *Matean Ashkharhavēp Handisarantsʻ*, ed. H.G. Margaryan (Erevan, 1983).

Mkhitʻar Ayrivanetsʻi. *Patmutʻiwn Hayotsʻ*, ed. N. Emin (Moscow, 1860).

Movsēs Daskhurantsʻi [or Kałankatuatsʻi]. Movsēs Kałankatuatsʻi, *Patmutʻiwn Ałuanitsʻ Ashkharhi*, ed. V. Arakʻelyan (Erevan, 1983). English translation by C.J.F. Dowsett, *The History of the Caucasian Albanians by Movses Dasxurancʻi* [London Oriental Series 8] (London, 1961).

Movsēs Khorenatsʻi. *Patmutʻiwn Hayotsʻ*, ed. M. Abełean and S. Yarutʻiwnean (Tiflis, 1913; repr. Delmar, NY, 1981). English translation by R.W. Thomson, *Moses Khorenatsʻi: History of the Armenians* [HATS 4] (Cambridge, MA, 1978). French translation by A. and J.-P. Mahé, *Histoire de l'Arménie par Moïse de Khorène* (Paris, 1993).

Narratio. See Secondary Literature, s.v. Garitte.

Nikephoros. C. Mango, *Nikephoros, Patriarch of Constantinople. Short History* [Dumbarton Oaks Texts 10] (Washington, D.C., 1990).

Pʻawstos. See s.v. *Buzandaran*.

Plutarch. *Life of Lucullus*.

Pseudo-Callisthenes. See s.v. *Alexander Romance*.

Pseudo-Epiphanius. G. Frasson, *Pseudo-Epiphanii Sermo de Antichristo* [Bibliotheca Armeniaca 2] (Venice, 1976).

Pseudo-Methodius. G.J. Reinink, *Die syrische Apokalypse des Pseudo-Methodius* [*CSCO* 540, 541, *Scriptores Syri* 220 (edition), 221 (translation)] (Louvain, 1993).

Pseudo-Shapuh Bagratuni. See s.v. *The Anonymous Story-teller*.

Pseudo-Yovhannēs Mamikonean. See s.v. Zenob.

Root of Faith. See Thomson, 'The Shorter Recension', s.v. Secondary Literature.

Seal of Faith. See *Knik' Hawatoy*.

Sebeos. *Patmut'iwn Sebēosi*, ed. G.V. Abgaryan (Erevan, 1979). References to page numbers of Sebeos are to this edition; they are marked in **bold** type in this translation.

Translation of Part III [the *History*] by F. Macler, *Histoire d'Héraclius* (Paris, 1904); C. Gugerotti, *Sebeos: Storia* [*Eurasiatica* 4, Quaderni del Dipartimento di Studi Eurasiatici, Universit degli Studi di Venezia] (Verona, 1990). Partial translation in H. Hübschmann, *Zur Geschichte Armeniens und der ersten Krieger der Araber* (Leipzig, 1875; repr. *REA* 13, 1978–79, 313–53). Unpublished translation by R. Bedrosian, *Sebeos. Patmut'iwn i Herakln*, (np, 1985).

Translation of Part I [the *Primary History*] in Gugerotti and in Thomson, *Moses Khorenats'i*, and of Part II in Gugerotti.

Seert Chronicle. Histoire nestorienne (Chronique de Séert), Deuxième partie, ed. and trans. A. Scher [*PO* 13.4] (Paris, 1919).

Shahnama. Le Livre des rois par Abou'lkasim Firdousi, 7 vols., trans. J. Mohl (Paris, 1876–1878).

Shepherd of Hermas, *Similitudes* (Loeb Edition, in *Apostolic Fathers*, II).

Socrates. *Sokratay sk'olastikosi Ekelets'akan Patmut'iwn ew Patmut'iwn Varuts' srboyn Silbestrosi episkoposin Hŕovmay*, ed. M. Tēr-Movsēsean (Ejmiatsin, 1897).

Sophronius, *Anacreontica. Sophronii Anacreontica*, ed. and trans. M. Gigante (Rome, 1957).

Spyridon. *La Légende de S. Spyridon, évêque de Trimithonte, Bibliothèque du Muséon* 33, ed. P. van den Ven (Louvain, 1953).

Step'annos Orbelean. *Patmut'iwn nahangin Sisakan*, ed. N. Emin (Moscow, 1861). French translation in M. Brosset, *Histoire de la Siounie par Stéphannos Orbélian* (St Petersburg, 1864; Introduction 1866).

Step'anos Taronets'i. *Step'annos Taronets'woy Patmut'iwn tiezerakan*, ed. S. Malkhasean (St Petersburg, 1885). French translation: E. Dulaurier, *Etienne Açoghig de Daron. Histoire universelle* (Paris, 1883) [Part I]; F. Macler, *Etienne Asolik de Taron. Histoire universelle* (Paris, 1917) [Parts II and III].

Strabo. *The Geography* (Loeb Edition).

Strategius. See s.v. Antiochus Strategius.

Synodicon Orientale, ed. J.B. Chabot (Paris, 1902).

Tabari. *The History of al-Tabari*, 35 vols., ed. E. Yar-Shater (Albany, New York, 1985–). German translation by Th. Nöldeke in *Geschichte der Perser und Araber zur Zeit der Sasaniden aus der arabischen Chronik des Tabari* (Leiden, 1879) = 'Tabari, tr. Nöldeke'.

Teaching. See s.v. Agat'angełos.

Theodore of Sykeon. See s.v. *Vie de Théodore*.

Theodore Syncellus. Sermon of Theodore Syncellus in *Analecta Avarica, Rozprawy Akademii Umiejetnosci, Wydzial Filologiczny*, series 2, vol. 15, ed. L. Sternbach (Krakow, 1900), 298–320.

Theon, *Progymnasmata. T'eovnay Yałags chartasanakan krt'ut'eanc' handerdz yoyn bnagrov*, ed. A. Manandyan (Erevan, 1938).

Theophanes. *The Chronicle of Theophanes Confessor. Byzantine and Near Eastern History AD 284–813*, trans. C. Mango and R. Scott (Oxford, 1997). References are to the pagination of the Greek text in the margin.

Theophanes Byzantius. Theophanes Byzantius ed. C. Müller in *Fragmenta Historicorum Graecorum* IV (Paris, 1851), 270–1.

Theophylact Simocatta. M. and M. Whitby, *The History of Theophylact Simocatta* (Oxford, 1986).

Timothy Aelurus. *Timotheus Aelurus des Patriarchen von Alexandrien Widerlegung der auf der Synode zu Chalcedon festgesetzen Lehre*, ed. K. Ter-Mekerttschian and E. Ter-Minassiantz (Leipzig-Ejmiacin, 1908).

T'ovma Artsruni. *Patmut'iwn Tann Artsruneats'*, ed. K. Patkanean (St Petersburg, 1887; repr. Tiflis, 1917; Delmar, NY, 1991). English translation by R.W. Thomson, *Thomas Artsruni: History of the House of the Artsrunik'* (Detroit, 1985).

Ukhtanēs. *Patmut'iwn Hayots'* (Vałarshapat, 1871). English translation by Z. Arzoumanian, *Bishop Ukhtanes of Sebastia. History of Armenia*, Part I (Fort Lauderdale, 1988), Part II (Fort Lauderdale, 1985).

Vardan. *Hawak'umn Patmut'ean*, ed. Ł. Alishan (Venice, 1862; repr. Delmar, NY, 1991). English translation by R.W. Thomson, 'The Historical Compilation of Vardan Arewelc'i', *DOP* 43, 1989, 125–226.

Vie de Théodore. French translation by A.-J. Festugière in *Vie de Théodore de Sykéôn, Subsidia Hagiographica* 48, vol. 2 (Brussels, 1970).

West-Syrian Chronicles. English translation by A. Palmer, *The Seventh Century in the West-Syrian Chronicles* [*TTH* 15] (Liverpool, 1993).

Yachakhapatum Chark' (Venice, 1954).

Yovhannēs Draskhanakertts'i [John Catholicos]. *Patmut'iwn Hayots'*, ed. M. Emin (Moscow, 1853; repr. Tiflis, 1912; Delmar, NY, 1980). English translation by K. Maksoudian, *Yovhannēs Drasxanakertc'i: History of Armenia* [OPP 3] (Atlanta, GA, 1987).

Zachariah Rhetor (of Mylitene). *Historia Ecclesiastica*, ed. E.W. Brooks [*CSCO Scriptores Syri*] (Louvain, 1919).

Zenob. *Patmut'iwn Taronoy*, with Yovhannēs Mamikonean, *Patmut'iwn Taronoy* (Venice, 1889). English translation of both by L. Avdoyan, *Pseudo-Yovhannē Mamikonean. The History of Taron* [OPP 6] (Atlanta, GA, 1993).

Zohrab. See s.v. Armenian Bible.

II. SECONDARY LITERATURE

Abgaryan. Without further qualification this refers to the Armenian text of Sebeos edited by G.V. Abgaryan and to his Introduction and notes. See Texts s.v. Sebeos and Note to the Reader.

Abgaryan, *Ananun* = G.V. Abgaryan, *Sebēosi Patmut'yunĕ ev Ananuni ařeltsvatsĕ* (Erevan, 1965).

Abgaryan, 'A propos' = G.V. Abgaryan, 'A propos de la republication de H. Hübschmann, *Zur Geschichte Armeniens* dans *REArm XIII*', *REA* 14, 1980, 478–80.

Abgaryan, 'Remarques' = G.V. Abgaryan, 'Remarques sur l'histoire de Sébéos', *REA* 1, 1964, 203–15.

Adontz/Garsoïan = N. Adontz, *Armenia in the Period of Justinian*, translated with Partial Revisions, a Bibliographical Note and Appendices, by Nina G. Garsoïan (Lisbon, 1970).

Ahrweiler, *Byzance et la mer* = H. Ahrweiler, *Byzance et la mer. La marine de guerre, la politique et les institutions maritimes de Byzance aux VIIe–XVe siècles, Bibliothèque byzantine, Etudes* 5 (Paris, 1966).

Akinean, *Baleshi Dprots'ē* = N. Akinean, *Baleshi Dprots'ē 1500–1704* (Vienna, 1952).

Akinean and Casey, 'Two Armenian Creeds' = N. Akinean and R.P. Casey, 'Two Armenian Creeds', *Harvard Theological Review* 25, 1931, 143–51.

Architettura Armena = *Architettura Medievale Armena* (Rome, 1968).

Armeniaca = *Armeniaca. Mélanges d'études arméniennes* (Venice, 1969).

Arutiunova-Fidanjan, '*I Smbatay*' = V.A. Arutiunova-Fidanjan, '*I Smbatay* or *I Spahan*?' in *From Byzantium to Iran*, 151–64.

Barfield, *Perilous Frontier* = T.J. Barfield, *The Perilous Frontier. Nomadic Empires and China* (Oxford, 1989).

Barthold, *Historical Geography* = W. Barthold, *An Historical Geography of Iran* (Princeton, 1984).

Beaucamp, 'Temps et Histoire' = J. Beaucamp, R.-Cl. Bondoux, J. Lefort, M.-F. Rouan, I. Sorlin, 'Temps et Histoire I: Le prologue de la *Chronique pascale*', *TM* 7, 1979, 223–301.

Blockley, 'Division' = R.C. Blockley, 'The Division of Armenia between the Romans and the Persians at the End of the Fourth Century A.D.', *Historia* 36, 1987, 222–34.

Blockley, *East Roman Foreign Policy* = R.C. Blockley, *East Roman Foreign Policy. Formation and Conduct from Diocletian to Anastasius* (Leeds, 1992).

Borkowski, *Alexandrie II* = Z. Borkowski, *Alexandrie II. Inscriptions des factions à Alexandrie* (Warsaw, 1981).

Brock, 'Christians' = S.P. Brock, 'Christians in the Sasanian Empire: a Case of Divided Loyalties', *Studies in Church History* 18, 1982, 1–19.

Brosset, *Rapports* = M. Brosset, *Rapports sur un voyage archéologique dans la Géorgie et dans l'Arménie exécuté en 1847–1848*. Premier livraison (St Petersburg, 1849).

Butler, *Arab Conquest of Egypt* = A.J. Butler, *The Arab Conquest of Egypt and the Last Thirty Years of the Roman Dominion* (Oxford, 1902).

Bryer/Winfield, *Pontos* = A. Bryer and D. Winfield, *The Byzantine Monuments and Topography of the Pontos*, [Dumbarton Oaks Studies, 20], 2 vols. (Washington, D.C., 1985).

Cameron/Conrad, *Problems* = Averil Cameron and L.I. Conrad edd., *The Byzantine and Early Islamic Near East I, Problems in the Literary Source Material* (Princeton, 1992).

Cameron, 'Disputations' = Averil Cameron, 'Disputations, Polemical Literature and the Formation of Opinion', *Disputation Poems and*

Dialogues in the Ancient and Medieval Near East, edd. G.J. Reinink and H.L.J. Vanstiphont (Leuven, 1991), 9–108.

Canard, 'Expéditions' = M. Canard, 'Les expéditions des Arabes contre Constantinople dans l'histoire et dans la légende', *Journal Asiatique* 208, 1926, 61–121. Reprinted in M. Canard, *Byzance et les musulmans du Proche Orient* (London, 1973).

Christensen, *L'Iran* = A. Christensen, *L'Iran sous les Sassanides* (Copenhagen, 1944).

Conrad, 'Conquest of Arwad' = L.I. Conrad, 'The Conquest of Arwad: A Source-Critical Study in the Historiography of the Early Medieval Near East', in Cameron/Conrad, *Problems*, 317–401.

Cowe, *Daniel* = S.P. Cowe, *The Armenian Version of Daniel* [UPATS 9] (Atlanta, GA, 1992).

Crone/Cook, *Hagarism* = P. Crone and M. Cook, *Hagarism. The Making of the Islamic World* (Cambridge, 1977).

Dabrowa, *Army* = E. Dabrowa ed., *The Roman and Byzantine Army in the East* (Krakow, 1994).

Dagron/Déroche, 'Juifs et chrétiens' = G. Dagron and V. Déroche, 'Juifs et chrétiens dans l'Orient du VIIᵉ siècle', *TM* 11, 1991, 17–273.

Dashian, *Leben und Sentenzen* = J. Dashian, *Das Leben und die Sentenzen des Philosophen Secundus des Schweigsamen in altarmenischer Übersetzung* [Denkschriften der kaiserlichen Akademie der Wissenschaften, Phil.-Hist. Kl., 44 Band, 3 Abhandlung] (Vienna, 1896).

de Blois, 'Calendar' = F. de Blois, 'The Persian Calendar', *Iran* 34, 1996, 39–54.

de Blois, 'Nagran martyrs' = F. de Blois, 'The date of the "martyrs of Nagran"', *AAE* 1, 1990, 110–128.

Dedurand, 'Citations patristiques' = M. Dedurand, 'Citations patristiques chez Etienne de Taron', *Armeniaca*, 116–24.

Dentzer, 'L'iconographie iranienne' = J.-M. Dentzer, 'L'iconographie iranienne du souverain couché et le motif du banquet', *IXème Congrès international d'archéologie classique, Annales archéologiques arabes syriennes* 21 (Damascus, 1971), 39–50.

Denzinger, *Enchiridion* = H. Denzinger, *Enchiridion Symbolorum*, 37th ed. (Freiburg im Breisgau, 1991).

Der Nersessian, 'Apologie' = S. Der Nersessian, 'Une apologie des images du septième siècle', *Byzantion* 17, 1944–1945, 58–87; reprinted in her *Etudes byzantines et arméniennes* (Louvain, 1973), I, 379–403.

Der Nersessian, *Armenian Art* = S. Der Nersessian, *Armenian Art* (np, 1977).

Dictionnaire de la Bible, 5 vols. (Paris, 1891–1892).

Donner, *Conquests* = F. McG. Donner, *The Early Islamic Conquests* (Princeton, 1981).

Dowsett, *Movsēs Dasxuranc'i*. See Texts, s.v. Movsēs Daskhurants'i.

Dunlop, *Khazars* = D.M. Dunlop, *The History of the Jewish Khazars* (Princeton, 1954).

Dvornik, *Political Philosophy* = F. Dvornik, *Early Christian and Byzantine Political Philosophy*, 2 vols. [Dumbarton Oaks Studies, 9] (Washington, D.C., 1966).

Eremyan, *Hayastanĕ* = S. Eremyan, *Hayastanĕ ĕst Ashkharhats'oyts'i* (Erevan, 1963).

Feissel, 'Inscriptions' = D. Feissel, 'Inscriptions chrétiennes et byzantines 532. Chypre. Soloi', *Revue des Etudes Grecques* 100, 1987, 380–1.

Fiey, 'Icho'denah' = J.M. Fiey, 'Icho'denah métropolite de Basra et son oeuvre', *L'Orient Syrien* 11, 1966, 431–450.

Flusin, 'L'esplanade du Temple' = B. Flusin, 'L'esplanade du Temple à l'arrivée des Arabes, d'après deux récits byzantins', in J. Raby and J. Johns edd., *Bayt al-Maqdis. 'Abd al-Malik's Jerusalem* I (Oxford, 1992), 17–31.

Flusin, *St Anastase* = B. Flusin, *Saint Anastase le Perse et l'histoire de la Palestine au début du VIIe siècle*, 2 vols. (Paris, 1992).

Foss, 'Persians' = C. Foss, 'The Persians in Asia Minor and the End of Antiquity', *EHR* 90, 1975, 721–47.

Foss, 'Sardis' = C. Foss, 'The Fall of Sardis in 616 and the Value of Evidence', *JÖB* 24, 1975, 11–22.

Frendo, 'Sebeos' = D. Frendo, 'Sebeos and the Armenian Historiographical Tradition in the Context of Byzantine-Iranian Relations', *Periteia* 4, 1985, 1–20.

Frolow, 'La vraie croix' = A. Frolow, 'La vraie croix et les expéditions d'Héraclius en Perse', *REB* 11, 1953, 88–105.

From Byzantium to Iran: Armenian Studies in Honour of Nina G. Garsoïan, ed. J.-P. Mahé and R.W. Thomson [OPP 5] (Atlanta, GA, 1997).

Garitte, *Agathange* = G. Garitte, *Documents pour l'étude du livre d'Agathange* [Studie Testi 127] (Vatican City, 1946).

Garitte, *Calendrier* = G. Garitte, *Le Calendrier palestino-géorgien du Sinaiticus 34 (Xe siècle)*, *Subsidia Hagiographica* 30 (Brussels, 1958).

Garitte, *Narratio* = G. Garitte, *La Narratio de Rebus Armeniae* [*CSCO* 132, Subsidia 4] (Louvain, 1952).

Garsoïan, 'City' = N.G. Garsoïan, 'The Early-Mediaeval Armenian City: an alien element', *The Journal of the Ancient Near Eastern Society* 16–17, 1984–1985 [*Ancient Studies in Memory of Elias Bickerman*], 67–83.

Garsoïan, *EH*. See Texts s.v. *Buzandaran*.

Garsoïan, 'The Locus' = N.G. Garsoïan, 'The Locus of the Death of Kings: Iranian Armenia – The Inverted Image', *The Armenian Image in History and Literature*, ed. R.G. Hovannisian [Studies in Near Eastern Culture and Society 3] (Malibu, CA, 1981), 27–64; reprinted in N.G. Garsoïan, *Armenia between Byzantium and the Sasanians* (London, 1985), no. XI.

Garsoïan, 'Prolegomena' = N.G. Garsoïan, 'Prolegomena to a Study of the Iranian Elements in Arsacid Armenia', *Handēs Amsorya, Zeitschrift für armenische Philologie* 90, 1976, 177–234; reprinted in N.G. Garsoïan, *Armenia between Byzantium and the Sasanians* (London, 1985), no. X.

Garsoïan, 'Separation' = N.G. Garsoïan, 'Some Preliminary Precisions on the Separation of the Armenian and Imperial Churches: I. The Presence of 'Armenian' Bishops at the First Five Oecumenical Councils', *Kathegetria, Essays Presented to Joan Hussey* (Camberley, 1988), 249–85.

'Quelques précisions préliminaires sur le schisme entre les Eglises byzantine et arménienne au sujet du concile de Chalcédoine: II. Le date et les circonstances de la rupture', *L'Arménie et Byzance, Histoire et Culture* [Byzantina-Sorbonensia 12] (Paris, 1996), 99–112.

'Quelques précisions préliminaires sur le schisme entre les Eglises byzantine et arménienne au sujet du concile de Chalcédoine: III. Les evechés méridionaux limitrophes de la Mésopotamie', *REA* 23, 1992, 39–80.

Gignoux, 'L'organisation administrative sasanide' = Ph. Gignoux, 'L'organisation administrative sasanide: le cas du *marzban*', *Jerusalem Studies in Arabic and Islam* 4, 1984, 1–29.

Gippert, *Iranica Armeno-Georgica* = J. Gippert, *Iranica Armeno-Georgica: Studien zu den iranischen Lehnwörtern im Armenischen und Georgischen* [Sitzungsberichte der Österreichische Akademie der Wissenschaften Bd. 606], 2 vols. (Vienna, 1993).

Göbl = R. Göbl, *Sasanian Numismatics* (Brunswick, 1971).

Golden, *Khazar Studies* = P.B. Golden, *Khazar Studies. A Historico-Philological Inquiry into the Origins of the Khazars*, 2 vols. (Budapest, 1980).

Goubert = P. Goubert, *Byzance avant l'Islam. I: Byzance et l'Orient* (Paris, 1951).

Gouillard, 'Gagik II' = J. Gouillard, 'Gagik II défenseur de la foi arménienne', *TM* 7, 1979, 399–418.

Greatrex = G. Greatrex, *Rome and Persia at War, 502–532* (Leeds, 1998).

Grierson, 'Consular Coinage' = P. Grierson, 'The Consular Coinage of "Heraclius" and the Revolt against Phocas of 608–610', *Numismatic Chronicle* series 6. 10, 1950, 71–93.

Grousset, *Histoire* = R. Grousset, *Histoire de l'Arménie des origines à 1071* (Paris, 1947).

Grumel = V. Grumel, *La Chronologie* [Bibliothèque byzantine, Traité d'Etudes byzantines 1] (Paris, 1958).

Gugerotti. See Texts, s.v. Sebeos.

Gyselen, *Géographie* = R. Gyselen, *La Géographie administrative de l'empire sassanide. Les témoignages sigillographiques* (Paris, 1989).

Haldon, *Byzantine Praetorians* = J.F. Haldon, *Byzantine Praetorians, Poikila Byzantina* 3 (Bonn, 1984).

Haldon, *Seventh Century* = J.F. Haldon, *Byzantium in the Seventh Century. The transformation of a culture* (Cambridge, 1990).

Hawting, *The First Dynasty* = G.R. Hawting, *The First Dynasty of Islam. The Umayyad Caliphate AD 661–750* (London and Sydney, 1986).

Heather, 'New Men' = P. Heather, 'New men for new Constantines? Creating an imperial elite in the eastern Mediterranean', in P. Magdalino ed., *New Constantines: the Rhythm of Imperial Renewal in Byzantium, 4th–13th Centuries* (Aldershot, 1994), 11–33.

Herrin, *Formation of Christendom* = J. Herrin, *The Formation of Christendom* (Oxford, 1987).

Herrmann, *Iranian Revival* = G. Herrmann, *The Iranian Revival* (Oxford, 1977).

Hewsen, *AŠX* = R.H. Hewsen, *The Geography of Ananias of Širak (Ašxarhac'oyc'). The Long and the Short Recensions* [Beihefte zum Tübinger Atlas des Vorderen Orients, Reihe B, nr. 77] (Wiesbaden, 1991).

Hewsen, 'Introduction' = R.H. Hewsen, 'Introduction to Armenian Historical Geography', *REA* 13, 1978–1979, 77–97.

Higgins, *Chronology* = M.J. Higgins, *The Persian War of the Emperor Maurice (582–602) I: The Chronology, with a Brief History of the Persian Calendar* (Washington, D.C., 1939).

Hinds, 'The First Arab Conquests' = M. Hinds, 'The First Arab Conquests in Fars', *Iran* 22, 1984, 39–53.

Honigmann = E. Honigmann, *Die Ostgrenze des byzantinischen Reiches* [vol. III of A.A. Vasiliev, *Byzance et les Arabes*] (Brussels, 1935).

Howard-Johnston, 'Al-Tabari' = J.D. Howard-Johnston, 'Al-Tabari on the Last Great War of Antiquity', in H. Kennedy ed., *Al-Tabari: a Medieval Muslim Historian and his Work* (Princeton, forthcoming).

Howard-Johnston, 'The Great Powers' = J.D. Howard-Johnston, 'The Great Powers in Late Antiquity: a Comparison', in Averil Cameron ed., *The Byzantine and Early Islamic Near East III, States, Resources and Armies* (Princeton, 1995), 157–226.

Howard-Johnston, 'Heraclius' Persian Campaigns' = J.D. Howard-Johnston, 'Heraclius' Persian Campaigns and the Revival of the East Roman Empire 622–630', *War in History* 6, 1999, 1–44.

Howard-Johnston, 'Official History' = J.D. Howard-Johnston, 'The Official History of Heraclius' Persian Campaigns', in Dabrowa, *Army*, 57–87.

Howard-Johnston, 'Procopius' = J.D. Howard-Johnston, 'Procopius, Roman Defences North of the Taurus and the New Fortress of Citharizon', *The Eastern Frontier of the Roman Empire*, ed. D.H. French and C.S. Lightfoot [BAR Int. Ser. 553] (Oxford, 1989), I 203–29.

Howard-Johnston, 'Siege' = J.D. Howard-Johnston, 'The Siege of Constantinople in 626', in C. Mango and G. Dagron edd., *Constantinople and its Hinterland* (Aldershot, 1995), 131–42.

Hoyland, 'Arabic, Syriac and Greek Historiography' = R.G. Hoyland, 'Arabic, Syriac and Greek Historiography in the first Abbasid century: an inquiry into inter-cultural traffic', *Aram* 3, 1991, 211–33.

Hoyland, 'Sebeos' = R.G. Hoyland, 'Sebeos, the Jews and the Rise of Islam', in R.L. Nettler, ed., *Medieval and Modern Perspectives on Muslim-Jewish Relations* (Oxford, 1995), 89–102.

Hoyland, *Seeing Islam as Others Saw It* = R.G. Hoyland, *Seeing Islam as Others Saw It. A Survey and Evaluation of Christian, Jewish and Zoroastrian Writings on Early Islam* [Studies in Late Antiquity and Early Islam 13] (Princeton, 1997).

Hübschmann, *AG* = H. Hübschmann, *Armenische Grammatik I. Etymologie* (Leipzig, 1895; repr. Hildesheim, 1962).

Hübschmann, *AON* = H. Hübschmann, *Die altarmenische Ortsnamen* (Strasbourg 1904; repr. Amsterdam, 1969).

Hübschmann, *Zur Geschichte Armeniens* = H. Hübschmann, *Zur Geschichte Armeniens und der ersten Krieger der Araber* (Leipzig, 1875; repr. *REA* 13, 1978–1979, 313–353).

Humphreys, *Islamic History* = R.S. Humphreys, *Islamic History. A Framework for Inquiry* (London and New York, 1991).

Hunt = E.D. Hunt, *Holy Land Pilgrimage in the later Roman Empire AD 312–460* (Oxford, 1982).

Johns, 'Southern Transjordan' = J. Johns, 'The *Longue Durée*: State and Settlement Strategies in Southern Transjordan Across the Islamic Centuries', in E.L. Rogan and T. Tell edd., *Village, Steppe and State. The Social Origins of Modern Jordan* (London and New York, 1994), 1–31.

Jones, *The Later Roman Empire* = A.H.M. Jones, *The Later Roman Empire 284–602*, 4 vols. (Oxford, 1964).

Justi = F. Justi, *Iranisches Namenbuch* (Marburg, 1895; repr. Hildesheim, 1963).

Kaegi, *Military Unrest* = W.E. Kaegi, *Byzantine Military Unrest 471–843. An Interpretation* (Amsterdam, 1981).

Kaegi, 'New Evidence' = W.E. Kaegi, 'New Evidence on the Early Reign of Heraclius', *BZ* 66, 1973, 308–30.

Kaplan, *Les hommes* = M. Kaplan, *Les hommes et la terre à Byzance du VIe au XIe siècle* (Paris, 1992).

Kelly, *Creeds* = J.N.D. Kelly, *Early Christian Creeds*, 2nd. ed. (London, 1960).

Kendall and Thomson, *David*. See Texts, s.v. Dawit' Anyalt'.

Kennedy, *Prophet* = H. Kennedy, *The Prophet and the Age of the Caliphates* (London and New York, 1986).

Khatchatrian, *L'architecture arménienne* = A. Khatchatrian, *L'architecture arménienne du IVe au VIe siècle* [Bibliothèque des Cahiers Archéologiques 7] (Paris, 1971).

Khatchatrian, *L'architecture arménienne* (1949) = A. Khatchatrian, *L'architecture arménienne. Essai analytique* (Paris, 1949).

Lampe = *A Patristic Greek Lexicon*, ed. G.W.H. Lampe (Oxford, 1968).

Lancaster and Lancaster, 'Tribal Formations' = W. Lancaster and F.

Lancaster, 'Tribal Formations in the Arabian Peninsula', *AAE* 3, 1992, 145–72.

Laurent/Canard = J. Laurent, *L'Arménie entre Byzance et l'Islam depuis la conquête arabe jusqu'en 886*. Nouvelle édition revue et mise à jour par M. Canard (Lisbon, 1980).

Leder, '*Khabar*' = S. Leder, 'The Literary Use of the *Khabar*: A Basic Form of Historical Writing', in Cameron/Conrad, *Problems*, 277–315.

Levy = R. Levy, *The Epic of the Kings* (Chicago, 1967).

Lewis/Niewöhner, *Religionsgespräche* = B. Lewis and F. Niewöhner edd., *Religionsgespräche im Mittelalter* (Wiesbaden, 1992).

Lombard = M. Lombard, *The Golden Age of Islam* (Amsterdam, 1975).

MacKenzie, *Pahlavi Dictionary* = D.N. MacKenzie, *A Concise Pahlavi Dictionary* (London, 1971).

Macler. See Texts, s.v. Sebeos.

Macler, *Apocalypses* = F. Macler, *Apocalypses apocryphes de Daniel* (Paris, 1895).

Madelung, *Succession* = W. Madelung, *The Succession to Muhammad. A Study of the Early Caliphate* (Cambridge, 1997).

Mahé, 'Critical Remarks' = J.-P. Mahé, 'Critical Remarks on the Newly Edited Excerpts from Sebēos', *Medieval Armenian Culture*, edd. T.J. Samuelian and M.E. Stone [UPATS 6] (Chico, CA, 1984), 218–39.

Mahé, 'Une légitimation scripturaire' = J.-P. Mahé, 'Une légitimation scripturaire de l'hagiographie: la Préface de Koriwn (443) à la *Vie de Maštoc'*, inventeur de l'alphabet arménien', *De Tertullien au Mozarabes. Mélanges offerts à Jacques Fontaine* [Collection des Etudes Augustiniennes. Série Antiquité, 132] I (Paris, 1992), 29–43.

Mahé, 'L'église' = J.-P. Mahé, 'L'église arménienne de 611 à 1066', in *Histoire du Christianisme*, ed. J.M. Mayeur, Ch. Pietri, A. Vauchez, IV (Paris, 1993), 457–547.

Mahé, 'Łewond' = J.-P. Mahé, 'Le problème de l'authenticité et de la valeur de la Chronique de Łewond', '*L'Arménie et Byzance* [Byzantina-Sorbonensia 12] (Paris, 1996), 119–26.

Mahé, *Moïse de Khorène*. See Texts s.v. Movsēs Khorenats'i.

Manandean, 'Invasions' = H. Manandean, 'Les invasions arabes en Arménie (Notes chronologiques)', *Byzantion* 18, 1948, 163–95.

Manandian, 'Les poids' = H. Manandian, 'Les poids et les mesures dans les plus anciennes sources arméniennes', *REA* 3, 1966, 315–46. [The second part appeared in *REA* 5, 1968, 369–419].

Manandjan, 'Marshruty' = J.A. Manandjan, 'Marshruty persidskikh pokhodov imperatora Iraklia', *Vizantiskij Vremennik* 3, 1950, 133–53.

Mango, *Byzantine Architecture* = C. Mango, *Byzantine Architecture* (London, 1986).

Mango, 'Deux Etudes' = C. Mango, 'Deux Etudes sur Byzance et la Perse sassanide', *TM* 9, 1985, 91–118.

Mango, 'Temple Mount' = C. Mango, 'The Temple Mount, AD 614–638', in J. Raby and J. Johns edd., *Bayt al-Maqdis. 'Abd al-Malik's Jerusalem* I (Oxford, 1992), 1–16.

Maraval = P. Maraval, *Lieux saints et pélerinages d'Orient* (Paris, 1985).

Markwart, *Südarmenien* = J. Markwart, *Südarmenien und die Tigrisquellen nach griechischen und arabischen Geographen* (Vienna, 1930).

Marquart, *Eranšahr* = J. Marquart, *Eranšahr nach der Geographie des Ps. Moses Xorenac'i* [Abhandlungen der Königlichen Gesellschaft der Wissenschaften zu Göttingen, Phil.-Hist. Klasse, N.F. III, 2] (Berlin, 1901; repr. Göttingen, 1970).

Marquart, 'Nachträge' = J. Marquart, 'Armenische Streifen. II. Nachtträge zu Eranšahr', *Huschardzan. Festschrift der MechitaristenKongregation in Wien* (Vienna, 1911), 300–2.

Marsden, *Greek and Roman Artillery* = E.W. Marsden, *Greek and Roman Artillery: Historical Development* (Oxford, 1969), *Greek and Roman Artillery: Technical Treatises* (Oxford, 1971).

Metzger, *Textual Commentary* = B.M. Metzger, *A Textual Commentary on the Greek New Testament* (Stuttgart, 1971).

Millar, 'Hagar' = F. Millar, 'Hagar, Ishmael, Josephus and the Origins of Islam', *Journal of Jewish Studies* 44, 1993, 23–45.

Mnats'akanyan, *Zuart'nots'* = S.Kh. Mnats'akanyan, *Zuart'nots'* (Erevan, 1971).

Morony, *Iraq* = M.G. Morony, *Iraq after the Muslim Conquest* (Princeton, 1984).

Nautin, 'L'auteur' = P. Nautin, 'L'auteur de la *Chronique de Seért*: Iso'denah de Basra', *Revue de l'Histoire des Religions* 186, 1974, 113–26.

Noth/Conrad = A. Noth and L.I. Conrad, *The Early Arabic Historical Tradition. A Source-Critical Study* (Princeton, 1994).

Nyberg, *Manual of Pahlavi* = H.S. Nyberg, *A Manual of Pahlavi. Part II: Glossary* (Wiesbaden, 1972).

Oikonomidès, 'A Chronological Note' = N. Oikonomidès, 'A Chronological Note on the First Persian Campaign of Heraclius (622)', *Byzantine and Modern Greek Studies* 1, 1975, 1–9.

Oikonomidès, 'Correspondence' = N. Oikonomidès, 'Correspondence between Heraclius and Kavadh-Siroe in the *Paschal Chronicle* (628)', *Byzantion* 41, 1971, 269–81.

Olster, *Usurpation* = D.M. Olster, *The Politics of Usurpation in the Seventh Century: Rhetoric and Revolution in Byzantium* (Amsterdam, 1993).

Ostrogorsky, *History of the Byzantine State* = G. Ostrogorsky, *History of the Byzantine State* (Oxford, 1968).

Reinink, *Pseudo-Methodius* = G.J. Reinink, *Die syrische Apokalypse des Pseudo-Methodius* [*CSCO* 540 (edition), 541 (translation), *Scriptores Syri* 220, 221] (Louvain, 1993).

Robin, 'La Tihama' = C.J. Robin, 'La Tihama yéménite avant l'Islam: notes d'histoire et de géographie historique', *AAE* 6, 1995, 222–35.

Robinson, 'Conquest of Khuzistan' = C.F. Robinson, 'The Conquest of Khuzistan: a historiographical reassessment', in L.I. Conrad ed., *History and Historiography in Early Islamic Times: Studies and Perspectives* (Princeton, forthcoming).

Rodinson, *Mohammed* = M. Rodinson, *Mohammed* (Harmondsworth, 1971).

Rubin, 'Reforms' = Z. Rubin, 'The Reforms of Khusro Anushirwan', in Averil Cameron ed., *The Byzantine and Early Islamic Near East III, States, Resources and Armies* (Princeton, 1995), 227–97.

Russell, *Zoroastrianism* = J.R. Russell, *Zoroastrianism in Armenia* [Harvard Iranian Series 5] (Cambridge, MA, 1987).

Sanjian, 'Contemporary Armenian Elegies' = A.K. Sanjian, 'Two Contemporary Armenian Elegies on the Fall of Constantinople, 1453', *Viator* 1, 1970, 223–61.

Sarkissian, *The Council of Chalcedon* = K. Sarkissian, *The Council of Chalcedon and the Armenian Church* (London, 1965; repr. New York, 1975).

Sarre and Herzfeld, *Archäologische Reise* = F. Sarre and E. Herzfeld, *Archäologische Reise im Euphrat – und Tigris – Gebiet* II (Berlin, 1920).

Schippmann, *Feuerheiligtümer* = K. Schippmann, *Die iranische Feuerheiligtümer* (Berlin, 1971).

Segal, *Edessa* = J.B. Segal, *Edessa 'The Blessed City'* (Oxford, 1970).

Sellwood, Whitting and Williams = D. Sellwood, P. Whitting and R.Williams, *An Introduction to Sasanian Coins* (London, 1985).

Sinclair, *Eastern Turkey* = T.A. Sinclair, *Eastern Turkey: an Architectural and Archaeological Survey*, 4 vols. (London, 1987–1990).

Sinclair, 'The Site of Tigranokerta' = T.A. Sinclair, 'The Site of Tigranokerta. I', *REA* 25, 1994–1995, 183–254.

Spuler, *Iran* = B. Spuler, *Iran in früh-islamischer Zeit* (Wiesbaden, 1952).

Stein, *Bas-Empire* = E. Stein, *Histoire du Bas-Empire* II (Paris, Brussels and Amsterdam, 1949).

Stein, *Studien* = E. Stein, *Studien zur Geschichte des byzantinischen Reiches vornehmlich unter den Kaisern Justinus II und Tiberius Constantinus* (Stuttgart, 1919).

Stone = M.E. Stone, *The Armenian Inscriptions from the Sinai* [HATS 6] (Cambridge, MA, 1982).

Stratos, *Seventh Century* = A.N. Stratos, *Byzantium in the Seventh Century*, 3 vols. (Amsterdam, 1968–1975).

Tallon, *Livre* = M. Tallon, *Livre des Lettres (Girk῾ T῾łt῾oc῾). Ier Groupe: Documents concernant les relations avec les Grecs* [Mélanges de l'Université Saint Joseph, 32, fasc. 1] (Beirut, 1955).

Tchukasizian, 'Echos' = B.L. Tchukasizian, 'Echos de légendes épiques iraniennes dans les "Lettres" de Grigor Magistros', *REA* 1, 1964, 321–9.

Ter-Ghévondian, 'Prince d'Arménie' = A. Ter-Ghévondian, 'Le 'Prince d'Arménie' à l'époque de la domination arabe', *REA* 3, 1966, 185–200.

Thierry, 'Héraclius' = N. Thierry, 'Héraclius et la vraie croix en Arménie', in *From Byzantium to Iran*, 165–86.

Thomson, *Agathangelos*. See Texts s.v. Agat῾angełos.

Thomson, *Armenian Version* = R.W. Thomson, *Rewriting Caucasian History. The Armenian Version of the Georgian Chronicles* (Oxford, 1996).

Thomson, 'Constantine and Trdat' = R.W. Thomson, 'Constantine and Trdat in Armenian Tradition', *Acta Orientalia* 50, 1997, 201–13.

Thomson, 'The Defence' = R.W. Thomson, 'The Defence of Armenian Orthodoxy in Sebeos', in I. Ševčenko and I. Hutter edd., *AETOS. Studies in Honour of Cyril Mango* (Stuttgart and Leipzig, 1998), 329–41.

Thomson, *Elishē*. See Texts, s.v. Ełishē.

Thomson, *Łazar*. See Texts, s.v. Łazar P῾arpets῾i.

Thomson, 'Maccabees' = R.W. Thomson, 'The Maccabees in Early Armenian Historiography', *JTS* 26, 1975, 329–41; reprinted in his *Studies in Armenian Literature and Christianity* (Aldershot, 1994).

Thomson, *Moses Khorenats'i*. See Texts, s.v. Movsēs Khorenats'i.

Thomson, 'Muhammad' = R.W. Thomson, 'Muhammad and the Origin of Islam in Armenian Literary Tradition', *Armenian Studies in Memoriam Haïg Berbérian*, ed. D. Kouymjian (Lisbon, 1986), 829–58; repr. in his *Studies in Armenian Literature and Christianity* (Aldershot, 1994).

Thomson, 'The Shorter Recension' = R.W. Thomson, 'The Shorter Recension of the *Root of Faith*', *REA* 5, 1969, 249–60.

Thomson, *Thomas Artsruni*. See Texts, s.v. T'ovma Artsruni.

Thomson, 'Transformation of Athanasius' = R.W. Thomson, 'The Transformation of Athanasius in Armenian Theology', *LM* 78, 1965, 47–69; repr. in his *Studies in Armenian Literature and Christianity* (Aldershot, 1994).

Thomson, 'Vardapet' = R.W. Thomson, '*Vardapet* in the Early Armenian Church', *LM* 75, 1962, 367–84.

Tommaséo. See Texts, s.v. Agat'angełos.

Toumanoff, *Dynasties* = C. Toumanoff, *Les Dynasties de la Caucasie chrétienne de l'antiquité jusqu'au XIXᵉ siècle. Tables généalogiques et chronologiques* (Rome, 1990).

Toumanoff, 'The Heraclids' = C. Toumanoff, 'The Heraclids and the Arsacids', *REA* 19, 1985, 431–4.

Toumanoff, 'The Mamikonids and the Liparitids' = C. Toumanoff, 'The Mamikonids and the Liparitids', *Armeniaca*, 125–37.

Toumanoff, *Studies* = C. Toumanoff, *Studies in Christian Caucasian History* (Georgetown, 1963).

Treadgold, *History* = W. Treadgold, *A History of the Byzantine State and Society* (Stanford, CA, 1997).

Wellhausen, *The Arab Kingdom* = J. Wellhausen, *The Arab Kingdom and Its Fall* (London and Totowa, NJ, 1973).

Whitby, 'A New Image' = Mary Whitby, 'A New Image for a New Age. George of Pisidia on the Emperor Heraclius', in Dabrowa, *Army*, 197–225.

Whitby, *Emperor Maurice* = Michael Whitby, *The Emperor Maurice and his Historian. Theophylact Simocatta on Persian and Balkan Warfare* (Oxford, 1988).

Whitby, 'The Persian King' = Michael Whitby, 'The Persian King at War', in Dabrowa, *Army*, 227–63.

Whitcomb, *Qasr-i Abu Nasr* = D.S. Whitcomb, *Before the Roses and Nightingales. Excavations at Qasr-i Abu Nasr, Old Shiraz* (New York, 1985).

Whittow, *Orthodox Byzantium* = M. Whittow, *The Making of Orthodox Byzantium 600–1025* (London, 1996).

Winkler, *Koriwns Biographie*. See Texts, s.v. Koriwn.

Winkler, 'Armenian Anaphoras' = G. Winkler, 'Armenian Anaphoras and Creeds,' *OCA* 254, 1997, 41–55.

Winkler, 'Eine bemerkenswerte Stelle' = G. Winkler, 'Eine bemerkenswerte Stelle im armenischen Glaubensbekenntnis: Credimus et in Spiritum Sanctum qui descendit in Jordanem proclamavit missum', *Oriens Christianus* 63, 1979, 130–62.

Winkler, 'Our Present Knowledge' = G. Winkler, 'Our Present Knowledge of the History of Agat'angelos and its Oriental Versions', *REA* 14, 1980, 125–41.

Yovhannēsean = M.V. Yovhannēsean, *Hayastani Berder* (Venice, 1970).

Zacos/Veglery = G. Zacos and A. Veglery, *Byzantine Lead Seals* I (Basel, 1972).

INDICES

INDICES

I. BIBLICAL QUOTATIONS AND ALLUSIONS

The page references are to the edition of the Armenian text by G.V. Abgaryan, Erevan 1979 (marked in bold in square brackets in the translation). The numbering of the Psalms follows that of the Armenian version and the Septuagint, not the Hebrew and the King James versions. The Armenian runs together Psalms 9 and 10 of the KJV; whereas the KJV runs together Psalms 146 and 147 of the Armenian. Therefore from Psalm 10, v.22 to Psalm 147, v.11 in the list below, add one to find the corresponding Psalm in the KJV.

Direct quotations within the text are marked with an asterisk [*].
Allusions within the text are in italics.
References made in the footnotes to the translation are unmarked.

2.5: **153***
6.16: **152***

II Timothy
1.9: *117*

Philemon
2.8: **153***

Hebrews
1.3: **120**
2.14: **154***
11.10: **120***
12.6: **119***
12.22–23: **119***
13.4: **159***

I Peter
1.2: **118***
2.17: *149*
2.24: **119***, **153***

I John
1.1: **152***, **153***
1.2: **152***
1.7: **153***
2.18: **164**
5.6–9: **153***

Revelation
12.9: *147*

II. TECHNICAL TERMS

Each entry presents the English term as it appears in the translation, the transcribed Armenian word, a brief commentary (if needed), the pages of the Armenian text (marked in **bold** in the translation) on which the term may be found and the total number of appearances of the term. This index is designed to provide an introduction only; it does not attempt to present an exhaustive analysis, etymological, bibliographical or otherwise.

'ancestral, customary' – *hayreni*
A rare term, used to qualify either religion (**85**), wealth (**129**) or kin (**174**). [Total: 5]

'Arab' – *Tachik*
Rarely used, and generally in a geographical sense. Its use in the treaty between Muawiya and Tʿēodoros Ṙshtuni (**164**) is unusual – in combination with 'army', *spay*, a word not otherwise attested in Sebeos. See also 'Hagarene'; 'Ismaeli'; 'Ismaelite'.
74, **75**, **164**, **171**, **174–176** [Total: 9]

'archbishop' – *arkʿepiskopos*
Applied by Modestos to Komitas in the formal heading of his letter to him (**116**); also used of Leontius of Caesarea (**155**). [Total: 2]

'archbishop/chief-bishop' – *episkoposapet*
Used of both the Nestorian Catholicos of Persia and Komitas, who is described as such in the formal heading to a letter.
70, **118** [Total: 2]

'arch-priest' – *erētsʿapet*
Used at **116** of Modestos, reflecting his rank in Jerusalem. [Total: 1]

'Armenia/Armenian' – *Hayastan*

Denotes the land or country of Armenia in combination with *erkir*, *ashkharh*, *kolmank'* or *sahmank'*, as well as Armenian nobles, princes etc. when qualifying an appropriate noun. Present throughout the text. Unlike *Hayk'*, it is never incorporated into a title. See 'Armenia/Armenian', *Hayk'*.

64, 66, 67, 86, 90, 91, 96–98, 104, 105, 110, 113, 114, 116, 129, 131, 143, 147–149, 173 [Total: 28]

'Armenia/Armenian' – *Hayk'*

More usual word to express 'Armenian', derived by M.K. from the eponymous ancestor of all Armenians. Although found in combination with 'land' and 'country' to express 'Armenia', and with other collective nouns, it is also found as a free-standing noun throughout the text, on 33 occasions. The title *ishkhan Hayots'*, 'prince of Armenia', is first encountered at **133**, in relation to Dawit' Saharuni. See 'Armenia/Armenian', *Hayastan*.

65–68, 70, 73, 76–78, 84, 87, 88, 90–92, 95, 101, 105, 107, 108, 111, 113, 116, 118, 126, 129, 132–134, 137, 138, 143–146, 148–151, 164–169, 171, 174, 175 [Total: 109]

'*aspet*/office of *aspet*' – *aspet/aspetut'iwn*

Derived from the Middle Iranian word for 'master of the horse' and used once in this Persian context (**71**). Otherwise this title is linked exclusively to the Bagratunik' house. It is used consistently to refer to Varaztirots', and later to his son Smbat, but was never applied to Smbat Bagratuni, Khosrov Shum. The relationship between this term and *sparapet* is difficult to discern, prompting some commentators to suggest that it was only ever a title and not an office. See 'commander', *sparapet*.

71, 94, 129, 132, 133, 138, 143, 144, 162, 163 [Total: 17]

'auditor' – *hamarakar*

The Vaspurakan auditor, a Persian administrator, became caught up in the rebellion of the Vahewunik' and negotiated with the rebels on behalf of Khosrov II. There is a solitary reference to the auditor of another Persian district (**96**), similarly targeted by rebel Armenians. He had fiscal duties but seems to have had responsibility for the storage and transport of revenue as well. See also 'investigator'; '*marzpan*'.

87, 88, 94, 96 [Total: 11]

'bishop/episcopacy' – *episkopos/episkoposut'iwn*
Derived from the Greek and used for both Armenian and non-Armenian bishops without discrimination. See also 'overseer'.
95, 100, 112, 118, 129, 148, 149, 150, 151, 154, 155, 156, 158, 167, 168
[Total: 42]

'boundary, territory' – *sahman*
65, 66, 78, 87, 102, 111, 113, 114, 126, 128, 130, 131, 135, 137, 139, 147, 155 [Total: 25]

'brigand' – *hēn*
Applied variously to Khosrov II, Khosrov king of Armenia and to the 'one of the south' i.e. the kingdom of Ismael.
65, 72, 73, 122, 141 [Total: 6]

'camp, army' – *banak*
Used in connection with Persian, Roman and Arab forces. It is only found in its plural form when denoting Arab forces. At **139**, the text refers to the 'royal forces', *ark'unakan banakawk'*, a phrase which seems to indicate caliphal control and command of the forces; see 'king', *ark'ay*. The variant *banakateln* does not appear to have any significance.
65, 79, 82, 102, 108, 109, 124, 125, 126, 132, 134, 135, 136, 138, 139, 141, 145, 173, 176 [Total: 33]

'capital' – *shahastan*
Used of Ahmatan/Hamadan and Bahl.
80, 91, 103, 112 [Total: 4]

'cathedral' – *kat'olikē*
Used of the main church in Dvin, at **121**. [Total: 2]

'Catholicos/Catholicosate (i.e. office of Catholicos) – *kat'olikos/kat'olikosut'iwn*
Title used for the head of the Armenian church. It renders the Greek 'metropolitan'. The office was split after the partition of Armenia in 591, reflecting the pro- and anti-Chalcedonian divisions within the church (**91, 112**). However it is also applied to the Nestorian church leader in Persia and Viroy of Aḷuank' (**70, 150**). See also 'patriarch'; 'archbishop'; 'arch-priest'; 'chief-priesthood'.

70, 91, 100, 112, 121, 129, 131, 132, 139, 144, 147, 148, 150, 156, 165–168, 174, 175 [Total: 46]

'census' – *shahrmar*
A Persian term, used at **67** to illustrate the inclusion of Siwnik' in the administrative structure of Atrpatakan rather than that of Armenia. At **176** the Armenian equivalent, *ashkharhagir*, is used, in a similar context. [Total: 1]

'chief-priesthood' – *k'ahanayapetut'iwn*
Used twice in an Armenian context (**129, 155**) and once generally when praising the Greek empire (**149**). [Total: 3]

'city' – *k'ałak'*
A walled urban centre. Within Armenia, it is applied to Vałarshapat, Dvin, Karin, Nakhchawan, Angł, Erginay and Dz'it'ařich. If any pattern is discernible, it is perhaps that the most recent entries in the text do not contain a comparable spread of cities to the earlier episodes. Furthermore, in these more recent entries, cities are increasingly cited by name without being identified as *k'ałak'*. See also 'town'; 'village'; 'walled village'.
65–70, 74–76, 84–91, 95, 100, 105–119, 121, 122, 124, 125, 127, 131, 133, 134, 137, 138, 140, 142, 143, 147, 149, 151, 158, 161, 164, 165, 169–172, 174, 175 [Total: 145]

'commander' – *hramanatar*
Found in a Persian context only, at **102, 129** and **130**. [Total: 3]

'commander' – *sparapet*
Derived from the Persian word for 'commander' and linked in the text to the Mamikonean house. It was an hereditary office, reflecting their dominant role in Armenian society. Yet only Vahan Mamikonean is called *sparapet* in the text, and three of the references have a Persian context. See also *'aspet'*; 'general'.
66, 73, 75 [Total: 4]

'community, residence, monastery' – *vank'*
Used of the Christians living at the court of Khosrov II under the protection of his wife Shirin (**85**), and of the community to which Yovhanik belonged (**121**). [Total: 3]

'contingent' – *gund*

The contingent formed around an individual prince; found consistently in a military context, although not applied to a named noble-led retinue. There is one reference to the region of *Vaspurakan gund* (**84**) and four references to the *Sephakan gund* (**145, 166**). The former term is met for the first time in the *AŠX*.

65, 66, 68, 74, 77, 84, 88, 90, 94, 99, 101, 136, 145, 166, 172 [Total: 19]

'*curator*' – *korator*

A Roman official, responsible for imperial estates.

89, 113, 133 [Total: 3]

'*curopalates*' – *kiwrapałat/kiwrapałatut'iwn*

A high Roman title, accorded by Heraclius to Dawit' Saharuni (**133**) in the mid 630s, and subsequently by Constans II to first Varaztirots' (**144**) and later Hamazasp Mamikonean (**175**). See also '*patrik*'. [Total: 4]

'district, province' – *gawar*

This term distinguishes smaller, individual districts, generally either Armenian or Persian. The fifteen Armenian *ashkharhk'* of the *AŠX* are subdivided into *gawark'*.

66, 68, 77, 84, 99, 101–104, 107–109, 111, 114, 115, 124, 126, 129, 134, 138, 141, 148, 165, 166, 174 [Total: 30]

'donative, salary' – *hrog*

Found in a Greek context at **122** and **164**, and derived from the Greek *roga*. Compare 'stipend', *rochik*, which has a similar meaning but in a Persian context. [Total: 2]

'eminent, greatest' – *metsametsk'*

Used infrequently as a general term with no obvious pattern of use.

64, 69, 80, 85, 114, 124, 133, 140 [Total: 8]

'eminent, senior' – *awag*

Used only once (**69**) in a Persian context. [Total: 1]

'emperor' – *kaysr*

Used exclusively in a Roman context, for Maurice, Heraclius and Constans. Intriguingly it is also used of T'ēodos, Maurice's eldest son who is reported by Sebeos to have survived the coup of Phocas, but not of Phocas himself. Infrequent use in respect of Constans II. See 'king', *ark'ay*; 'king', *t'agavor*.

65, 76, 81, 84, 86–88, 90, 91, 95, 105, 106, 110, 111, 114, 122–125, 128, 131, 133, 135, 136, 139, 143, 158, 163, 164 [Total: 36]

'empire, principality, authority' – *ishkhanut'iwn*
Used in a variety of senses, as the definition implies. See 'lordship'; 'prince'.

64, 66, 67, 76, 84, 95, 96, 101, 109, 128, 132, 133, 143–145, 151, 165, 172, 174, 175 [Total: 27]

'flag' – *drawsh*
Found only in combination with 'contingent'. When T'ēodoros Ṙshtuni receives a standard from Muawiya (**169**), a different word for 'flag', *vaṙ*, is used.

77, 94, 101 [Total: 4]

'fortification' – *amrut'iwn*
By contrast to 'inaccessible', *amur*, this term indicates an artificial, constructed defensive work. Used of only two sites. Also used of armour (**103**). See also 'fortress', *amur*; 'fortress', *berd*; 'fortress, *amrots'*.

103, 109, 136 [Total: 6]

'fortress, stronghold' – *amrots'*
Found in a generic sense at **70** and **144**. See also 'fortification'. [Total: 2]

'fortress' (n.) and 'inaccessible, secure' (adj.) – *amur*
Indicates remoteness or isolation contributing to the strength of the location as much as any man-made construction. It is particularly linked with the land of Gełum and the country of Media. See also 'fortification'.

89, 91, 95, 96, 98, 99, 125, 172, 173 [Total: 15]

'fortress' – *berd*
Describes a man-made defensive feature. This term is frequently coupled with the name of the fortress. Dvin itself is occasionally referred to as a *berd*, although this may refer to a fortress nearby; see **100**. At **100** and **110**, the (Persian) official in charge of a *berd* is defined as *berdakal*. In the treaty between Muawiya and T'ēodoros Ṙshtunik' (**164**), a rare

plural of *berd*, *berdorayn* appears in apposition to *amirays*, a word otherwise unattested in this text. See also 'fortification'.

75, 100, 103, 105, 108–110, 138, 141, 145–147, 164–166, 174 [Total: 37]

'general, commander' – *zawravar/zawravarut'iwn*
Used of Persians, Greeks and Armenians but never of Arabs. It appears regularly in the text until **148**, but not thereafter. At **131**, Mzhēzh Gnuni is entitled the commander of the Greeks and Dawit' Saharuni replaces him in this office at **133**. At **137** Mushel Mamikonean is called the 'Armenian general', the first occasion on which this phrase appears. At **138** the office 'general of the country of Armenia' appears, belonging to T'ēodoros Řshtuni. See also '*aspet*'; 'commander'; and '*stratelat*'.

70, 88, 89, 105–109, 114, 115, 122, 125, 126, 131–133, 136–140, 143–146, 148 [Total: 40]

'governor' – *sahmanakal*
Found in the lists of governors; interchangeable with *marzpan*.

71, 105 [Total: 2]

'Greek' – *Yoynk'*
Used frequently throughout the text. Occasionally the singular *yoynn*, 'the Greek', appears by itself, at **90, 110, 113–115, 123, 147, 171, 174**. However 'the Aluan', *Aluann* and 'the Siwni', *Siwnin* are also used in a similar way (**166**). See also 'Roman'.

65, 67, 68, 71, 74, 75, 79, 80, 84, 86, 88, 89–92, 97, 104–111, 113–115, 123, 124, 128, 131–136, 141, 143, 144, 147, 148, 150, 164, 171, 173–176 [Total: 75]

'guard, bodyguard' – *p'ushtipan*
Used to denote the royal guard of the Persian king. On one occasion, it is found in combination with *ostikan* (**83**). Linked with 'auxiliary', *hamaharz*.

74, 75, 81, 83 [Total: 6]

'Hagarene' – *Hagarats'ik'*
Rare generic term for Muslims, referring to their descent from Hagar, a maidservant of Abraham by whom he had a son, Ismael. More

commonly called 'Ismaelites' or 'sons of Ismael'. The text never refers to them as Saracens or as 'foreigners', *aylazgik'* (the most usual Armenian term). See also 'Arab'; 'Ismaeli'; 'Ismaelite'.

139, 170 [Total: 2]

'hall' – *dahlich*
The gathering place at the royal court for the greatest Persian nobles. See also 'palace'.

75, 103, 127, 149 [Total: 4]

'head of a family, patriarch' – *nahapet*
Noticeable for its infrequent use. It is applied specifically to Vahan Mamikonean and Sahak Artsruni; the other two references are impersonal, relating to the heads of the tribes participating in the Arab conquests. Given its Biblical context – specifically its identification with Abraham the patriarch – it may have the sense of the founder of the family, or at least of that particular line or branch. See also 'lord'; 'noble'; 'prince'; 'tanutēr'.

65, 112, 135 [Total: 4]

'house, family' – *tun*
Used in the sense of both family and literally of a building – see for example **139** 'a house of prayer'. Interestingly, the other Armenian term for family or house, *tohm*, is not found.

65, 75, 77, 84, 94–96, 99, 129, 135, 139, 145, 165–167, 170, 174 [Total: 20]

'inhabitants' – *bnakich'k'*
Used of both districts and cities, one of the rare expressions for the local community, as opposed to the great number of terms denoting the leadership of those communities. See also 'ordinary people'.

108, 111, 112, 115, 117, 131, 136, 137, 142, 162, 170 [Total: 16]

'investigator' – *k'nnoł*
A Persian administrative official (**102**). [Total: 1] See also 'auditor'; *'marzpan'*.

'Ismael' – *Ismayeli*
Applied to Muslims, denoting common descent from the son of

Abraham and Hagar. Its use in combination with 'king' and 'prince' is mentioned in the relevant entries. See below and also 'Arab'; 'Hagarene'.

65, 131, 134, 135, 137, 139–141, 145–147, 164, 165, 169, 171–176 [Total: 38]

'Ismaelite' – *Ismayelats'ik'*
Less common than *Ismayeli*; used generically and never of an individual. See above and also 'Arab'; 'Hagarene'.

139, 141, 145–147, 163–165, 169, 171, 172, 175 [Total: 21]

'king' – *ark'ay*
A title restricted to Persian and other non-Roman kings until **128**, when it is applied to a Roman emperor, Heraclius, for the first time. Thereafter it is used infrequently in a Roman context. It is also used to designate the caliph, *ark'ay Ismayeli*, at **164, 169, 170, 172** and **176**. The Armenian word *amirapet*, found in later histories, is never used in Sebeos. The title *ark'ay ark'ayits'* is applied on three occasions to the Persian king, at **82** and **88**. See also 'king', *t'agavor* and 'emperor'.

65–70, 73–76, 80–85, 88, 89, 94–97, 99–113, 115, 123, 124, 126–129, 141, 143, 144, 146, 147, 149–151, 155, 157, 158, 161, 163–166, 168–170, 172, 175, 176 [Total: 146]

'king' – *t'agavor*
Found in both Persian, Greek and other contexts, this title appears very frequently throughout the text. Used repeatedly for Heraclius after **131** and no fewer than 37 times for Constans II. This contrasts with the use of *kaysr* for Constans on only three occasions. At **176** and **177**, it is used to designate the caliph; see also 'king', *ark'ay* and 'emperor'.

65, 68–71, 73–76, 79–88, 90–95, 97, 99–101, 103–107, 111, 113–116, 122–124, 129–134, 136, 137, 139, 141–144, 147–151, 155, 158, 160, 162, 163, 165, 167, 168, 171, 174–176 [Total: 184]

'kingdom, kingship' – *t'agavorut'iwn*
Used throughout, in both Persian and Greek contexts, though never to reflect the Arab conquests. The Muslim domination is described in terms of their 'authority', *ishkhanut'iwn*, or their 'lordship', *tērut'iwn*.

64, 66, 67, 69, 73, 74, 76, 78, 80, 84, 89, 90, 94, 95, 97, 100, 104, 106, 111–115, 121, 122, 124, 126–130, 132, 133, 136, 137, 139, 141–143, 149, 151, 152, 161, 164, 165, 168, 169, 175 [Total: 97]

'land, country' – *ashkharh*

Used in a political or administrative, as opposed to a geographical, sense to denote a particular land. Thus titles are linked to *ashkharh* and not *erkir*. The fifteen regions of Armenia in the Armenian Geography (*AŠX*) are called *ashkharhk'*.

64, 65–67, 70, 72–78, 80, 84–88, 90–92, 94, 95–100, 105, 106, 111, 113, 116–119, 123, 125, 129, 130, 132, 137, 138, 143, 144, 147–151, 155, 162, 164–168, 170, 172–175 [Total: 104]

'land, country' – *erkir*

A general term denoting geographical extent, although occasionally it refers to the earth in general.

67–70, 72, 73, 76–79, 84, 86–92, 95, 96, 98, 100–103, 106, 109, 110, 113–115, 123, 126, 128, 131, 132, 134–138, 141–143, 147, 151, 152, 156, 161–164, 166, 169, 170–174, 176, 177 [Total: 111]

'letter, official letter' – *hrovartak*

Regularly used throughout the text, particularly in relation to high-level diplomatic correspondence.

73, 74, 77, 78, 92, 94, 99, 100, 103, 113, 123, 124, 128, 148 [Total: 21]

'lord' – *tēr*

A title used both of Jesus Christ (40 occasions) and of the head of a family (43 times). The text indicates that there could only be one *tēr* of a house at any one time. However in the contemporary notices, both Mushel (**166, 173, 175**) and Hamazasp (**169, 174, 175**) Mamikonean are given the title *tēr Mamikonēits'*. This marks a significant change; the appearance of two rival leaders of the same house suggests that the period after 640 was a time of greater social fluidity, when customary social practices began to disintegrate. See also 'head of a family'; 'tanutēr'.

67–70, 72, 77, 87, 88, 94, 99, 101, 116–120, 123, 124, 129, 137–139, 143, 145, 146, 148, 152, 156–166, 169–177 [Total: 83]

'lordship, dominion' – *tērut'iwn*

Used of both Arsacid, Greek, Persian and Ismaelite lordship.

64, 67, 77, 83, 90, 99, 106, 122, 134, 151, 163–165 [Total: 13]

'*Magistros*' – *Magistros*
  A Greek title, applied to T'ēodoros (**133**) and to Gēorg (**162**, **163**). [Total: 7]

'magus' – *movpet*
  A priest of the Persian state religion. The head of the organization is entitled *movpetan movpet*, 'movpet of movpets'.
  69, **85** [Total: 4]

'*marzpan*/ office of *marzpan*' – *marzpan/marzpanut'iwn*
  Found only in a Persian context. Its original sense was 'governor of a border region'. It is used of Persian governors of Armenia, of the Persian command that Smbat Bagratuni held in Vrkan between 599 and 606/607, and of the Armenian office accorded to his son Varaztirots' by Kawat in 628. See also 'auditor'; 'investigator'.
  67, **70**, **71**, **96**, **98–101**, **111**, **129** [Total: 15]

'metropolitan' – *metropawlit*
  Used twice, once of Komitas when addressed by Modestos (**116**) and once of Kamyishov of Beth Dasen (**151**). See also 'Catholicos'; 'patriarch'. [Total: 2]

'noble, free' – *azatk'*
  A general meaning of noble, as distinct from the third estate, the *anazatk'* or unfree. One reference to *azatagund* (**79**), which denotes a military formation.
  79, **81**, **134** [Total: 3]

'noble' – *nakharar*
  Found 17 times in a Persian context and 15 in an Armenian context. The term is used both collectively and individually. It indicates nobility in both societies, and is applied to all members of the same family. The distribution of the term in the text is very uneven, there being only four references after the death of Khosrov II (**128**) and none after **149**. This implies that it obtained definition only in and through Persian society; after the Persian withdrawal from Armenia and the subsequent Sasanian collapse, the term ceased to have meaning and was therefore replaced in the contemporary notices with the term 'prince', *ishkhan*.

64, 65, 73–75, 77, 80, 83, 84, 90–92, 94, 95, 101–104, 127, 128, 137, 144, 148, 149 [Total: 32]

'noble' – *sepuh*
Used only once, at **89**, in relation to the members of the rebellious Vahewunik' house, none of whom is accorded the title 'lord', *tēr*. Hence it describes the junior members of a house. [Total: 1]

'ordinary people' – *ṙamik*
A rare term, reflecting those neither noble nor ecclesiastical. See also 'inhabitants'; 'peasant'.
115 [Total: 1]

'ostan' – *ostan*
Originally this referred to the royal domain of the Arsacid kings of Armenia. Subsequently it was applied to the core domain or capital of the major families. Linked exclusively to Dvin (**111, 113**). It denotes the Persian administrative and strategic centre around Dvin. [Total: 2]

'overseer, bishop' – *tesuch'*
A literal translation of the Greek 'epi-skopos' (**100**). See also 'bishop'. [Total: 1]

'pact, covenant' – *ukht*
Used of both secular agreements – that between Constans and Muawiya at **143** for example – and of the clergy, at **91** and **114**, 'the covenant of the church, the clergy'. There is no sense of 'oath of fealty' or vassalage.
68, 76, 91, 114, 129, 143, 164 [Total: 8]

'palace' – *ark'unik'*
Rare but found in both a Persian and a Roman context.
79, 143, 160 [Total: 3]

'palace' – *kayeank'*
Found only in relation to the palace of the Persian king.
68–70, 84, 85, 95 [Total: 6]

'palace' – *palat*
Found in a Greek context to denote the imperial residence in Constantinople.
   84, 88, 92, 93, 104, 114, 133, 136, 146, 149, 156 [Total: 12]

'palace' – *tachar*
Denotes the palace of the Persian king and also the temple of Solomon in Jerusalem (**139**).
   104, 130, 139, 155 [Total: 4]

'patriarch / office of patriarch' – *hayrapet / hayrapetut'iwn*
This term is applied in an Armenian context specifically to saint Gregory, the 'Illuminator' of Armenia, and saint Sahak, a famous head of the Armenian church in the fifth century. The contemporary heads of the Armenian church are all entitled 'Catholicos' rather than 'patriarch'; see entry above. The other references to patriarch are either to the patriarch of Jerusalem or the patriarch of Constantinople.
   100, 112, 116, 121, 124, 129, 142, 143, 148, 149, 151, 155 [Total: 14]

'*patrik*, patrician' – *patrik*
The Greek title, used of both Greeks and Armenians. It is not found after **139**; this may coincide with the award of 'prince of Armenia', *ishkhan Hayots'* and / or '*curopalates*' to Armenians. See 'prince'; '*curopalates*'.
   67, 74, 77, 82, 83, 104, 105, 132, 139 [Total: 9]

'pavilion' – *mashkapachēn / mashaperchan*
The quarters of the Persian king on campaign (**69, 82**). [Total: 2]

'peasant' – *shinakan*
Used only once (**172**), illustrating the lack of interest on the part of the author in the third estate. [Total: 1]

'people, race, kin' – *azg*
Used in a variety of contexts. At **130** and **174**, it is applied to an individual family, giving the meaning of kin or extended family.
   64, 65, 70, 74, 76, 81, 86, 90, 97, 102, 115, 130, 134, 135, 160, 172, 174 [Total: 18]

'possession, property' – *kaluats*
Hereditary entitlement based upon kinship with Abraham through Ismael. Not used in a specific, individual sense and not of any land-holding in Armenia. Muawiya's triumph in the first Arab civil war is described in terms of him ruling over the 'possessions of the sons of Ismael'.
136, 139, 176 [Total: 3]

'prefect, governor' – *ostikan*
Used once in respect of a court official (**83**), but more often as 'governor', for example of Jerusalem (**115**). In the tenth century, it was the title of the Arab governor of Armenia, but there is no mention of governors of Armenia in the text. Compare '*marzpan*'.
83, 115, 149, 169 [Total: 5]

'priest' – *erēts'*
Used interchangeably with *k'ahanay*, with no obvious pattern. See also 'youth', *manuk*.
89, 97, 99, 114, 116, 121, 149, 167 [Total: 11]

'priest / office of priest' – *k'ahanay/k'ahanayut'iwn*
Used interchangeably with 'priest', *erēts'*. Derived from Syriac. See also 'youth', *manuk*.
85, 97, 114, 119, 120, 154, 168 [Total: 8]

'primate, pastor / leadership' – *aṙajnord/aṙajnordut'iwn*
Used four times to denote those responsible for spiritual guidance (**100, 117, 158, 160**) and twice to designate secular leadership (**75, 129**). See also 'archbishop'; 'Catholicos'; 'patriarch'. [Total: 6]

'prince, official' – *ishkhan*
Used in Persian, Armenian, Roman and Arab contexts, both indivi-dually and generically. In a Persian or Roman context it implies an offi-cial or officer, someone with authority or the power of compulsion. It is used frequently to refer to the members of the Armenian noble houses. At **133** a new title, *ishkhan i veray amenayn ashkharhats'n*, 'prince over all the countries', is granted to Dawit' Sahaṙuni and at **138**, the title *ishkhan Hayots'*, 'prince of Armenia', is awarded to T'ēodoros Ṙshtuni; a similar title was later confirmed to him by Muawiya (**169**) but its remit

was extended to include Iberia, Ałuank' and Siwnik'. At **164, 169, 170** and **176**, Muawiya is entitled *ishkhan Ismayeli*. He is distinguished from the caliph, who is either *ark'ay Ismayeli* or *t'agavor Ismayeli*; see 'king'. See also 'noble'.

66, 67, 73, 83, 84, 86, 88, 90, 94–96, 101, 102, 106, 107, 109, 115, 122, 128–134, 137, 138, 140, 142–147, 149, 150, 155, 162–176 [Total: 88]

'queen' – *bambishn*

Applied to the Sasanian queen at **69, 85** and **130**, where it designates Bor, daughter of Khosrov II, who briefly held power in her own right. [Total: 3] See also 'wife'.

'region, district, side' – *kołmn*

A very general term for a region, which can also refer to one side (of two) or to a particular direction.

65–67, 69, 73, 76–78, 80, 84, 88–92, 95–98, 101, 104, 106–110, 112–114, 121, 124, 126–130, 132, 134, 136, 138, 142, 143, 145–147, 149–151, 155, 162, 163, 165, 166, 168–173, 175, 176 [Total: 127]

'Roman' – *Hoŕom/Hŕovmayetsi'*

Used increasingly towards the end of the text, but apparently interchangeable with the more common 'Greek', *Yoynk'*.

77, 83, 106, 123, 134, 147, 148, 162, 164, 165, 167, 169, 170 [Total: 20]

'*Sephakan*' – *Sephakan*

Traditionally derived from *sepuh* and defined to mean 'hereditary'. In the text of Sebeos, the term is used only in combination with 'contingent', *gund* and has a geographical meaning: see **145** and **166**, 'the regions of the *Sephakan gund*'. [Total: 4]

'stade' – *asparēz*

A measure of distance, linked to the length of a stadium, traditionally 606 feet or one eighth of a Roman mile.

86, 171 [Total: 2]

'stipend' – *ŕochik*

Denotes the financial remuneration for services rendered to the Persian king (or queen, for which see **85**). Usually in combination with *yark'unust*, 'royal treasury'. Found exclusively in a Persian context except at **143** when the text portrays Constans in a similar role, but uniquely through Persian vocabulary. See also 'donative'.

85, 94, 105, 110, 143 [Total: 5]

'stratelat, general' – *stratelat*
Used only of the Greek commander, at **77** and **105**. [Total: 2]

'submission' – *tsarayut'iwn*
A term indicating recognition of the authority of another. It is found in both an individual and a collective context; thus numerous cities submit to Khoream at **111–115**. However it only applies in the text of Sebeos to the ultimate overlord – either the Persian or Roman king, or later the Arab caliph – and does not refer to any relationship of service at a lower level within Armenian society.

66, 67, 74, 77, 84, 88, 92, 96, 104, 110–113, 115, 123, 133, 136, 142, 144, 151, 164, 166, 169, 170, 172, 173–175 [Total: 53]

'tanutēr, headship' – *Tanutērakan/tanutērut'iwn*
Traditionally defined to mean senior member of a house and used interchangeably with *nahapet* or *tēr*. At **76** and **84**, it appears in combination with *ishkhanut'iwn* and *tun*. Both these references occur in the conditions of the 591 treaty between Maurice and Khosrov II which redefined the partition of Armenia; on both occasions, they define an area of Armenia. See 'head of the family'; 'lord'.

76, 84, 95, 101, 129, 144 [Total: 6]

'tent' – *khoran*
Used of Khosrov's quarters on campaign, and once (**124**) in a similar context for those of Heraclius.

79, 82, 83, 109, 124 [Total: 11]

'throne, cushions' – *gahoyk'*
These played an important role in the strictly hierarchical Sasanian, and, by extension, Armenian social structure. Their appearance in the text is associated with either plunder or gift-giving. There is no reference to the order of 'dignity', *gah* or 'position', *bardz*, amongst the nobles, a subject which absorbed other Armenian historians.

75, 79, 132, 144, 155, 175 [Total: 6]

'town' – *awan*
Clearly distinct from 'city', *k'ałak'*, although much less common. The difference between the two may be related to the presence or absence of walls. At **138**, Dvin is categorized as an *awan*, which is very unusual. See also 'city'; 'village'; 'walled village'.
84, **125**, **126**, **138** [Total: 6]

'tribunal' – *atean*
On both occasions at **150**, used in a Persian context. [Total: 2]

'tribute' – *hark*
A general term for tax or tribute. Although only four references are given, these have either a Persian or Arab context; no reference is made to direct Roman financial impositions upon Armenia.
66, **96**, **123**, **172** [Total: 4]

'tribute-collector' – *harkapahanj*
Found only at **172**. Both references indicate that they collected money and not goods in kind. [Total: 2]

'tutor, guardian' – *dayeak*
The arrangement for the up-bringing of noble-born sons in the family of another noble was common in both Persian and Armenian society. Found only in a Persian context (**73**). [Total: 1]

'*vardapet*, spiritual instructor' – *vardapet*
Used once in an expressly Armenian context, of the Catholicos (**100**) and on three occasions in connection with famous teachers of the early church.
100, **158**, **161** [Total: 4]

'vicar, locum-tenens' – *tełapah*
A title applied to Modestos (**116**), reflecting his intermediate status in Jerusalem after the forced exile of the patriarch Zak'aria. Also applied to the emperor as God's vice-regent on earth (**133**). [Total: 2]

'village' – *gewł*
Identified as a small settlement, without defences, although one has a 'small fort', *berdak*, within it; this settlement is defined further as a

'walled village/komopolis', *giwłak'ałak'* (**102**). Villages are usually named in the text. See also 'city'; 'town'; 'walled village'.

70, 71, 98, 102, 104, 108, 109, 112, 125, 137, 148, 166 [Total: 17]

'walled village/komopolis' – *giwłak'ałak'/k'ałak'agiwł*
A small, defended settlement.
88, 101, 102, 108 [Total: 4]

'wife, lady' – *tikin*
Used twice of Shirin, wife of Khosrov II (**85**) and once in the plural (**127**) for the wives of Khosrov. At **85** Shirin is also entitled 'queen of queens', *tikinats' tikin*, the corollary of 'king of kings', *ark'ay ark'ayits'* (**82, 88**). See also 'queen'. [Total: 3]

'youth, cleric' – *manuk*
Found in its usual context – both Khosrov II (**82**) and Constans (**147**) are described as young men, to explain their inexperienced behaviour – and collectively, to specify the clergy (**91, 154**).
82, 91, 107–109, 112, 115, 147, 154 [Total: 9]

III. ARMENIAN PERSONAL NAMES BY FAMILY

The direct references in this appendix are to the following works: *The Epic Histories (Buzandaran Patmut'iwnk')* [HATS 8] (Cambridge, MA, 1989) ('*EH*') by N.G. Garsoïan, which contains an extensive commentary on these families; and *Studies in Christian Caucasian History* (Georgetown, 1963) ('*Studies*') by C. Toumanoff. The numbers in brackets identify the numbering of the person in the lists in the five-volume study by H. Achar̄ean, *Hayots' Andznannuneri Bar̄aran* (Erevan, 1942–1962; repr. Beirut, 1972). This work remains untranslated. The figures in bold supply the first reference only to that individual in the text of Sebeos, and follow the page numbers in the Abgaryan edition of the text (incorporated in the same way into the body of the translation) and not the page numbers of this book.

Amatuni [house in Vaspurakan and Aragatsotn]: *EH* 346–7; *Studies* 197–8
    Kotit [no.1]: **87**
    Shapuh [no.4]: **138**
    bishop of Amatunik' [Matt'ēos no.6]: **150**
Apahuni [house in Turuberan, north of Lake Van]: *Studies* 199
    Artavazd [no.17]: **101**
    Hmayeak [no.8]: **101**
    Manuēl [no.8]: **101**
    Vstam [no.3]: **101**
        See also region Apahunik'
Ar̄anean [house in Ayrarat]: *Studies* 199
    165
Ar̄awełean [house in Ayrarat]: *Studies* 199
    165
    Khach'ean [no.1]: **138**
Artsruni [house in Vaspurakan]: *EH* 350; *Studies* 199–200
    Sahak [no.28]: **112**

Musheł [no.17]: **165**
Sahak [no.29]: **92**
Vahan [no.17]: **66**
Vard [no.1]: **67**
Vardan, the 'Red' [no.6]: **65**
Vardan, II [no.11]: **67**
Vasak [no.10]: **70**
bishop of Mamikoneankʻ [Komitas, no.1]: **150**
Mokatsʻi [house south of Lake Van]: *Studies* 182
Vardik [no.1]: **138**
See also region Mokkʻ
Ṙshtuni [house south of Lake Van]: *EH* 402; *Studies* 213
Tʻēodoros [no.6]: **129**
bishop of Ṙshtunikʻ [Abraham, no.9]: **100**
See also region Ṙshtunikʻ
Sahaṙuni [house in Ayrarat]: *EH* 404; *Studies* 214
Dawitʻ [no.16]: **133**
Siwni [house in northeastern Armenia]: *EH* 408–9; *Studies* 214
166
Grigor [no.29]: **137**
Pʻilippos [no.1]: **70**
Sahak [no.30]: **95**
Stepʻanos [no.16]: **87**
Vahan [no.19]: **67**
See also region Siwnikʻ
Spanduni [house in Ayrarat]: *Studies* 221
165
Tayetsʻi [house in northern Armenia]:
Sargis [no.7]: **101**
See also region Taykʻ
Trpatuni [house in Vaspurakan]: *Studies* 221
Sargis [no.9]: **101**
Tʻēodoros [Tʻēodos, no.1]: **87**
Vahewuni [house in Tarawn]: *Studies* 215
Grigor [no.35]: **166**
Khosrov [no.13]: **94**
Nersēs [no.18]: **89**
Samuēl [no.8]: **87**
Sargis [no.5]: **89**

IV. PERSONAL NAMES

For Armenian family names, see the separate Index III, Armenian Personal Names by Family. There is great variation in the spelling of names in the Armenian text. Normally the Armenian form is reproduced in the translation, though standard forms may be found in the commentary and indices.

V. GEOGRAPHICAL INDEX

There is great variation in the spelling of names in the Armenian text. Normally the Armenian form is reproduced in the translation, though standard forms may be found in the commentary and indices. The page references are to the pages of the Armenian text, marked in **bold** in the translation.

VI. LIST OF HISTORICAL NOTES

[Section 1]

[Section II]

[Section III]

MAPS

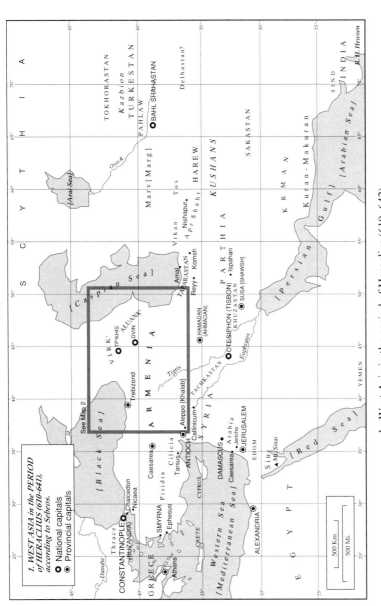

1. West Asia in the period of Heraclius (610–642)

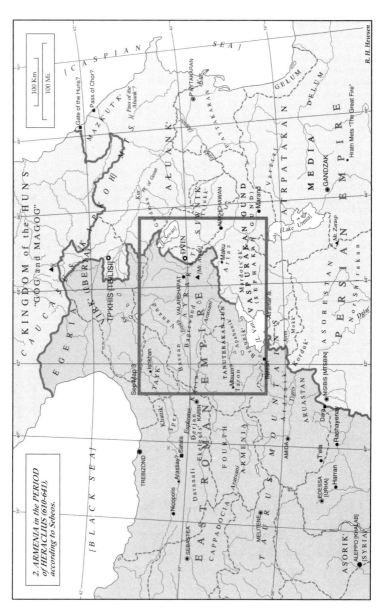

2. Armenia in the period of Heraclius (610–642)

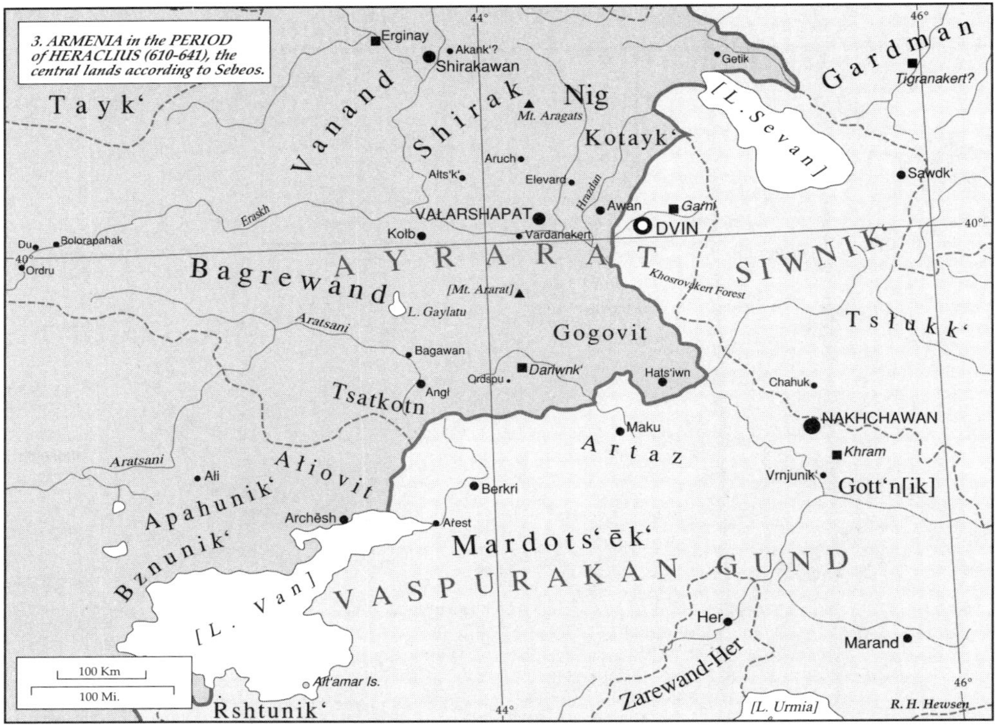
3. ARMENIA in the PERIOD of HERACLIUS (610-641), the central lands according to Sebeos.
Tayk‘
Vanand
Erginay
Shirakawan
Akank‘?
Shirak
Nig
Mt. Aragats
Kotayk‘
Getik
[L. Sevan]
Gardman
Tigranakert?
Sawdk‘
Aruch
Alts‘k‘
Elevard
Hrazdan
Awan
Garni
DVIN
VAŁARSHAPAT
Eraskh
Kołb
Vardanakert
Du
Bolorapahak
Ordru
Bagrewand
AYRARAT
SIWNIK‘
Khosrovakert Forest
[Mt. Ararat]
L. Gaylatu
Aratsani
Gogovit
Tsłukk‘
Bagawan
Darawnk‘
Ordspu
Hats‘iwn
Chahuk
Angł
Tsatkotn
NAKHCHAWAN
Maku
Artaz
Khram
Aratsani
Ali
Ałiovit
Vrnjunik‘
Gott‘n[ik]
Berkri
Apahunik‘
Archēsh
Arest
Mardots‘ēk‘
Bznunik‘
VASPURAKAN GUND
[L. Van]
Her
Marand
Zarewand-Her
Alt‘amar Is.
100 Km
100 Mi.
Rshtunik‘
[L. Urmia]
R. H. Hewsen
44°
46°
40°

3. Armenia in the period of Heraclius: the central lands

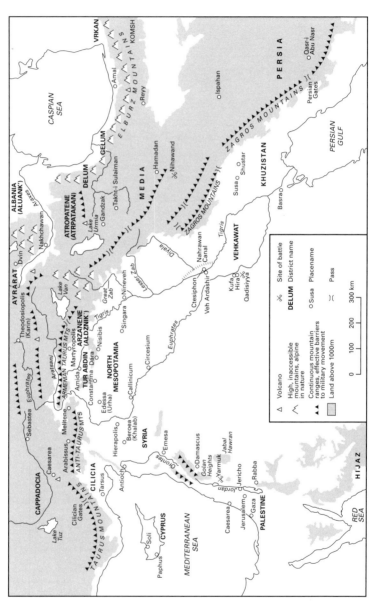

4. The Near East (topography)

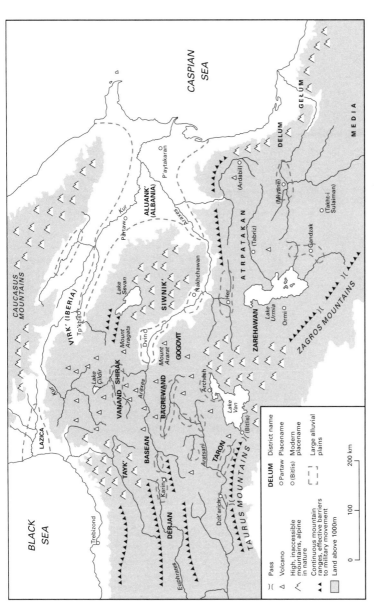

5. Armenia and neighbouring lands (topography)